TO engage boys and girls

Steve Mynard

ISBN 978-1-905538-66-9

A catalogue record for this book is available from the British Library.

Printed in China by 1010

Published by Optimus Education, a division of Optimus Professional Publishing Limited.
Registered office: 33-41 Dallington Street, London EC1V 0BB.
Registered number: 05791519
Tel: 0845 450 6406
Fax: 0845 450 6410

Written by Steve Mynard

Edited by Giles Flitney

Design and illustration by Stewart Henson and Tom Kington

www.optimus-education.com

Contents

Introduction

Section 1 – Adventurous activities in context

Section 2 – The activities

Introduction

Why are adventurous activities important?

We live in peculiar times! Many children do not have the opportunity to play outside other than at school. Children do not climb trees, build dens and rope swings and so on as they did when I was growing up in the late 1960s and 1970s. Many children get their entertainment from the television through programmes, DVD films or games. No matter how hard the television companies work to make programming educational, the fact remains that many children are simply sitting staring at a box in the corner of their living room for a lot of the time. Game playing may help hand/eye coordination, but so many more additional skills can be developed through adventurous play. A growing number of children are overweight: obesity is on the increase and 30 years down the line there will be a diabetes epidemic. We need to do something!

The adventurous activities in this book are practical and often cross-curricular tasks or projects with a real purpose and outcome that children can relate to. They are not a panacea, but they will bring some of the movement back into children's learning. They will stretch young brains by giving them something to work on.

Knowing how children develop physically, emotionally, sociologically and intellectually is key to knowing what learning opportunities to give them. A solid understanding of pedagogy should underpin all teaching. Whether you are a fan of Piaget or Vygotsky, Bruner or Skinner, giving children adventurous learning opportunities will enhance the natural progression of skill development that all children need in order to become fully functioning adults.

Boys have had a bit of a rough ride over the years with our girl-friendly approach to learning – sit still, listen to me, do as you are told and now do a written assessment – it just doesn't suit many boys and so they underachieve. Adventurous activities will not solve the problem of boys' underachievement on its own, but it will at least help them to enjoy their schooling and feel motivated to discover more for themselves through reading and writing, problem solving, design and scientific experimentation.

Girls aren't left out, though! Boys desperately need adventurous activities in order to progress. Many girls are already efficient and effective learners – they may not *need* these activities, but they will *want* them.

The recent changes that the Early Years Foundation Stage guidance have ushered in will gradually spread through Key Stages 1 and 2. There will be a less prescriptive approach to the curriculum and more freedom to bring the type of activities promoted in this book into your day-to-day teaching. The emphasis will be much more on enquiry-based learning and learning in the outdoor classroom.

Who is this book for? Aims and purposes

During nearly 20 years of teaching I have always tried to make learning practical, exciting and fun. Many teachers have asked me for advice on doing the activities that are in this book. I have run training courses on some of the themes here. This book is an attempt to put the ideas into a written form that will be accessible to all teachers.

The only thing stopping you from cooking on an open fire with your children or building a rope bridge, for example, may be unfamiliarity. You haven't done it before and you are a bit apprehensive about having a go. You are worried what your headteacher might have to say about it, let alone the parents! I have experienced all these feelings at different times. The thing that has kept me going is that when I was a boy I loved climbing trees and getting muddy – and I learned a great deal through doing these things! As a parent I know that my daughters have benefited from this approach to using our leisure time together. When I do practical activities with children I see real learning happening – and so will you.

If you are a school leader, the aim of this book is to get you to initiate change in your school and bring these activities into your curriculum. You know you want a more creative curriculum; this book will help you achieve that.

This book aims to:

- get teachers excited about adventurous activities so they will get children excited about this way of learning
- get children moving all their muscles – including their mental muscles
- help usher in a creative curriculum
- provide detailed advice to help you overcome any apprehension you might feel about this approach
- provide information to help you link up with organisations that can support you in this.

How to use this book

Overview of contents

The book is divided into two sections and concludes with useful appendices to help you continue developing the theme of adventurous activities in your school.

Section 1 – Adventurous activities in context

This section looks at research on how children learn and why boys and girls need to be given different opportunities in order to be treated equally. There are full references for the research evidence if you wish to pursue the pedagogical implications of using these activities. Also included in this section is information on leadership in the context of these activities– how to make them part of a whole-school approach. There is detailed advice on planning at a whole-school and class level. Information on assessment, progression and differentiation ensures that the needs of the individual child are met.

Section 2 – The activities

The majority of the book is made up of 75 adventurous activities, which are laid out in such a way that you will be able quickly to identify activities you want to try. I recommend that you read through Section 1 before embarking on the activities.

Appendices

These provide a wealth of practical information that will allow you to find all the resources and support you need to make your school an adventurous school.

Using the book

This is a book of ideas. No pathway through the activities is suggested. In keeping with the spirit of adventure and discovery that this book seeks to promote, you are free to select individual activities to do randomly when you feel like it or construct your own whole-school plan that says which classes will do which activities. There is some advice on doing this in the leadership and planning sections.

The activities in the book are arranged in themes to help you quickly locate the activities that will fit in with your class work. Each theme section opens with an introduction. There are details of National Curriculum links and general health and safety advice for that section. There are also literacy links. Part of the philosophy of the book is that reading and writing, speaking and listening should emerge from practical and exciting learning experiences. The literacy links show you how to do this.

Each individual activity contains the following information:

- Rationale – explains why you might choose to use this activity
- Learning objectives – details what aspects of the curriculum Early Years and Key Stage 1 children will cover through the activity
- Resources – tells you what you will need
- Introducing the activity – suggests practical ways of getting the children interested in the subject of the lesson
- Conducting the activity – gives step-by-step directions as to how to do the activity
- Health and safety – highlights any key points you will need to take into consideration

- Follow-up activities – suggests where you might go once you have completed this activity
- Teaching points – in the margin of each activity you will find interesting facts related to the subject of the activity
- Diagrams – many of the activities include step-by-step diagrams to ensure that following the instructions is as straightforward as possible.

Curriculum change

Over the last 20 years there has been almost continual change to the curriculum we deliver to our children. Whatever changes may come our way in the future, rest assured that all the activities in this book are timeless. They are the kind of activities that children have engaged with for generations. You will find a place for adventurous activities in any curriculum.

Health and safety statement

This book is intended as a guide and stimulus to creative learning. While health and safety guidance is given for each activity it is ultimately your responsibility to ensure your children are kept safe.

Before leading any adventurous activity you must ensure that your intended schedule and activities comply fully with the health and safety policies of your own school and those of your own local authority.

Section 1

Adventurous activities in context

Leadership, planning and assessment

Leadership for adventurous activities

If you are a headteacher or member of the senior leadership team, you have an important role to play in the development of an adventurous approach to the curriculum.

Why adopt a whole-school approach?
Your individual teachers may adopt some of these activities as individuals in their class teaching, but if you adopt a whole-school approach you will reap huge learning rewards. The key benefits I have found are that adventurous activities:

- Help engage boys in learning
- Bring a creative dimension to the curriculum
- Help develop cross-curricular links
- Are enjoyable for children and staff.

A creative dimension to the curriculum shifts is often cross-curricular and brings a fresh focus on the bedrock of learning such as thinking skills, problem solving, cooperative learning and enquiry as opposed to knowledge-focused learning where specific information is the key.

Other benefits to adventurous activities are that they give new and valuable experiences to many children who would otherwise not have the opportunity, hopefully give children a long-lasting love of the outdoors that will help lead to a healthy and fulfilling lifestyle as a adult, and give children views on the natural world, raising awareness of issues of sustainability and conservation.

Getting started
You can initiate change yourself by borrowing a class for an afternoon and dipping into this book to select an activity. You may then feel motivated to encourage your teachers to try out a few activities.

When you reach the stage where people are getting fired up about adventurous activities you can adopt a more formal approach. Make adventurous activities the focus of a staff meeting and discuss with your staff how they want to roll out this approach.

You might decide to stage an Adventurous Activities Week in the same way you would run a Science Week or Art Week. The whole school goes adventurous for just one week and you use the experience to help integrate adventurous activities into your curriculum on a more regular basis.

Your school may choose to have an Adventurous Activities Coordinator; someone with an enthusiasm for this approach who then inspires and encourages other members of staff.

You may decide to run some additional afterschool clubs such as a Nature Club or Survival Club and bring adventurous activities into your school that way.

Target setting

Adventurous activities do not fit neatly into a tick box or sub-level approach to assessment and this can make it more challenging to set targets that are recognisable to your school improvement partner or Ofsted.

I still find SMART a useful acronym for target setting, even after all these years. Make your targets for using adventurous activities in your school:

- Specific
- Measurable
- Achievable
- Realistic
- Time-related.

In terms of planning for adventurous activities, you might set a target such as 'During the summer term each teacher will plan and carry out three adventurous activities'.

Targeting whole-class and individual pupil progress in adventurous activities is more challenging but you can link it in with your other target-setting work on literacy or numeracy. Use the literacy links in each section of this book to help expand your children's horizons when it comes to writing. The activities in the design and technology and gardening sections are particularly suited to enhancing children's shape, space and measure skills. Make the use of adventurous activities one of a range of targets aimed at raising standards in literacy and numeracy in your school improvement plan.

Planning for learning

Planning for learning is a key part of our work as teachers. This is particularly so when it comes to adopting an adventurous approach to the curriculum as these activities will need to be carefully planned in to your current schemes of work. While we do have a National Curriculum and the units within the QCA schemes of work can sometimes feel like a straightjacket, we do actually have considerable freedom in how we deliver the curriculum. As a class teacher you can choose to insert adventurous activities into your termly and weekly planning. As a member of the leadership team you can choose to plan for an adventurous curriculum and map out a whole-school long-term planning grid that emphasises this.

A structured approach

Each school will have its own system of grids and charts mapping out the curriculum. There is, however, an underlying structure, which it is worth acknowledging:

- **Long-term planning** covers the whole year. It is where you map out the curriculum you have to cover in each year group. A long-term planning grid will detail what you are going to cover in which term.
- **Medium-term planning** gives further details on the themes and curriculum content you will be covering in a term. It is where you map out your weekly agenda over a period of five to eight weeks.
- **Short-term planning** shows what your class are going to cover each week or fortnight, depending on how your school approaches this level of planning. This is where you give a greater level of detail on each activity – what your objectives are, how you are going to deliver them, what resources you will need and what outcome you are aiming for.

Adventurous activities, the National Curriculum and QCA

When the National Curriculum was introduced in the late 1980s many schools continued with their topic-based approach to planning and delivering the curriculum. The elements of the National Curriculum were shaped and crafted to fit existing themes such as The Ancient Egyptians or People Who Help Us. Learning remained cross-curricular to a large extent.

This worked well for many schools, but with national testing and the introduction of the literacy and numeracy strategies pressure increased to deliver each subject individually in what could be described as a more secondary model. The unit structure of the QCA schemes of work reinforces this.

After nearly 20 years of change we have what feels like an extremely rigid curriculum. While government ministers are keen to emphasise that much of this is non-statutory or simply guidance, it is still very much the case that Ofsted want to see results. It is a brave headteacher who abandons the QCA schemes of work. Even with the current climate of curriculum change these activities are as relevant today as they were when I was a child over 30 years ago.

Adventurous activities and the creative curriculum

Having worked in many schools around the country, I see it as a sad reflection of our education system that almost every Year 6 child in the country will make a slipper in design and technology.

They will only make one slipper – two would at least be useful! Why not make a glove or a hat? And this approach is everywhere, in all subjects at all ages. Whether it is designing and evaluating a sandwich, improving the view from the classroom window or memorising the names of Henry VIII's wives, we have become obsessed with every child doing the same thing.

Some schools are adopting a more creative approach and this is where adventurous activities will come into their own. In planning for a cross-curricular thematic or topic-based approach, schools are not going back to the 1970s or 1980s. Educational evolution is not a cyclical process; it is more like an upwards spiral. We can now revisit cross-curricular planning with the objective-focused advantages that the literacy and numeracy strategies encouraged us to follow.

Topic-based learning in the 1980s could be a bit woolly, with different elements of the curriculum crow-barred into place to make it all fit. The sharper focus of recent years means that we can take responsibility for the curriculum – we know more now about effective planning, monitoring, assessment and subject leadership.

Some schools are venturing forth into the age of the creative curriculum. They are looking at the curriculum afresh and repackaging it. Some use QCA units where they want to and write their own units where they feel they can do a better job.

If your school is moving down this line then make the case for including the adventurous activities in this book within your new style curriculum.

Yearly planning (long-term)

This will be at a whole-school level and details what each year group has to cover in each of the National Curriculum subjects over the year. A school that is thinking along the lines of adventurous activities could highlight specific areas for each year group to approach in an adventurous way.

If you are just starting out on an adventurous approach as a class teacher, earmark one or two curriculum subjects and themes where you think you might like to try introducing some of the activities in this book.

Termly planning (medium-term)

This is the first layer of planning that is at the teacher level. This is where you get the chance to make your curriculum adventurous if yours is not yet an adventurous school. Your yearly long-term grid will show in which term you are going to cover which subjects and themes. At the medium-term level you get to decide on the approach you will adopt to those themes. If your school follows the units of the QCA schemes of work there is still considerable opportunity for adventurous activity. On the following three pages the grids show the adventurous activities described in this book assigned to the QCA units for Year1 and Year 2.

NC subject	QCA theme	Adventurous activity
Art and design	**Unit 1A** Self-portrait	
	Unit 1B Investigating materials	Art: A living willow dome Make an Iron Age pot
	Unit 1C What is sculpture?	Art: A living willow dome Found art
	Unit 2A Picture this!	
	Unit 2B Mother Nature – designer	Art: Natural dyes
	Unit 2C Can buildings speak?	
Citizenship	**Unit 01** Taking part – developing skills of communication and participation	Woodcraft: Cooking on a campfire Build a shelter Leave a trail Codes and signals Hiking
	Unit 02 Choices	
	Unit 03 Animals and us	Gardening: Keeping chickens
	Unit 04 People who help us – the local police	
	Unit 05 Living in a diverse world	Gardening: African gardens Our wonderful world: Festivals around the world
	Unit 06 Developing our school grounds	Our wonderful world: Improving our local environment
Design and technology	**Unit 1A** Moving pictures	
	Unit 1B Playgrounds	Design and technology: Build your own adventure course Woodcraft: Tying knots
	Unit 1C Eat more fruit and vegetables	Design and technology: Cultural cooking
	Unit 1D Homes	Design and technology: Big construction Build an igloo Nature: Give a hedgehog a hibernation home Build a bird box
	Unit 2A Vehicles	Design and technology: Cotton reel car Build a go-kart
	Unit 2B Puppets	Design and technolo gy: Junk dragon puppets
	Unit 2C Winding up	Design and technology: Cotton reel car
	Unit 2D Joseph's coat	

NC subject	QCA theme	Adventurous activity
Geography	Unit 1 Around our school – the local area	Our wonderful world: Making landscapes Our local geography
	Unit 2 How can we make our local area safer?	
	Unit 3 An island home	
	Unit 4 Going to the seaside	Nature: Rock pooling and beachcombing
	Unit 5 Where in the world is Barnaby Bear?	Our wonderful world: Travel the world Woodcraft: Making and reading maps
History	Unit 1 How are our toys different from those in the past?	Role-play: Knights and castles Pirate Day Small world play: Superhero HQ
	Unit 2 What were homes like a long time ago?	Our wonderful world: Local history timeline
	Unit 3 What were seaside holidays like in the past?	Our wonderful world: Historical drama days
	Unit 4 Why do we remember Florence Nightingale?	Our wonderful world: Living history – frozen pictures
	Unit 5 How do we know about the Great Fire of London?	Role-play: Fire!
Science	Unit 1A Ourselves	Role-play: Emergency ward
	Unit 1B Growing plants	Gardening: Create a vegetable garden Growing potatoes Growing vegetables from seeds Plant a mini-orchard Nature: Grow your own tree Estimate the height and age of a tree Bark casting Role-play: Garden centre Small world play: The Underwater Kingdom
	Unit 1C Sorting and using materials	Science: Make a magnetic compass
	Unit 1D Light and dark	Nature: Make a moth trap Science: The night sky Make a sundial Make a pinhole camera Make a periscope Small world play: Lost in Space Woodcraft: Finding north and telling the time by the sun

Science (continued)	Unit 1E Pushes and pulls	
	Unit 1F Sound and hearing	Nature: Nature games
	Unit 2A Health and growth	
	Unit 2B Plants and animals in the local environment	Gardening: Make a wormery Make your own compost bin Keeping chickens Nature: Become a nature detective Take a plaster cast footprint Bird feeding station Build a bird hide to watch birds up close Indoor wildlife pond Pond-dipping expedition Making mini habitats for minibeasts Ant town Rock pooling and beachcombing
	Unit 2C Variation	Nature: Minibeast trail Life cycles – butterflies Life cycles – frogs
	Unit 2D Grouping and changing materials	Science: Make your own paper Build an erupting volcano Small world play: The Pirates of Volcano Island
	Unit 2E Forces and movement	Design and technology: Making and flying kites Science: Weather – recording, predicting and enjoying Make an electromagnet Woodcraft: Build a rope bridge
	Unit 2F Using electricity	Design and technology: Light up a lighthouse

If you are teaching in Reception the EYFS guidance gives you even greater freedom. In following table you can see how I included adventurous activities in my medium-term planning for a term of work on Africa with a Reception class using the EYFS guidance. Just two of the areas of learning and development are included here as examples. This was in a school that had not adopted an adventurous approach to the curriculum, so it was a matter of me as class teacher making sure that I made time for these activities.

EYFS: Creative development **Term: Five** **Class: Oak**

Development matters 40 to 60+ months	Spontaneous learning opportunities and ongoing	Planned activities	Events, outings and visitors
Being creative 1. Talk about personal intentions, describing what they were trying to do 2. Respond to comments and questions, entering into dialogue about their creations 3. Make comparisons and create new connections. **Exploring media and materials** 4. Explore what happens when they mix colours 5. Choose particular colours to use for a purpose 6. Understand that different media can be combined to create new effects 7. Experiment to create different textures 8. Create constructions, collages, paintings and drawings 9. Use ideas involving fitting, overlapping, in, out, enclosure, grids, and sun-like shapes 10. Work creatively on a large or small scale. **Creating music and dance** 11. Begin to build a repertoire of songs and dances 12. Explore the different sounds of instruments 13. Begin to move rhythmically. **Developing imagination and imaginative play** 14. Introduce a storyline or narrative into their play 15. Play alongside other children who are engaged in the same theme 16. Play cooperatively as part of a group to act out a narrative.	• Collage with different fabrics, papers, foods and materials • Painting (finger, bubble, hand, splatter) with different sized brushes, different types of paint on different sized, shaped and textured paper • Printing with string, shapes, food, leaves, etc • Drawing with pencils, pens, crayons, charcoal on different papers • Modelling with junk, clay, dough, construction, etc • Look at paintings and other forms of art and discuss • Recreate and make up new characters and stories through imaginative and small world play • Make music through singing, body sounds, classroom objects and musical instruments • Listen to wide range of music from around the world and from different times • Respond to music through painting, drawing, moving and writing.	**Music and dance:** • Drumming – syllable clapping • Rumble in the Jungle – noises and sounds. **Pattern:** • African clothing and beads • Animal skin patterns on salt dough models • Making and decorating African pots. **Painting and drawing:** • Handa's Surprise – observational drawing of fruit • Class picture of Elmer. **Small world play:** • African safari. **Assessment:** • Colour mixing circles • Notes in learning journey on choice of colours during observational drawing.	

EYFS: Knowledge and understanding of the world **Term: Five** **Class: Oak**

Development matters 40 to 60+ months	Spontaneous learning opportunities and ongoing	Planned activities	Events, outings and visitors
Exploration and investigation 1. Notice and comment on patterns 2. Show an awareness of change 3. Explain own knowledge and understanding, and ask appropriate questions of others. **Designing and making** 4. Construct with a purpose in mind, using a variety of resources 5. Use simple tools and techniques competently and appropriately. **ICT** 6. Complete a simple program on a computer 7. Use ICT to perform simple functions, such as selecting a channel on the TV remote control 8. Use a mouse and keyboard to interact with age-appropriate computer software. **Time** 9. Begin to differentiate between past and present 10. Use time-related words in conversation 11. Understand about the seasons of the year and their regularity 12. Make short-term future plans. **Place** 13. Notice differences between features of the local environment. **Communities** 14. Gain an awareness of the cultures and beliefs of others 15. Feel a sense of belonging to own community and place.	• Explore textures such as wet/dry sand, dough, shaving foam, cooked spaghetti, etc • Make DT models using junk • Explore surroundings, indoors and out – outdoor play, welly walks, etc • Access construction independently, build and develop new techniques • Develop cutting and sticking, joining and fixing skills • Use computers, calculators, programmable toys, tape recorders, cameras confidently • Discuss changes, patterns similarities, differences – calendar, weather, etc • Share learning journeys with families, talk about photos of themselves as babies, in school, active and doing things, now and in past • Develop language of time through sequencing events and daily routines.	**Getting to know Africa:** • Maps, atlases and globes • Jigsaws of the world and Africa • Looking at and discussing photos of people and animals • Foods from Africa – make hot chocolate and fruit salad. **Culture:** • Drumming and songs • Storytelling • Make African houses • Cooking on an open fire. **Travel:** • Turn role-play corner into a travel agent's shop • Build an aeroplane in front of interactive whiteboard with rows of chairs and a doorway and travel to Africa • Make passports • In-flight entertainment – *The Lion King*. **ICT:** • Espresso – African documentaries and news • Google maps – zoom in on Africa and look at aerial photos. **Assessment:** • Find Africa on a map of the world • Retell an African story • Drumming photos and notes in learning journey.	

Weekly planning (short-term)

This is the delivery level and planning needs to detail what you aim to achieve with your activity (the learning intention) and how you will differentiate for individual children. The resources you need to deliver the lesson and what you will actually do are recorded for each activity in the pages of this book and there is no need to copy that out. If your headteacher requires detail, simply photocopy the page and attach it to your short-term planning sheet.

On your school weekly planning grid, indicate the times of the week when you will deliver different activities. For each adventurous activity in this book there is detailed lesson plan. Use the adventurous activity planning sheet on p17 to record the activity you are going to do, its links to the National Curriculum and any differentiation issues.

There is an evaluation section at the bottom of the adventurous activity planning sheet. It is important to monitor your planning to make sure it is effective. For each activity record what went well and what could be improved. Do this as soon as possible after completing the activity while it is fresh in your mind. Ask the children for their feedback and include this in your evaluation.

Adventurous activity planning sheet
Title of activity:
National Curriculum links:
Learning intentions:
Differentiation: More able Less able Individual children
Use of additional adult support:
Evaluation:

Assessment, progression and differentiation

The tide is turning in favour of ongoing teacher assessment for young children's learning. This suits the creative and flexible approach that adventurous activities require. It is important to be able to show progression in learning and the approach outlined here will help you achieve this. It also has to be appreciated that young children vary in their abilities for many reasons. A key benefit of the activities detailed in this book is that they allow learning to take place at many different levels. Differentiation within the activities will stretch your more able children and support your less able. It fact, you will be pleasantly surprised how your perception of who is less or more able will be turned on its head through using these activities.

Assessment

The Early Years Foundation Stage (EYFS) has encouraged us to adopt an ongoing observational approach to assessing young children's development. I would encourage you to extend this approach into Year 1 and Year 2.

In Reception many practitioners now have a learning journey record book for each child. This can be a spiral bound A4 booklet made up of blank pages with a couple of pages for each of the six areas of the curriculum – personal, social and emotional development, creative development and so on. Teachers, teaching assistants, any other adult helpers and parents can all write comments in the appropriate section based on their observation of the child. This becomes an ongoing record and is very valuable when assessing progress at the end of the year before children move into Year 1. It is also a very helpful tool for report writing.

With the more formal curriculum of Key Stage 2, many schools already have in place assessment grids to record children's progress in key literacy and numeracy skills, with sub-level indicators and so on. Other subjects are more often left to individual teachers to record progress. It is worth Year 1 and Year 2 teachers keeping an ongoing observational record similar to the Reception learning journey. You might do this with subject names for each section or you might carry the Reception curriculum areas on into subsequent years. Some schools that are adopting a more creative curriculum have opted for sections based on key learning skills such as thinking skills, problem-solving skills or research skills.

Another approach is to assess children's skills in the adventurous activities you are using – a sample record sheet is shown on p20. This has always been my approach to group activities and it works well. I have a record sheet on a clipboard while engaged in an activity and record quick notes about the skills the children are using, who is doing OK with the activity and who is struggling. I also like to include how I would adapt and improve the activity. Keep these record sheets in a section in your assessment folder and they will help you build up a picture of your children over the year.

Progression

If your school adopts an adventurous approach to the curriculum it would support progression in adventurous skills if a year-by-year plan were drawn up to show which activities will be undertaken by which class and when.

In terms of progression within the year for your own class, include references to individual adventurous activities within your long-term planning. Use your assessment records to adapt future activities based on how the children managed with each activity and include these adaptations in your medium- and short-term planning.

Differentiation

These activities are multi-skilled and will bring out different abilities in different children. You may be surprised to find that one of your less able boys is an expert on worms, for example, because his dad is a keen fisherman. You may find that one of your quiet little girls is a fantastic tree climber and den builder. I have found this myself!

There are two key approaches for you to adopt to extend and support different children. Firstly, try not to pigeonhole children based on assumptions about what they will be good at and what they will struggle at. Give everyone a chance and see how they get on. Make a note of any surprises and include opportunities to extend these children in your short-term planning. Secondly, be on the lookout for children's own creative ideas about where to take the activity next. These activities are ideally suited to giving children the opportunity to extend their own learning.

You will also find that the cooperative nature of many of these activities leads to children supporting each other as they learn together. You will often find the self-esteem of your less able children grows as they are able to tackle activities that their normally more able peers struggle with.

Adventurous activity assessment record sheet
Title of activity:
National Curriculum areas:
Learning intentions:
Skills: Tick key skills you want to focus on with this activity and add a note of what you are specifically looking for Cooperation   Gross motor skills Problem-solving   Fine motor skills Construction   Communication Imagination   Role-play Creativity   Following instructions Initiative   Subject knowledge
Assessment: Who coped very well with this activity? Who was fine with this activity? Who struggled and why?
Differentiation: How could I extend this activity to stretch the more able? How could I adapt this activity to support the less able?

Adventurous activities and child development

Adventurous activities are a practical and exciting way to enthuse and motivate all children, and particularly reluctant learners. This approach is underpinned by learning theory developed during the 20th century by the two giants of child development and psychology – Piaget and Vygotsky. In my experience these two names are rarely mentioned in staffrooms these days: it is worth reacquainting ourselves with the complementary approaches they developed. This will provide the solid bedrock of educational philosophy that underpins your work on adventurous activities.

Another issue is that of differences in the social, emotional, intellectual and physical development of boys and girls and how this will impact on their learning. Our education system with its over-structured learning outcomes and a rigid testing system is 'girl-friendly' at present. In this section we explore the developmental differences between boys and girls and ask how we can address these to ensure learning is accessible to all.

Learning theory

A sound understanding of learning theory brings a whole new dimension to teaching. It provides a foundation for you to build your practice on. You will see the children's actions and words in a whole new light and it will help you to tailor your teaching more closely to their learning.

Piaget

The Swiss psychologist Jean Piaget (1896–1980) did more than any other researcher to investigate the development of intelligence in children. During the early 1920s Piaget conducted research on intelligence tests. Frustrated by the simplicity of some of the testing methods, he began using psychiatric interviewing techniques in an endeavour to learn more about how children reasoned. Piaget became increasingly interested in the development of thinking and, as there was little work going on in this area, he gave it a name, **genetic epistemology**, meaning the study of the development of knowledge.

Piaget's theory of cognitive development

Piaget noticed that all babies are born with similar **biological equipment**. He called these **structures** and identified these as the senses, the brain and reflexes such as sucking and grasping.

At the start of life, a baby has a set of basic reflexes and a set of innate schema. A **schema** is a store of information about previous experiences and can be used to evaluate future experiences and make decisions about them.

Piaget proposed two ways in which schema become more complex:

- Assimilation is the process by which new information and experiences are fitted into existing schema
- Accommodation is the process by which schema are changed when new information cannot be assimilated.

Assimilation and accommodation are forms of **adaptation**, whereby the developing intellect makes changes as it learns new information.

Piaget's view stands between nature and nurture. The child is born with certain innate abilities and these develop and mature in a set sequence under the influence of the environment in which the child grows up.

Piaget proposed four stages of cognitive development:

Stage one: the sensorimotor stage (0 to 2 years)

Everything starts with reflexes – innate behaviour that occurs without conscious thought or planning. Sucking and throwing out arms and legs when startled are examples of innate reflexes.

Steadily the child begins to coordinate sensory information with motor information (such as seeing its own hand moving) and new schemas develop.

An important development in this first stage is **object permanence** – understanding that an object still exists even if it cannot be seen.

Stage two: the pre-operational stage (2 to 7 years)

This stage begins when the child starts to use symbols and language. The child is still unable to use operations, logical mental rules such as the rules of arithmetic, hence the title of the stage.

The pre-operational stage is divided into two sub-stages:
Preconceptual sub-stage (2 to 4 years): During this sub-stage the child's cognitive development becomes increasingly dominated by symbolic activity. He/she is able to use symbols to stand for actions; a toy doll stands for a real baby or the child role-plays mummy or daddy. Language also develops rapidly during this stage.

Intuitive sub-stage (4 to 7 years): This sub-stage is characterised by the way in which children base their knowledge on what they feel or sense to be true, yet they cannot explain the underlying principles behind what they feel or sense.

This is the sub-stage that Piaget studied most intensively. He identified three principal cognitive structures employed by the child during the intuitive sub-stage.

Egocentrism is concerned with viewing the world from a self-centred, subjective point of view.

Centration is about focusing on one aspect of a situation or task and ignoring other, possibly relevant, aspects. Conservation is an example of a logical rule that children in this sub-stage are unable to use: if a child is shown two balls of modelling clay of the same size and they agree that they are the same size, they are unable to see that they remain the same size when one is rolled out into a sausage shape.

Irreversibility is the inability to work backwards to your starting point.

Stage three: the concrete operational stage (7 to 11 years)

Intuition is replaced by the use of logical rules. Conservation is a good example. The concrete operational child is able to comprehend the concept of conservation where the pre-operational stage child is not.

Piaget considered that a child's understanding is still limited by actual experience of the 'concrete' world and believed that at this stage children struggle to grasp ideas that are hypothetical or abstract.

Stage four: the formal operational stage (12 years onwards)

The child is capable of abstract and systematic thought and will construct a plan of action when confronted with a problem to solve. They will take into account various factors and explore possibilities.

Reflect on your own experience of child development and you will be able to identify these stages and processes in the children you know. I have found that matching the theory to reality in this way has helped to embed this learning in my own mind and that has made a difference to the way I teach.

Vygotsky

Piaget took the view that the child was like a **scientist**, discovering and inventing the world anew for themselves. Vygotsky's view was of the child as an **apprentice**, benefiting from the accumulated experience of the culture by which he or she is surrounded.

Vygotsky's theory of social-cultural cognitive development

Vygotsky died at the age of 38, before his theory was fully developed. Since his death, Vygotsky's ideas have been worked into a coherent theory and this focuses on three areas.

Cultural aspects

Vygotsky took a social-cultural approach. Children do not start afresh, learning everything for themselves; they can draw on the accumulated wisdom of previous generations.

'Each generation stands on the shoulders of the previous one', is how Vygotsky portrayed this. The intellectual, material, scientific and artistic achievements of the previous generation are taken over by the current generation, developed further and then handed on to the next generation.

Vygotsky called the things that are handed on **cultural tools**. He identified language as the most essential cultural tool for three reasons:

1. Language is the main way in which society's experience is passed on from generation to generation
2. Language enables children to regulate their own activities
3. As it becomes internalised, language becomes the principal tool of cognitive functioning – the child moves from talking to themselves when engaged in play or problem-solving to thinking for themselves.

Interpersonal aspects

This is the area in which Vygotsky has had the most profound influence. He recognised that cognitive development results from interacting with another more knowledgeable and more competent person. This is the key to cognitive progress.

Intellectual competencies emerge through internalising problem-solving strategies first encountered while working with another person on a joint task. Cognitive development progresses from joint regulation (we do it together) to self-regulation (I do it for myself).

Vygotsky saw the best indicator of a child's potential as being what he or she could achieve when working with the support and encouragement of a more competent person.

To develop this idea further, Vygotsky proposed the Zone of Proximal Development (ZPD). In this context proximal simply means 'next'. The ZPD represents the gap between what the child already knows and what they are capable of learning with assistance. These are the 'buds of development' rather than the 'fruits'. Tasks in the ZPD are those that the child currently finds too difficult to accomplish alone but which can be accomplished with the support and encouragement of a more skilled person.

Individual aspects

Unlike Piaget, Vygotsky paid little attention to the role of the individual. He did not focus on the stages of development or the ages at which these might occur. Like Piaget, he did see the child as an active participant in learning rather than a passive recipient of information from other people.

Vygotsky in the classroom

Vygotsky's ideas are widely used in classrooms – often without practitioners being fully aware of their origins. The most commonly applied is the **scaffolding** of learning.

Scaffolding is a term that most of us have heard from time to time. Essentially it means that a more experienced person offers support, encouragement and guidance to a learner, as appropriate. The key term is 'as appropriate'. Guidance can be given in two forms:

1. When the learner runs into difficulty, **specific** instructions are given
2. When the learner is coping well, only **general** encouragement is given.

The 'scaffold' is provided by the expert and this allows the child to climb higher. Scaffolding is a powerful technique employed quite naturally and unconsciously by many good parents and teachers. An awareness of these definitions may help you to be more aware of when this is happening in your setting.

The important thing is for the adult to remain flexible and constantly modify what they are offering in response to what the child is doing. Scaffolding emphasises the social-interactive nature of learning and describes quite clearly the conditions most suitable to learning. It is also crucial to remember that, in time, we all learn to scaffold for ourselves – self-instruction. The goal of learning is to become an independent learner. Scaffolding can help achieve this.

Children also learn from each other and two phrases are employed to describe the different ways in which this can be promoted:

- **Collaborative learning** involves children who are at similar levels of competence working together in pairs or in groups
- **Peer tutoring** involves a more knowledgeable child providing guidance to another child in order to bring him/her up to a higher level of competence in a task. Research has shown that this not only benefits the child who is receiving the guidance; it also promotes learning in the child expert.

Variety is essential in developing this approach in the classroom. If children only ever work with the same children in groups or pairs it severely limits the scope for them to learn from each other.

Applying learning theory to adventurous activities

Many of the activities in this book will give you the opportunity to see Piaget and Vygotsky's theories in action. Particularly, if you have the chance to teach across the EYFS and KS1, you can place individual children alongside Piaget's stages of development, which will help your own understanding. Being aware of where individual children are developmentally will help you in your planning and assessment.

Scaffolding is key to children's learning in adventurous activities. As you plant potato tubers with children and share your knowledge of soil, weeds, worms and so on, they will move into new Zones of Proximal Development.

Boys and girls are different

When I trained as a teacher in the early 1980s we were encouraged to see all children, boys and girls, as the same; we had to treat them exactly the same and give them exactly the same provision. I am now convinced that this philosophy is at the heart of the problem we are currently facing with boys' attainment.

A few years ago, when I first started to look in detail at boys' learning, some people would say to me, 'Yes, but intra-gender differences are greater than inter-gender differences, so we shouldn't spend too much time on different curricula for boys and girls'. It took me a little while to get my head around this! What they were basically saying is that the differences within a gender are wider than those between genders, so let's carry on as normal! I disagree with this assessment and believe that it allows us to ignore the issue.

Let's take a look at the statistics: Foundation Stage Profile Results for England for 2007/2008 show that girls continue to outperform boys in all 13 assessment scales. The gap is particularly wide in the following areas:

- Social development (10 percentage points difference between boys and girls)
- Emotional development (11 percentage points)
- Linking sounds and letters (11 percentage points)
- Reading (11 percentage points)
- Writing (18 percentage points)
- Creative development (14 percentage points).

A 2007 report by the Joseph Rowntree Foundation entitled 'Tackling Low Educational Achievement' found that these early gender differences reflect a pattern that can continue right up to the age of 16: boys outnumber girls by 20 per cent as low achievers at GCSE.

There may be as much difference between the most and least able girl as there is between the most and least able boy, but there are more underachieving boys than underachieving girls. We need to acknowledge this and do something about it.

The Department for Children, Schools and Families now agrees with this. In 2008 it published a booklet called 'Confident, Capable and Creative: Supporting Boys' Achievements' targeted at practitioners in the Early Years Foundation Stage. The booklet states that, 'The qualities and skills that are most valued by schools, the ability to communicate orally and represent ideas on paper, are often the very aspects of learning that boys find most difficult.' I agree! Furthermore, by trying to force young boys into a girl-style learning approach, where they sit nicely, listen carefully and answer politely, we are actually turning them off learning at the very start of their learning journey.

I am not saying that all girls are 'compliant and passive recipients of new skills and knowledge', nor that all boys are 'active learners and problem solvers', to take a couple of quotes from the booklet. What I am saying is that they are different and we need to treat them differently.

The Organisation for Economic Co-operation and Development (OECD) backs up this view in a report entitled, 'Starting Strong'. The report asserts, 'We know that to give boys and girls equal rights in the Early Years means to give them different and specific opportunities. It is not sufficient to say that everything... is open to all children, since at this age children choose gender-specific activities.'

Social differences

In the classes I have taught over the years the girls are friendlier towards each other. The boys tend to be more antagonistic. The girls generally try to resolve any disagreement over access to resources amicably. If they can't then they ask an adult to get involved and each side will explain the situation in the expectation that the adult will sort the matter out. Most of the boys will try to resolve a disagreement by the use of force – grab, shove, shout.

A nationwide report on Australian students' social development found that while many boys and girls get along well with others, more girls than boys feel that it is important to relate well to others, contribute to community wellbeing and adhere to rules and conventions. The study concluded that, 'Boys are less concerned with these aspects of social development than are girls.' (Ainley et al, 1998). The gap gets wider as children get older. The report goes on, 'Empathy may operate as a brake on aggressive behaviour. Much of the research into empathy has reported a consistent gender pattern, with girls showing higher levels of empathy than boys.' It is these empathic skills that allow girls to reach the higher levels of our EYFS assessment scales.

While there is some evidence of a link between differences in brain structure in boys and girls and the development of social skills, there is plenty of evidence that social conditioning plays a big part, too. Parents just don't seem to be able to help themselves! Girls are actively encouraged to be 'kind and friendly' (ie, be passive) and boys are taught to 'stand up for yourself' (ie, be aggressive).

There will, of course, be other factors in the social development of young children. Being an only child, for example, seems to be significant in difficulties with the development of skills needed to manage conflict. Position in the family, degree of attachment to carer, before and after school care arrangements may all play a role. Gender, however, is an important difference that teachers need to take into account in the planning of activities to promote and develop social interaction.

Emotional differences

Around the age of four to five some very interesting changes take place in children's ability to understand, control and express emotions. At this age children acquire the ability to alter their emotional expression. They may feel hurt on the inside after a disagreement, but they smile and say it doesn't matter. This is an important skill for children to develop from the point of view of social interaction. This is reflected in the EYFS assessment scales with 'consideration of the consequences of words and actions on themselves and others' being a higher-order skill.

The ability to feel one way inside and express it outwardly in a different way is known as 'display rules' and they are complex. In the *Encyclopedia of Childhood and Adolescence* (Kagan, 1996), Janice Zeman of the University of Maine says that this skill 'requires that children understand the need to alter emotional displays, take the perspective of another, know that external states need not match internal states, have the muscular control to produce emotional expressions, be sensitive to social contextual cues that alert them to alter their expressivity, and have the motivation to enact such discrepant displays in a convincing manner.'

There is evidence that a group of neurons in the brain called the amygdala have a strong influence on emotions, particularly on the memory of emotional reactions. There are physiological differences in the amygdala between boys and girls. Girls appear to be able to talk about their feelings sooner than boys because they develop the connection between the amygdala and the cerebral cortex much earlier than boys. The cerebral cortex plays a key role in thought and language.

Children who have difficulties with their emotions may play up or they may withdraw from situations. In my own classes I have seen that boys tend to behave in negative ways during emotional situations. In the context of display rules they have not yet learned how to feel one way and express themselves in another, more socially acceptable way.

Intellectual differences

The evidence from the EYFS profile shows that the difference between boys and girls is greater in reading and writing, but much less so in numeracy and physical development and lowest of all in knowledge and understanding of the world.

Research into the physical structure of the brain does show differences between boys and girls, which may go some way to explaining differential attainment. Girls have consistently shown an advantage over boys in verbal abilities and this is related to differences in the organisation of the brain. Girls acquire language earlier than boys and have a greater ability to concentrate for longer during a conversation. Girls have better memories and can retrieve information more quickly from the memory. Boys tend to be more visually and spatially aware and are better at throwing and catching, for example. They are better at mental manipulation of images, which may benefit problem-solving, design and construction skills (Hamaan, 2005).

There is also evidence that different rates of hearing development are more likely to benefit girls, who develop clearer hearing earlier than boys (Ismail and Thornton, 2002).

While there is increasing evidence for a genetic influence on gender differences in intellectual development, the influence of nurture and environment is still strong. The debate now is less about nature versus nurture and more about what percentage each contributes to the various differences.

Family and social influence have an impact, with girls' rights as learners having been more strongly asserted in recent decades. Girls now outperform boys across the board academically. One of the reasons we can be a little squeamish about discussing gender differences and the impact this is having on boys' underachievement may be that we don't want to downplay the successes in female emancipation in recent times.

Physical differences

Gross motor skills such as running, jumping and climbing tend to develop slightly faster in boys. Fine motor skills, including the ability to hold and use a pencil, develop faster in girls. This may be one factor in giving girls an advantage in school.

There is also some evidence that boys' physically aggressive, impulsive play and risk-taking behaviour may be linked to brain development. The male hormone testosterone causes brain development in the left hemisphere of the growing foetus to slow and allows the right hemisphere to dominate. The right brain is associated with visual-spatial functions and the left brain with language. It is, of course, far more complex than this and individual differences within gender may be greater than the difference between genders when it comes to brain function. It is also important to understand that while some functions of the left or right brain may be preferred by individuals, the word 'dominate' is probably overused. In reality the two hemispheres of the brain cooperate much more than is generally believed (Nikolaenko, 2005. Sax, 2006).

Putting this complexity to one side, those of us who work with young children know that boys are more active and physical and 'take up a lot of space on the playground', whereas girls will sit down and get on with a task.

Are gender differences important?

Brain research is not absolutely conclusive. Neither are behavioural studies looking at the impact of nurture and environment on the social, emotional, intellectual and physical development of young children. What we do know from personal experience is that boys and girls are different. While there are boys who like to sit and write and girls who like to build space rockets, it is generally true that boys and girls have different approaches to learning. As teachers we must provide different opportunities in order to ensure that the needs of all are met.

In looking at developmental differences it is clear that in most areas boys will develop the learning skills that girls have; it just takes them longer. If this is the case, why the large gap at age 16? Surely boys would have caught up by then? We need to think in terms of the impact of getting it wrong at a young age on the future development of the learner. If we are not providing boys with adventurous activities that meet their needs when they are three, four or five, they are more likely to disengage from school and learning. This pattern becomes ingrained and they carry it with them through the rest of their school lives. This is why the early years are so important.

Applying knowledge of gender differences to adventurous activities

It is this research on the impact of gender differences that provided the impetus for the writing of this book. It is my belief that we do need to treat boys and girls differently in order to give them equal opportunities. Having said that, all the activities in this book are accessible to both boys and girls – it is just that the boys *really* need these activities whereas most of the girls would tick along OK without them.

When you are planning adventurous activities, be aware of the social, emotional, intellectual and physical differences between boys and girls. Boys will need support in sharing resources and the more practical activities you do, the more chance they will have to develop these. Boys are not particularly empathetic – no matter how much circle work we do – but they can develop empathy if they work on gardening and wildlife projects where they come into contact with the diversity of life and the need for us to take responsibility for other living things. Boys do need space to run around and climb. They just do! Boys need different types of experiences from girls in order to show their creative side.

When you are assessing children's learning, be aware of these developmental differences. Give boys the opportunity to show that they can do the things that they are supposed to be able to do at certain ages by offering them a greater range of 'boy-friendly' activities.

And finally

It is OK to acknowledge that boys and girls are different – we don't have to accept a 'one-size-fits-all' approach to the curriculum. Once you have got over that hurdle you will find your boys make good progress in their learning.

References

Ainley, J et al (1998) *Schools and the Social Development of Young Australians.* Australian Council for Educational Research, as quoted in 'Just boys, just girls and just schooling: Curriculum behaviours (including bullying) and gender', professional development discussion paper, South Australia Department of Education, Training and Employment (2001).

Cassen, R and Kingdon, G (2007) *Tackling Low Educational Achievement*, Joseph Rowntree Foundation, *www.jrf.org.uk/publications/tackling-low-educational-achievement*

DCSF (2008) *Confident, Capable and Creative: Supporting Boys' Achievements* *http://nationalstrategies.dcsf.gov.uk/node/88188*

DCSF: Foundation Stage Profile Results in England, 2007/08 *www.dcsf.gov.uk/rsgateway/DB/SFR/s000812/index.shtml*

Hamann, S (2005) 'Sex Differences in the Responses of the Human Amygdala' in *The Neuroscientist,* vol 11, no 4, 2005.

Ismail, H and Thornton, ARD (2003) 'The Interaction Between Ear and Sex Differences and Stimulus Rate' in Hearing Research, vol 179, no 1, May 2003. Elsevier.

Nikolaenko, N (2005) 'Sex Differences and Activity of the Left and Right Brain Hemispheres' in *Journal of Evolutionary Biochemistry and Physiology,* vol 41, no 6, November 2005. MAIK Nauka/ Interperiodica.

OECD (2006) *Starting Strong: Curricula and Pedagogies in Early Childhood Education and Care*

Sax, L (2006) *Why Gender Matters*, Broadway.

Zeman, J (1996) *The Gale Encyclopedia of Childhood and Adolescence,* ed J Kagan, Gale Cengage Learning.

Section 2

The activities

Theme: Nature

Nature: Introduction

When I was a small boy I was fascinated by the natural world around me. I grew up on a housing estate on the edge of a dormitory town in Essex so the natural world was a little thin on the ground. Fortunately my primary school had a field surrounded by a large, old hawthorn hedge which we would scurry under during break time in search of bugs and beasties. Our teachers encouraged us with the kind of activities that were prevalent in primary schools in the late 1960s and early 1970s: we kept tadpoles and watched them turn into froglets, we had a nature table and every now and then someone would bring in an abandoned bird nest or a broken blackbird egg they had found on their way to school and the whole morning's schoolwork would switch to focus on that. I also had parents who took me and my sisters out into the countryside for walks on Sundays and encouraged us to take an interest in nature. The natural world is still important to me and I encourage my own children to take an active interest in the insects, birds, mammals, trees and flowers with which we share this wonderful world. The habits we learn in childhood we carry through into adult life.

You don't have to live in the sticks to enjoy nature. In fact, many of our wild animals and plants can be spotted more easily in the city than out in the countryside. Your local park, a disused railway line that has been converted into a cycle track, a canal tow path and children's back gardens will provide opportunities for most of these activities.

In my experience children have an almost instinctive love of nature and certainly many adults spend their leisure time engaged in activities such as bird watching or walking in the countryside. I think the key to this human interest in nature is in its diversity, its beauty and in its endless fascination. This awareness is strong in young children and our role as teachers is simply to encourage and nurture it.

The following activities will help you do just that. I have been using these techniques for over 20 years in school and out of school. It has always been a source of great pleasure to me to see the look of wonder on a young child's face when they discover something new for themselves in the natural world.

Learning objectives

Here is an overview list of learning objectives for nature activities in general. Specific learning objectives are given for each activity.

Early Years Foundation Stage

Personal, social and emotional development

- Be confident to try new activities, initiate ideas and speak in a familiar group.
- Respond to significant experiences, showing a range of feelings when appropriate.

Communication, language and literacy

- Interact with others, negotiating plans and activities and taking turns in conversations.
- Sustain attentive listening, responding to what they have heard with relevant comments, questions and actions.

- Extend their vocabulary, exploring the meanings and sounds of new words.
- Attempt writing for different purposes.

Problem solving, reasoning and numeracy
- Count reliably up to ten everyday objects.
- In practical activities and discussion, begin to use the vocabulary involved in adding and subtracting.
- Use language such as 'more' and 'less' to compare two numbers.
- Use language such as 'greater', 'smaller', 'heavier' or 'lighter' to compare quantities.
- Use everyday words to describe position.

Knowledge and understanding of the world
- Investigate objects and materials by using all of their senses as appropriate.
- Find out about, and identify, some features of living things, objects and events they have observed.
- Look closely at similarities, differences, patterns and change.
- Ask questions about why things happen and how things work.

Physical development
- Use a range of small and large equipment.

Creative development
- Respond in a variety of ways to what they see, hear, smell, touch and feel.

Key Stage 1

The key curriculum area for the nature theme is science. Where there are links to other curriculum areas these are highlighted for each activity. With the dominance of QCA guidance in primary teaching it is sometimes forgotten that there is a sound National Curriculum underlying our work. Here are the relevant extracts from the science curriculum.

Sc1 Scientific enquiry
Knowledge, skills and understanding
Ideas and evidence in science
1. Pupils should be taught that it is important to collect evidence by making observations and measurements when trying to answer a question.

Investigative skills
2. Pupils should be taught to:

Planning
a. ask questions (for example, 'How?', 'Why?', 'What will happen if ... ?') and decide how they might find answers to them
b. use first-hand experience and simple information sources to answer questions
c. think about what might happen before deciding what to do
d. recognise when a test or comparison is unfair

Obtaining and presenting evidence

e. follow simple instructions to control the risks to themselves and to others
f. explore, using the senses of sight, hearing, smell, touch and taste as appropriate, and make and record observations and measurements
g. communicate what happened in a variety of ways, including using ICT (for example, in speech and writing, by drawings, tables, block graphs and pictograms)

Considering evidence and evaluating

h. make simple comparisons (for example, hand span, shoe size) and identify simple patterns or associations
i. compare what happened with what they expected would happen, and try to explain it, drawing on their knowledge and understanding
j. review their work and explain what they did to others.

Sc2 Life processes and living things
Knowledge, skills and understanding

Life processes

1. Pupils should be taught:

a. the differences between things that are living and things that have never been alive
b. that animals, including humans, move, feed, grow, use their senses and reproduce
c. to relate life processes to animals and plants found in the local environment.

Green plants

3. Pupils should be taught:

a. to recognise that plants need light and water to grow
b. to recognise and name the leaf, flower, stem and root of flowering plants
c. that seeds grow into flowering plants.

Variation and classification

4. Pupils should be taught to:

b. group living things according to observable similarities and differences.

Living things in their environment

5. Pupils should be taught to:

a. find out about the different kinds of plants and animals in the local environment
b. identify similarities and differences between local environments and ways in which these affect animals and plants that are found there
c. care for the environment.

Literacy links

There are many opportunities to develop children's writing skills through the activities within this nature theme section.

A wildlife journal

I still have my own wildlife journals from 30 years ago. I didn't start keeping one until I was 15. I wish I had kept some sort of record from my earliest days of wildlife exploring. Keeping a wildlife journal with details of the date, time and location of observations and findings is an important skill for any wildlife detective to develop.

Identification cards

Draw up a simple record card format including species name, size, colour, food and habitat for each animal and plant you spot in your school grounds. Store these in a box and other budding naturalists will be able to use them to identify the wildlife they see. Don't forget to include a picture of the species.

Research

Using the school library to find out more about the species they are spotting is not just something for children who can read and write effectively. I have done some very interesting research into underwater life with reception children using the illustrations on front covers of books as a means of selecting them. We have used illustrations in the books to generate questions we want to find the answers to and then I have read the book to the children while they listen out for the answers.

Older children can practise their non-fiction writing skills. You might like to produce class books on different habitats such as woodland or rivers. You could do books on groups such as birds or insects.

Nature watch blackboard

Fix a blackboard on a wall in your outdoor classroom so children can write on it any plants or animals they spot, with the date and time of their observation. You often see this at nature reserves and it is a way for naturalists to share information.

Health and safety

Many of these nature activities involve a certain amount of mud! Hand-washing is the primary health and safety issue. Some of the activities that require a degree of construction using scissors or a sharp knife will need adult supervision. Additional health and safety information is given for each activity where necessary. The key thing I always stress to children when we are out and about studying nature is – don't put anything in your mouth!

1. Become a nature detective

What is a nature detective?

A nature detective is someone who can tell the story of the activities of wildlife without actually seeing the living animal.

Why become a nature detective?

This is a great way to hone observational skills; it really gets children looking, listening, sniffing and touching. Tracking wildlife develops children's sense of awareness of the animals they share their world with.

Learning objectives

The main focus for learning with this activity for both EYFS and KS1 is to fully use the senses (except taste). Questioning skills is another key area. If we simply tell children that this is a fox footprint or this is a blackbird nest, we miss opportunities to get them talking about what they think the clues might tell us. Who left this footprint? Is the bird that made this nest big or small? Why do you think that?

Resources

- Magnifying glass
- Collecting pots and tubs
- Rubber gloves
- Tweezers
- Field guides such as the Field Studies Council's fold-out guides to animal tracks and signs and owl pellets.

Introducing the activity

Discuss the work of a real detective investigating a crime. Suppose there has been a burglary. You might like to start with a Burglar Bill book for an amusing introduction (*Burglar Bill*, Allan and Janet Ahlberg, 1999, Puffin). What clues would Burglar Bill leave behind? He might drop a glove. He might leave a footprint or finger print. Animals leave clues as they go about their daily or nightly activities. We don't often see mammals such as foxes or badgers but we can find clues that will tell us they have been there. We see lots of birds. They also leave tell-tale signs of where they have been such as the broken snail shells from a song thrush's meal.

Conducting the activity

While you are out and about on a walk in the countryside, at a local park or in the school grounds look for the following signs of wildlife:

Footprints: Around the muddy edge of a pond or along a muddy path is the best place to go searching for bird and mammal tracks. When you find some tracks, step back so you don't crush them with your own footprints. Take a look at the shape of the print. Can you see claw marks? Is it a bird or a mammal? How can you tell? Look at the pattern of the trail. The distance between each print will tell you if it is a big or small animal. If just the toe has touched the ground it may be a running animal. If the print is clear and deep with crisp edges the animal may have stopped here for a while and stood still.

Paths: Animals such as rabbits and foxes use the same paths over and over again. If you spot a thin path running through the grass or woodland floor, follow it. If the path runs under a fallen tree or under a fence you will know it is an animal path and not one made by humans. Keep following the path and it might take you to the animal's home. You could draw a sketch map of where the paths go.

Hair, fur and feathers: Where paths go under barbed wire fencing hair is often caught on the barbs. If the fur is reddish coloured, it is a fox. Grey for a rabbit and black/white for a badger. Feathers can often be found below where a bird is nesting; if you find a feather, look up and see if you can spot a nest in a nearby tree.

Feeding: Look for nuts with little holes drilled into them by the teeth of mice. Chewed leaves and bark may show that a deer has passed by. Broken snail shells next to a stone show that a song thrush has been feeding.

Bedding: If you are lucky enough to find a badger sett in woodland (look for a huge pile of earth outside a large hole) you may find piles of bracken or grass nearby. This is the old bedding that the badgers have chucked out – they are very house proud animals.

Nests: Late autumn is the time to go searching for old nests in the bare trees. Don't take the nest away – the bird might want to use it again next year.

Burrows: Mice and voles make small holes, rabbits and foxes make medium sized ones and badgers make really large ones. A fox's earth will have a strong musty smell around it. Place a stick over the entrance to the hole and return the next morning to see if the stick has been moved. This will tell you if the animal is using the hole or not. If you want to try to watch the animal at its home you will need to know this.

Faeces or dung (let's call it poo, shall we?): Bird poo, fox poo, rabbit poo – you will come across lots of it. Look but don't touch – it is a very valuable sign left by the birds and animals that have passed by. Rabbit poo is small and round and dark grey in colour; quite fibrous. If you find slightly larger poo and it is blacker in colour with a smooth gloss to it and a slight taper to one end this will probably be deer poo. Deer regularly make use of the same paths through woodland so look out for tracks if you find their poo on a path. Fox poo will be full of hair from its prey and is a green/grey colour. Badgers have a specific toilet place near their sett. They dig a shallow hole and use it again and again.

Pellets: You might see a buzzard or a kestrel or, if you are extremely lucky, an owl. Watch to see where it lands. Birds of prey have favourite places where they perch; on a fence post, telegraph pole or dead tree. Often they will cough up and spit out a pellet, which is made up of the bones, feathers and fur of their prey. Once the bird has moved on, look around on the ground below where you saw it perching to see if you can find any of these pellets. Back at school you can unpick the pellet using tweezers and wearing rubber gloves. You will find all manner of tiny bones from mice, voles and shrews.

Health and safety

The main point to emphasise is that some of the clues animals leave may carry germs and could cause illness. This shouldn't stop you from becoming a nature detective; learning to take risks in a responsible way is an important part of growing up.

- Always wear rubber gloves when handling bird pellets
- Don't touch poo! Just look.

Follow-up activities

If you become an effective nature detective it will help you see the actual animal or bird. If you find a song thrush's feeding site you might hide in a nearby bush and see if you can see the song thrush breaking open snail shells on its chosen rock.

The clues you find when out and about detecting nature can make an interesting display back in school. This activity will also fire up children's enthusiasm for research. This may be as simple as finding a picture of a dormouse to draw and place beside a display of nibbled nuts. For year two children it might involve making their own tracks and trails identification chart.

Teaching points

Encourage children to move quietly as you search for clues. The bird or mammal you are tracking may be close by and you may get a lucky glimpse.

Children can carry a small sketch pad with them to record the clues they find.

2. Take a plaster cast footprint

What is a plaster cast footprint?

This activity uses plaster of Paris to mould a mammal or bird footprint you have found embedded in mud.

Why make a plaster cast footprint?

Using plaster of Paris to cast the footprint of a mammal or bird is an exciting technique that allows you to keep a permanent trophy of your wildlife tracking. Children can compare the footprints of different mammals and birds. They can compare the footprints of wildlife to their own: 'Hey, I've got the same number of toes as a badger!'

Learning objectives

The taking of a plaster cast footprint is delicate work involving the physical skill of using simple tools and equipment. For EYFS children, this makes it a physical development (PD) activity. In knowledge and understanding of the world (KUW), it covers looking closely at similarities, differences, patterns and change. For KS1 children, this activity will help them to appreciate the diversity of living things.

Resources

- Plaster of Paris (can be bought at a chemist)
- Plastic bottle of water
- Strips of card 4cm wide and several different lengths – 20cm, 30cm and 40cm
- Paperclips
- A container for mixing the plaster
- A mixing stick
- An old knife
- A soft brush
- Newspaper to wrap the cast in for carrying back to school
- Black and white powder paint.

Introducing the activity

This activity grows out of the previous one on tracking wildlife and will be used when you find mammal or bird prints in mud. If you want to introduce the theme of footprints specifically, a fun way to do this is as follows. Sprinkle a fine dusting of plain white flour across your classroom carpet. Walk across the carpet in a big pair of boots and then again alongside in a pair of ordinary shoes. When the children arrive in the classroom this will provide the stimulus for a discussion about footprints: Who made these prints? How many people were there? Where are they going? What does the tread pattern tell us about the kind of footwear the person was wearing?

Conducting the activity

- Find a print – ideally, know in advance where some will be
- Fold a strip of cardboard around the print so it is big enough to fully encircle the print with a margin of about 2cm all round

- Use a paperclip to hold the cardboard circle
- Press the cardboard circle into the mud so it encloses the print
- Quickly mix the plaster of Paris to a thick but runny consistency (like treacle) with no lumps and pour carefully into the mould
- The plaster of Paris needs to be 2.5cm deep or it might break when dry
- Leave the plaster of Paris to dry for about 30 minutes
- When it is dry, carefully lift up the mould – some mud will come up with it
- Wrap the mould in newspaper and return to school
- Leave the mould to fully dry overnight
- Carefully remove mud from the print with an old knife and a soft brush
- Paint the raised footprint with black powder paint and the surrounding plaster of Paris with white powder paint
- Use reference books, field guides and the internet to identify the print and make a label to be displayed with it.

Health and safety

Just make sure the children wash their hands after making their plaster cast print and keep the plaster of Paris away from mouths.

Follow-up activities

Once the print cast is fully dry you can use it to make a reverse print in Plasticine. Spread petroleum jelly over the cast to prevent sticking and press the print into the Plasticine.

Display the prints on your class nature table with a picture of the mammal or bird that made it and some written research.

Make your own footprints by painting children's feet with powder paint and pressing onto sheets of sugar paper. This can lead into work on measuring footprints and comparing to the height of the individual.

Teaching points

After making one or two plaster casts children will be able to estimate how much plaster they need to mix for the size of footprint.

3. Bird feeding station

What is a bird feeding station?

For many people, feeding the birds might involve throwing some stale bread for ducks at the local park. For teachers and children there is a wide range of feeding strategies including bird tables and puzzles such as hidden food to test birds' ingenuity.

Why feed birds?

There are lots of myths around feeding birds and a good place to get accurate information is the website of the Royal Society for the Protection of Birds. This will tell you the times of year that birds appreciate feeding and what to feed them. We feed birds for two main reasons: firstly because our modern way of life has deprived many birds of valuable sources of food, and secondly because it provides the opportunity for us to study our feathered friends up close.

Learning objectives

Identifying and comparing bird species is a good way to develop the skills of discrimination (making and seeing distinctions) for EYFS children. This is another opportunity to look closely at similarities and differences (KUW). Two birds may be the same size and shape, but a different colour (a greenfinch and a house sparrow, for example). Another two (a blackbird and a crow, for example) are the same colour, but one is much bigger. KS1 children are looking at living things in their environment.

Resources

For the seed feeder:

- An empty one-litre plastic milk bottle
- A knife to cut through plastic (adult assistance)
- A marker pen
- A long, thin piece of rounded wood (dowelling).

For the bird cake:

- 500g of lard or suet
- A saucepan and stove (adult assistance)
- 1kg of mixed seeds, broken nuts, dried fruit, oatmeal, bits of cheese or cake crumbs
- Small yoghurt pots
- String.

Introducing the activity

On a cold winter's day ask the children what they had for breakfast. Ask them what the birds outside the window might be having for their breakfast. Get children to watch the birds over the course of the morning from the classroom window in pairs. They can record the kind of things the birds are eating – berries, worms, snails and insects.

Talk about your results. Do the children think the birds are finding life easy or difficult in this bad weather? What can we do to help them?

Conducting the activity

Make a seed feeder

- Mark out a rectangle across the face of the bottle about 1.5cm up from the bottom and on the opposite face to the handle. Make your rectangle 3cm tall and the same width as the bottle.

- Cut out the rectangle of plastic with a sharp knife (adult assistance)
- Cut two small holes opposite each other in the sides of the bottle and push a length of dowelling through so that the extending wood on each side acts as a perch for visiting birds
- Pour birdseed into the feeder from the top and replace the lid to stop rain getting in
- Hang on a tree in your school grounds where it can be seen from a classroom window – make sure it is in a cat-proof position.

Make a bird cake

- Melt the fat in a saucepan (adult assistance)
- Add a mixture of seeds, nuts, etc and stir well
- Lay a piece of string 15cm long in each yoghurt pot so one end touches the bottom and one end dangles over the edge
- Pour the fat/seed mixture into the yoghurt pot and arrange the string so it rises from the middle of the mixture
- Allow the mixture to set firmly overnight and then gently remove the bird cake from the mould
- If the cake breaks up, don't worry – just pop it on your bird table and the birds will still enjoy it
- Hang your bird cake on the tree with your seed feeder.

Teaching points
Teach children to use a saw safely to cut the dowelling for the bird feeder.

Health and safety

As these activities involve some cutting and heating it is important to carry them out in small groups with adult assistance.

Follow-up activities

Birds need water, not just for drinking but also for bathing, which helps maintain the health of their feathers. Provide a birdbath alongside your feeding area.

Keep a record of the birds that visit your feeding station and bird bath. A clipboard with a pencil attached by a piece of string kept on a windowsill will allow children speedily to write the name or draw a picture of the birds they see visiting.

A rota of children watching in pairs for ten minutes each over an hour-long period will provide the data for a bar chart to show frequency of visitors.

On the last weekend of January every year the RSPB organises the Big Garden Birdwatch and schools can take part too. Visit the RSPB website for details. (*www.rspb.org.uk*)

4. Build a bird hide to watch birds up close

Why build a bird hide?

Birds are highly visible and they fly, both of which make them exciting for children. They are also very nervous and difficult to get close to. Building a bird hide is the solution. Opportunities to watch birds will help children practise their observational skills. Identifying a bird and putting a name to it will bring a real sense of achievement. Recognising that species next time the child sees it reinforces the pleasure.

Learning objectives

Identification is the key skill and that involves careful looking as well as comparison. Is the bird I can see on the bird table the same as the one on the poster? Is it the same colour? Is it the right size? What is its beak like? What is its name? This covers similarities and differences for both EYFS and KS1. Counting and comparing birds and describing where they are will allow number, comparison and spatial awareness skills to develop for EYFS children. 'The blackbird is bigger than the blue tit. The greenfinch is hanging on the bird feeder under the bird table. The starling likes to strut on top of the table. We saw three goldfinches today; that's one more than yesterday.'

Give Year 2 children data-handling projects involving counting the birds that visit the table over the course of a week.

Resources

For the hide:

- Camouflage clothing – greens, greys and browns
- A large cardboard box
- Powder paints – green, grey and brown
- Camouflage netting – available from camping shops or army surplus stores
- Old sheets and blankets in camouflage colours
- Long bendy poles such as willow or hazel – about three metres long
- String
- Scissors to cut the string
- Old cushions.

To watch birds:

- Binoculars – toy plastic ones can give a reasonable magnification and discount supermarkets will sometimes sell proper adult binoculars for under £20
- Bird identification guides
- Pencil and notebook to record observations.

Introducing the activity

If you have a well established bird feeding table that attracts a lot of visitors you may want to get closer. If you have a bird nesting box in the school grounds or you have found a nest in a tree you may want to see the baby birds having their first flight. Explain to the children that these are the exciting observations you can make using a bird hide.

Ask the children what you will need to do if you want to get close to birds – be very quiet, move slowly, don't make any sudden movements, blend in with the environment, hide. How can we achieve these things?

Conducting the activity

Start with camouflage clothing. Ask children to bring in clothes in greens, greys and browns. Dress a child up and try to make them as camouflaged as possible. Face painting and a hat are a good idea. Get the child to sit close to your bird table or feeder – by a bush or with their back to a tree helps break up the outline of the child. Other children can watch from the classroom window and see if any birds visit the feeder while the child is sitting there.

Next take a large cardboard box – large enough for a child to sit in. Paint it in greens, greys and browns and place the box near the feeding station. Two children walk to the box. One goes in and the other child walks back holding a coat at arms length. This tricks the birds into believing that two people have walked away from the hide. Again, see how many birds visit the table while the child watches from the hide.

The highlight of this activity is building a proper bird hide – the kind wildlife cameramen like Simon King use to get close to an osprey on *Springwatch*.

A simple hide can be made by tying camouflage-coloured sheets and blankets between trees and bushes.

A stand-alone hide can be built by pushing eight poles of willow or hazel into the ground in a circle. Bend the tops of the poles over and tie together with string. Drape camouflage netting over the structure. Place some old cushions in the hide to make it comfortable and then children will be able to spend longer in there. This is the kind of hide you could make near a bird box on a fence post. It is a real achievement and a privilege to be able to sit just three or four metres away from a family of tits while the young practise their flying skills and leave the nest.

Health and safety

Be careful with the scissors while building the hide.

Follow-up activities

Send the data that you collect from your observations to your local wildlife trust. This information is important to them in the work that they do to support the wildlife of your local area. You can often do this online, which gives children a real purpose to their computer use.

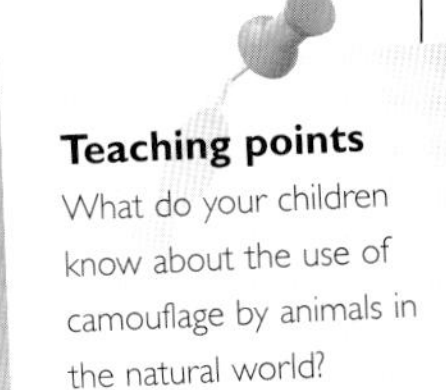

Teaching points

What do your children know about the use of camouflage by animals in the natural world?

5. Indoor wildlife pond

What is an indoor wildlife pond?

This is a practical way to overcome the challenges of the British weather and involves creating the environment of an outdoor habitat indoors.

Why make an indoor wildlife pond?

An indoor wildlife pond will allow children to marvel at the wonders of underwater life in the comfort of their own classroom.

Learning objectives

This activity allows you to give KS1 children a greater understanding of life processes. Key points are the way in which different underwater animals are adapted to their environment, the way they move and how they feed. EYFS children can practise their counting skills (PSRN) and looking at similarities and differences (KUW).

Resources

- Large transparent plastic water table on a stand
- Hosepipe
- Rocks
- Mud
- Pond plants
- A bucket of pond water.

Preparation

Set your transparent water table up a week before you plan to do this activity and fill with tap water using the hosepipe. Tap water needs a week to lose its chlorine content and make it suitable for pond life to live in. Gather your other resources together over the next week.

Your pond water should come from a real pond; you can get your pond plants here too. Visit the website of your local wildlife trust to find a nearby nature reserve with a pond. Phone the trust to ask if they would mind you taking a bucketful of water and a couple of handfuls of pond plants. They probably have an education officer who will visit your school and talk to the children.

Introducing the activity

Set up your indoor pond with the children on a miserable, wet day. This will really bring the message home to the children that we can find alternatives and solve problems when situations aren't in our favour.

You might like to start by telling the children how you were hoping to spend some time outside studying wildlife, but unfortunately the weather is too bad. Give them just a moment to express their disappointment and then announce your alternative. Or tell them you would still like to study pond life and ask them to come up with alternatives to solve the problem.

Conducting the activity

- Ask the children what is needed to make a wildlife pond and as they name possible 'ingredients' bring them out from a bag; let the children add them to your indoor wildlife pond
- Place the rocks first and then pour in a little mud – maybe a quarter of a bucket. You could time how long the mud takes to settle
- Next add your pond plants
- Finally, pour in your bucket of pond water
- Leave your indoor wildlife pond to settle down.

When the children want to study pond life they can kneel down next to the transparent water table and look through the side.

Only keep your indoor wildlife pond for a week as the bugs and beasties would really prefer to be in a real pond. Carefully remove rocks and plants then let the water run out of the bottom tap of your water table through a sieve into a bucket. This will allow you to save the bugs and beasties and pour the strained water down the drain. Save a bucket of water at the end and tip the contents of your sieve into it plus the mud from the bottom of your indoor wildlife pond. This can all be returned to the pond where you collected your bucketful of pond water.

Health and safety

You might like to tape up the tap of your indoor wildlife pond with strong duck tape. It only takes one or two little twists of a naughty hand for you to end up with wildlife all over the classroom floor!

Follow-up activities

When children are familiar with the unusual tails, legs, faces and antennae of water minibeasts it can be great fun to design your own imaginative creatures. Use Plasticine or wire covered in papier mâché and see who can invent the strangest bug.

Teaching points

Allow children to spend as long as they like observing pond life – it may be a source of endless fascination for some of your more reluctant learners.

6. Pond-dipping expedition

Why go on a pond-dipping expedition?

Having an indoor wildlife pond to study pond life up close and in comfort is great, but there is nothing quite like an expedition to a real pond. Pond-dipping is a good opportunity to instil in children a respect for other creatures. It is importance to return your catch to the same place where it was found.

Learning objectives

For many children pond-dipping is their first experience of a proper wildlife expedition. Use this activity to reinforce the messages of respect and taking care – of the wildlife and of themselves. This will be part of your PSHE curriculum. KS1 children will be focused on variation and classification in the science curriculum. EYFS children will be trying a new activity and responding to significant experiences (PSED).

Resources

- Nets – household sieves and home-made nets using net curtains work well
- Magnifying glasses/hand lens
- Trays and pots – large for storing the catch and small for individual specimens (white plastic is best as aquatic minibeasts will stand out against it)
- Dropping pipettes
- Plastic forceps
- Small paint brushes
- Plastic teaspoons
- Weed hook and drag line – made from bent wire coathangers and a long piece of string
- Identification guides
- Pencil, paper and clipboard.

Introducing the activity

Lay out your pond-dipping equipment on the classroom floor in the middle of a circle of seated children. Name each item and explain how it is used. This should ensure that when you go to the pond the children can get down to the exciting business of pond-dipping more quickly. Talk about appropriate clothing for a pond-dipping expedition.

Conducting the activity

When you reach your pond, the first thing to do is give the children clear safety instructions. If children kneel by the pond edge and don't overreach with their net they will stay safe. You need to model this appropriate behaviour for them.

Fill a large bucket with pond water and pour into the trays the children are sharing. Keep these trays about two metres back from the pond edge.

Children can then dip with their nets. A slow swish just below the surface will capture certain pond life and a poke around in the bottom will haul a different catch. Empty the contents of the net into the tray.

Children can now endeavour to catch individual specimens from their trays using a plastic teaspoon or dropping pipette and transfer these to smaller pots where they can be studied closely using a magnifying glass. Use the fine paint brushes to move small sticks and stones aside to see what is hiding behind and underneath.

An adult can use the weed hook and drag line to pull in weed from the middle of the pond, which will be full of life.

Children can sketch and make notes about the invertebrates they catch.

Health and safety

Children **must** be fully supervised at all times when near water and should **not** be allowed in the water. Dipping from the bank is perfectly safe. Make sure you have a good ratio of adults to children. Your local authority will offer guidance on this. One adult to two children is ideal for foundation stage and one adult to four children for Key Stage 1.

Follow-up activities

Stream-dipping is also fun, though I would restrict this to Year 2 children. With a good preparation talk Year 2 children can be allowed into **very shallow** water if there is good access from the bank. By this I mean a gently sloping bank and a shallow gravel and sand edge, so that they can walk step by step into the shallow water. And by shallow water I mean no deeper than 10cm. Only one child at a time, accompanied by an adult, should enter the stream, with another adult supervising the group on the bank.

Stream-dipping technique:

- Stand in the water and place your net downstream of you
- Shuffle your feet about among the stones on the stream bed to loosen anything clinging there. The water animals will be swept into your net by the current
- Transfer your catch to a shallow tray half filled with stream water on the stream bank and study individual specimens in the same way you did with the pond life.

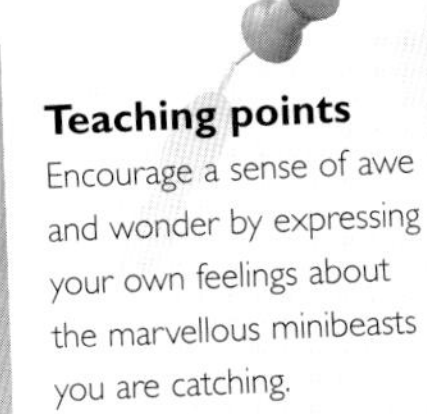

7. Nature games

What are nature games?

The children think they are playing, but really they are learning, not that there is a difference! These are activities that will help children to experience their wonderful world in quite deep and meaningful ways.

Why play nature games?

Some of these games involve cooperation. Some require children to concentrate on their own thoughts and feelings. All involve the intense use of the senses.

Learning objectives

There is a lot of personal skill development in here for EYFS children, such as self-confidence and self-discipline (PSED). These games are good for developing and refining personal and interpersonal skills. KS1 children will gain the same benefits and you can extend their scientific vocabulary through discussing their discoveries.

Resources

Resource requirements are given for each individual activity.

Setting the scene

Over 20 years ago, when I was training as a teacher, I came across an inspiring book full of practical ways to enthuse children about the world around them. The book is called *Sharing Nature with Children* by Joseph Bharat Cornell (1979). My copy is dog-eared and dirty as it has been used so much.

Cornell is a naturalist and author who founded the Sharing Nature Foundation in 1979. The foundation 'uses creative nature activities to give people joyful and inspiring experiences of nature'. The aim is to change the way people look at the world around them and to give them a deeper and more profound experience of nature.

The book contains a whole range of nature games designed to get children using all their senses to explore the natural world. The great thing about these games is that they can be used anywhere. Whether your school is in the middle of the city or deep in the country, you will find these practical techniques useful.

Before describing the games Cornell makes some suggestions for teachers regarding good practice and it is worth repeating them.

Teach less and share more: A lot of learning about nature involves giving names to things. Try to share more your own thoughts and feelings with children about the plants and animals you come across. Discuss how they live and what they do.

Be receptive: Be aware and listen – to the children and what they are expressing about the experience and also to what is going on around you as you explore a place.

Focus the child's attention without delay: Talk to them before you go out about using all their senses. As soon as you walk out of the door start doing that immediately by drawing children's attention to sights, sounds and smells. This sets the tone for any outing.

Look and experience first; talk later: Don't worry about knowing the names of everything. Just take it all in and then sit down and reflect; share the experience.

A sense of joy should permeate the experience: This may be through spontaneous enthusiasm or calm, quiet reflection.

Conducting the activity

The following games can all be played in your school grounds, in a local park or out in the wilds on a day trip. They require minimal preparation and equipment.

Meet a tree

This game is best played in a woodland setting. A local park will work well as long as there is a variety of trees. Put the children in pairs. One is blindfolded and their partner carefully leads them on a circuitous route to a tree. The blindfolded child explores the tree thoroughly with their hands. They can also hug the tree to get a sense of its size. The child is then led back by another route to the starting point. The blindfold is removed and the child has to try to find their tree using sense of direction and feel. Suddenly what was just a bunch of trees becomes a collection of individual trees with one special one waiting to be found.

Blindfold trail

Lay out a long piece of string, maybe 25 metres, through the place you want to explore, running it over fallen logs, round trees, over stony ground and through long grass. Make the string rise and fall by attaching it to low-hanging branches or weighting it down with a stone. The whole class is blindfolded and each child takes hold of the string and sets off on an adventure to experience a familiar place in an unfamiliar way. Retrace the trail without blindfolds to help put the experience into perspective.

Unnature trail

Without the children seeing, lay out a collection of about 10 unnatural or unexpected objects along a 50-metre stretch of path: hang a salt cellar or a metal spoon in a tree, place a banana in the long grass, a toy car, a plastic ball, an inflated balloon and so on. Slightly hide the objects so the children really have to look for them. Make some of them more conspicuous than others. Don't tell them how many there are; simply ask the children to walk along the path and look out for anything that doesn't really belong there. Once everyone has walked along the path, find out who spotted the most objects. Discuss each object: what is unnatural about it, how well is it camouflaged? Follow this game with a search for camouflaged minibeasts.

Duplication

This fun game helps develop memory skills. Collect 10 natural objects from the surroundings and lay them on a tray under a cloth. Tell the children they have 30 seconds to look at the objects and then they have to go off into the surroundings and find 10 identical objects. When they return, compare what they have found to what was on the tray.

Still hunting

This is an immensely powerful experience. I have always used it after plenty of preliminary work using other nature games so the children are already beginning to experience nature in a deep way.

Explain to the children that they are going to be given a place to sit in silence and simply take in everything around them. Bring the group or class together in a large circle. Everyone holds hands above head height and together you 'draw down the veil of silence'. From this point no one can talk until the veil is lifted. Lead the children off, still holding hands in a long chain, into the wood or across the field or along the stream or wherever you are working and point to a spot to indicate that the first child in the line should sit down. At a distance of 10 metres or so point to another spot, and so on until every child has their own special place to sit.

Leave the children sitting for five or 10 minutes and then gather them up, still in silence, and come back into a circle. Clasp hands and 'lift the veil of silence'. At this point the children are free to talk and you will be amazed at the rush of excited chat as they share what they saw, heard, smelled and touched in the place where they were sitting. I have done this with some very challenging children and it has always reminded me exactly why I am a teacher.

Health and safety

In all of these games it is important to establish boundaries with the children so they know where they can and can't go before they set off to explore. It is also important to emphasise safety, especially that nothing that the children find should be tasted unless an adult has said that it is fine to do so.

Teaching points

Encourage a sense of awe and wonder by expressing your own feelings about the marvellous minibeasts you are catching.

8. Grow your own tree

Why grow your own tree?

Probably more than any other environmental activity, planting a tree is a hopeful and positive act. Planting a tree gives a child a stake in the future. Trees that I planted with children when I first started teaching are coming up for 20 years old now and when I revisit the school of my first teaching post it gives me great pleasure to see those birch and ash trees over 20 feet tall. I hope the young adults on the estate where I taught still visit them from time to time and that they will take their own children to see them.

Learning objectives

The emphasis here is on PSHE and Citizenship for KS1 children and PSED for EYFS children; it is about caring enough about the future to do something active to help our beleaguered planet. Discussion around this point will encourage a sense of responsibility.

Resources

Growing trees from seed

- Yogurt pots to collect seeds
- Plant pots and compost
- Hand trowels.

Transplanting tree saplings

- Tree saplings. You can grow them yourself or buy them from a specialist grower such as the one listed in the website section on p232. One sapling per child prevents arguing.

Introducing the activity

Discuss with the children the important part that trees play in all our lives. On a practical level they provide us with wood for construction, paper for writing and food such as almonds and apples. They also contribute to the global environment by absorbing and storing carbon dioxide and releasing oxygen, which we need to breathe. They affect the weather system in a major way and are a significant component of the water cycle. Water that is absorbed by tree roots and exhaled by the tree leaves evaporates to join the clouds of the water cycle. Forested hillsides help prevent rapid run-off of rainfall and can prevent flooding

Conducting the activity

Growing trees from seed

Take the children out for a walk in the local area on an autumn day and collect whatever tree seeds you find. Even on a housing estate you are likely to find rowan and ash trees. On housing estates built from the 1970s onwards planners often allowed old hedgerows to continue growing between streets so you will find a greater variety of seeds there.

The seeds of some native tree species will not germinate if plonked straight into the ground. Nuts such as hazel and oak can go straight into pots filled with earth. With berries, such as holly or hawthorn, it is best to remove the soft flesh and leave the seed in a pot of sand outside over winter. This begins to break down the seed coat and allows germination.

To plant your tree seeds, place some stones in the bottom of a plant pot to aid drainage and fill with a mixture of soil and compost. Children can dib a 4cm to 5cm-deep hole in the soil, drop in the seed and cover. Label the pots with the name of the child and the name of the tree species and leave in a corner outside. Sunlight is not necessary for germination to take place, but move the pot to a sunnier place once the seedling has broken through the soil.

Transplanting tree saplings

Tree saplings can be bought as bare-rooted or pot-grown. Bare-rooted trees have to be transplanted during the winter months, that is from November to February. Pot-grown trees can be transplanted at any time, but in the winter when they are dormant is still best. Pot-grown trees are also more expensive and that is often a factor for schools. If you have grown your own tree saplings from seed, you won't need to worry about the cost.

Dig a hole of a depth, length and width of about one spade-length. Place your tree sapling in the hole so that the root collar is level with the ground surface. This is important. The root collar is a mark on the stem between the roots and the trunk. This needs to be level with the ground surface so that the part of the tree that is used to being underground is underground. This will allow the tree to get off to a good start in its new home.

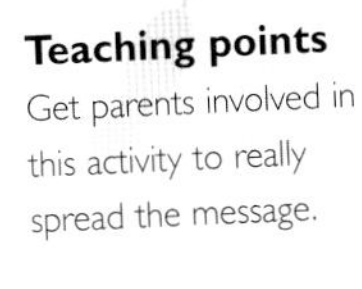

Teaching points

Get parents involved in this activity to really spread the message.

Carefully refill the hole with the soil and press it down firmly to ensure good contact between soil and roots.

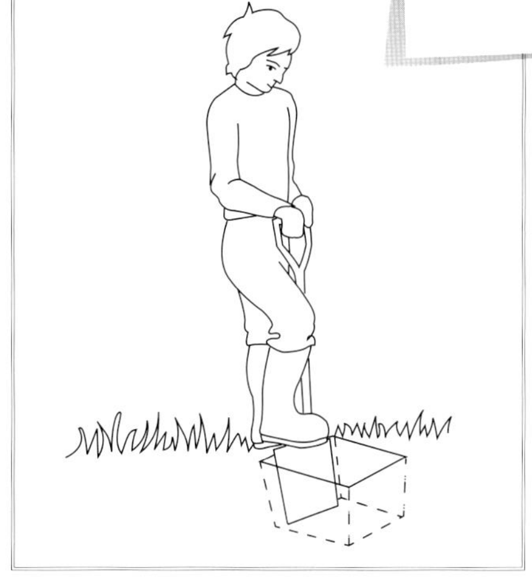

Water your tree.

Measure and record the height of the tree.

Health and safety

Be careful with the spades when transplanting tree saplings.

Follow-up activities

Caring for your trees is the most important follow-up activity. Young trees don't like competition so you will need to weed around the base of the tree or surround the base with a mulch (such as old carpet cut into squares 50cm by 50cm). In hot, dry weather they will need watering, and a young tree can drink a lot of water.

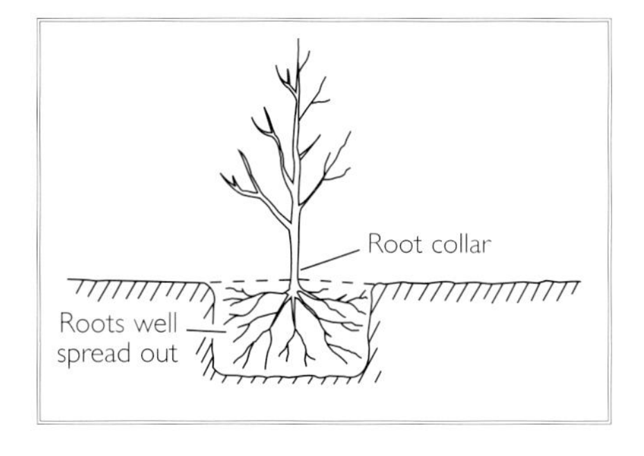

The other follow-up activity is for each child to visit their tree once a year for the duration of their time at the school and measure it. This will give them a real sense of achievement as they see their tree getting bigger.

9. Estimate the height and age of a tree

Why estimate the height and age of a tree?

This is an activity I learned to do myself when I was a boy scout many years ago. It doesn't seem to have much point to it (unless you want to become an arboriculturist – someone who studies trees), but it is fun and offers some practical maths opportunities.

Learning objectives

EYFS children can explore PSRN concepts and use language such as bigger and smaller, taller and shorter. KS1 children will be using more detailed maths such as measuring in metres. They will also gain an understanding of perspective and scale.

Resources

- Tape measure in feet and inches
- Chalk
- Pencil
- Long tape measure in metres.

Introducing the activity

Ask the children to come up with ideas about how they could estimate the height and age of trees in the school grounds or nearby.

Conducting the activity

Estimate the age of a tree

Most activities in this book give measurements in centimetres and metres. This activity deals in feet and inches and there is a very good reason for that. The person who originally worked out this technique did it in feet and inches and if you try to do it in metres and centimetres it becomes quite complicated!

Mark a point on the bark of the tree with chalk four feet six inches from the ground.

At this point, measure the girth of the tree (all the way round).

However many inches the girth of the tree is will be approximately the age of the tree. A tree that measures six feet eight inches around will be approximately 80 years old.

Estimate the height of a tree

There are several ways to do this. Here is the easiest.

One person stands by the base of the tree and their partner walks away from the tree holding a pencil.

The person walking needs to find a point where they can do the following: hold up the pencil at arm's length so that it looks like the tree is the same size as the pencil.

Next, the person holding the pencil turns it one right angle to either side of the tree with one end of the pencil at the base of the tree. The pencil will look like it is lying on the ground.

The person holding the pencil tells their accomplice to walk away from the tree until it looks like they are standing at the other end of the pencil.

With your long tape measure, measure the distance between the base of the tree and the person standing at the other end of the pencil.

This distance will be approximately the height of the tree.

Health and safety

There are no health and safety implications with this activity.

Follow-up activities

If, for any reason, a tree is being cut down in your school grounds or nearby then you can test out the technique for estimating the age of the tree. Before the tree is cut down, calculate your own estimate of its age. After it is cut down count the annual growth rings across the cut stump. How close were you?

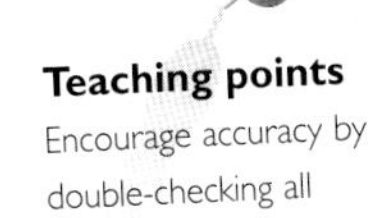

Teaching points

Encourage accuracy by double-checking all measurements and calculations.

10. Bark casting

What is bark casting?

This activity uses a similar technique to that of taking a plaster cast of an animal footprint to create a lasting memento of a trip into the countryside.

Why make bark casts?

Many children will have taken bark rubbings and you can do that as a prelude to this activity. Taking a bark casting is just that little bit more exciting and also allows you to recreate the shape of the curved tree trunk.

Learning objectives

Spending time focusing on the bark of a tree in this way gives you the opportunity to discuss a part of the living tree with children. In the EYFS this activity will help children understand the features of living things. It also allows children to look closely at similarities and differences in the pattern of bark on different trees. With KS1 children you can discuss the role that bark plays in protecting the tree and how the under layer of bark is involved in the movement of water and food around the tree. This covers life processes and green plants.

Resources

- Plasticine
- Plaster of Paris
- Water
- A pot to mix plaster
- A mixing stick
- Powder paints.

Introducing the activity

Ask children to name the parts of a tree. Ask them if they know what each part does. This may well be a complete mystery to children – what *do* the leaves *do*? Get the children to take a deep breath. Tell them that the leaves of a tree breathe. Have a glass of water to hand and take a sip yourself. Ask the children how trees drink? Through their roots. Ask your children what the purpose of our skin is. Ask them what a tree has instead of skin.

Take the children out to meet some trees. Just touch the bark and experience its roughness or smoothness depending on the species. Compare different trees. Then take your bark castings.

Conducting the activity

- Knead the Plasticine until it is soft.
- Shape the Plasticine into a thick slab and press it firmly on to the bark of the tree.
- Peel off the Plasticine slab and you will see the impression of the bark on it.
- Back in the classroom, lay the Plasticine print on a table with the bark impression facing upwards.

- Bend the Plasticine slab into a downward curve and build up a rectangular wall of Plasticine around it. This will act as a dam when you pour in the plaster of Paris.
- When you are sure you have blocked up any holes in your mould, pour in the plaster of Paris.
- Leave the cast to dry. This will take longer than for a footprint as it is bigger.
- When the plaster is dry remove all the Plasticine to reveal your bark cast.
- Children will see how the curve you made has given the cast a curve like real bark.
- Paint your bark cast and try to recreate the different colours of the different trees you took casts from.
- Display with a label alongside bark casts from other trees for comparison purposes.

Health and safety

Any activity such as this is a good opportunity to reinforce the message that we need to take particular care with powders and liquids that are not food. Getting this message across when children are young is good training for future scientific experimental work.

Follow-up activities

Experiment with taking plaster casts of twigs, leaves and acorns. Press these into Plasticine and fill with plaster.

Use Modroc (plaster of Paris bandages) and wire to make miniature trees of your own to adorn a small world play forest.

Teaching points

Use a magnifying glass to see what the bark looks like close up.

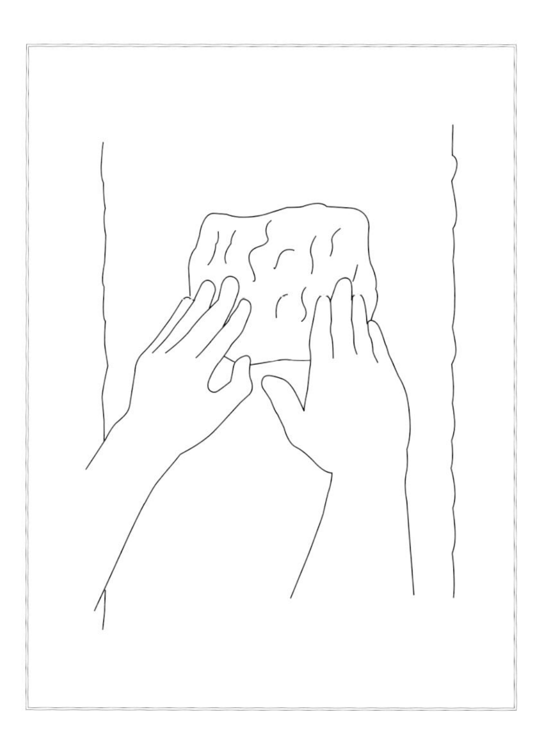

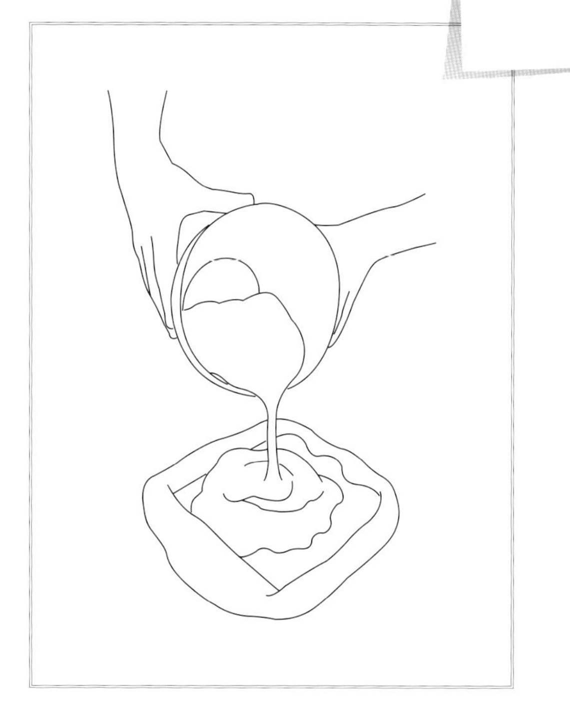

11. Give a hedgehog a hibernation home

Why give a hedgehog a hibernation home?

Hedgehogs have quite a hard time of it. Many gardeners are overly tidy and there are fewer piles of old leaves and logs lying around for hedgehogs to hibernate under. Traffic levels on our roads have increased dramatically in recent years – just getting around town is a life and death expedition for a hedgehog. Well-meaning people put out bread and milk for hedgehogs, but this just gives them diarrhoea – cat food is better. Helping hedgehogs gives children a sense of responsibility for other living things.

There are some quite fancy designs around for making a hedgehog house. These can work out to be expensive and would probably be too complicated for a class to undertake (unless their teacher was a woodwork enthusiast). This activity will allow you to explore the needs of a hedgehog though constructing a hibernation home.

Learning objectives

This activity is about taking responsibility for helping other living things and links in with the PSHE curriculum for KS1 children and PSED for EYFS children.

Resources

- Three logs about 30cm to 50cm long and about 15cm across
- A big pile of twigs
- Straw.

Introducing the activity

Explore the website of Tiggywinkles, the world's busiest wildlife hospital, at *www.sttiggywinkles.org.uk* with your children. Read some of the statistics about the number of injured hedgehogs the hospital treats each year. Read about the difficulties hedgehogs experience finding food and safe places to hibernate in the modern world. Discuss what role people have played in making life difficult for hedgehogs – roads and traffic are a big danger and overly tidy gardens mean fewer places for hedgehogs to hibernate.

Read Dick King-Smith's marvellous book *The Hodgeheg* (2003, Puffin) to your class. Dick King-Smith has a gift for being anthropomorphic without being patronising towards animals.

In a hall session you could role-play being a hedgehog preparing for winter. Talk the children through the search for food – it's important to get fattened up for the winter. The search for a suitable place to hibernate. The fear of a dog barking. The feeling of cold as the nights grow longer. Exploring the life of a hedgehog through role-play will give children a greater insight and will stimulate ideas for a discussion on how you can construct a hibernation home that would meet the needs of a hedgehog.

Conducting the activity

- In a sheltered and quiet corner of your school grounds (maybe under a bush) lay your logs in a hedgehog-sized horseshoe shape on the ground.

- Lay some large twigs carefully over the logs to create a roof.
- Pile all the other twigs on top of this small den structure.
- Make sure you leave an opening through the pile into the cosy confines of the log home.
- Leave a couple of handfuls of straw under the bush – a visiting hedgehog may use this for winter bedding.

Health and safety

It is a good idea to wear gardening gloves when handling logs and twigs in case there happen to be any thorns – though you will want to try to avoid making your hibernation home out of thorny twigs.

Follow-up activities

You may never know whether a hedgehog took up residence in your hibernation home over winter or not. You certainly shouldn't disturb the home during the winter. What you can do is wait until early May and then carefully remove the twigs. If there is what looks like a little bed in between the logs then a hedgehog may well have taken up residence. Explain to the children that sometimes when we help wildlife we don't always get the pleasure of seeing them – sometimes it is enough to know that we *might* have made a difference.

Draw fun hedgehog homes with hedgehog bathrooms and kitchens, hedgehog cars and televisions. Doing this in a pair or a group of up to four children generates all sorts of creative ideas.

Teaching points

While you are constructing the hedgehog home, talk about how a hedgehog might do this for themselves.

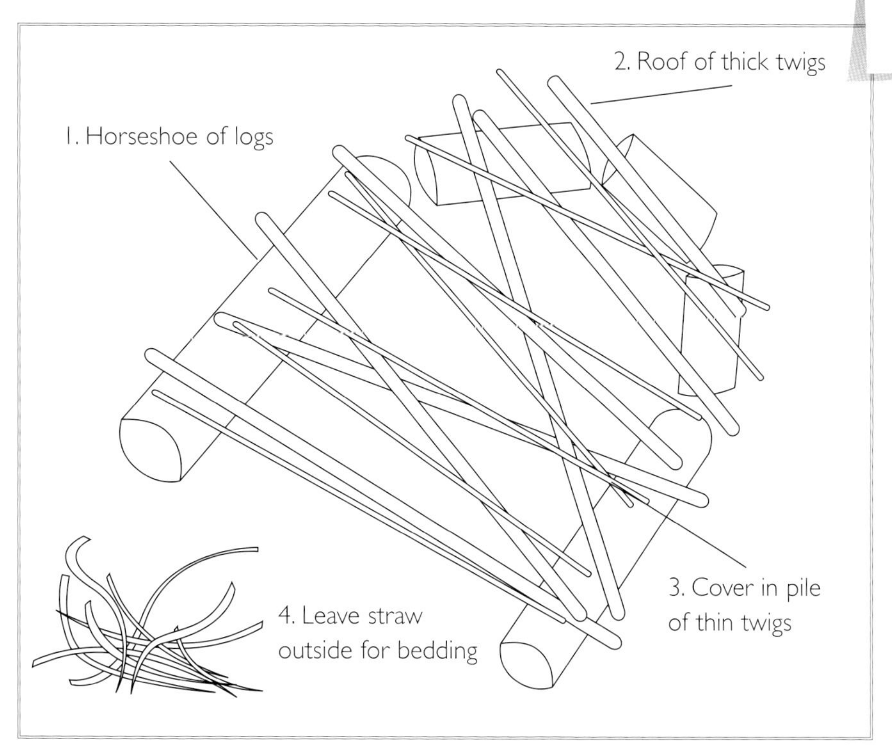

12. Minibeast trail

What is a minibeast trail?

We are used to following paths when we go out and about – paths to the shops and paths around the local park. A minibeast trail is a path through the miniature world of the bugs and beasties with which we share our wonderful world.

Why go on a minibeast trail?

This activity will get children right down among the grass roots so they can discover the fascinating variety of activities going on down there. It will give them an insight into the world of the very tiny.

Learning objectives

Taking turns and working together can be stressed during this activity and will benefit EYFS children through PSED. It is very exciting and some children might find it a challenge to share the activity with their partner. Limiting resources to one between two is a good way to ensure children have to cooperate. KS1 children are working with life processes and variation and classification in the science curriculum.

Resources

- Magnifying glasses – one for each pair of children
- Pieces of string cut to two metres in length – one for each pair of children.

Introducing the activity

In class explore magnifying glasses. Ask children to look at the back of their hand or their fingernail up close. Look at a friend's ear. Point out to children just how interesting it is to see things really close up. Tell the children you are going to take them out to look at the world of the very small in nature. Explain that you don't have enough magnifying glasses for one each so they will have to share – briefly discuss the implications of this.

Conducting the activity

- Take the children out into the school grounds.
- Distribute the resources – string and magnifying glasses – and tell children you are going to shrink them down to the size of an ant.
- Ask children to find a space in the area where you are working – you don't want them bumping into each other when they are down on their hands and knees following a trail.
- The children lay the piece of string out in either a straight or wiggly line.
- They lie down on their fronts or kneel to explore the route of the string with the magnifying glass. It really is amazing what is down there in the roots of the grass.
- Once everyone has had a go, sit in a circle and talk about what the children saw.
- Ask children who can find the most interesting place to lay out their trail – they could make a trail that runs over several different patches, maybe some grass, a path, a dry and bare mud patch.

Health and safety

As children are crawling around on the ground, look out for anything you might not want them to crawl through!

Follow-up activities

Back in class children can draw sketches of the minibeasts they found and display them alongside a piece of string and a magnifying glass, mounted on a small display board.

Children can zoom in on minibeasts and look for body parts such as legs, eyes and antennae.

Teaching points

Encourage children to move slowly along their trail – they will see more.

13. Life cycles – butterflies

Why study the life cycle of a butterfly?

Life cycles are an important part of the science learning of any young child.

Learning objectives

Life cycles are the key learning point with this activity and it is worth repeating the 'egg – caterpillar – pupa – butterfly – egg' mantra over and over again while you are engaged with this activity just to make sure children have really got it. EYFS children are in the realm of the KUW curriculum and KS1 children are learning about life processes.

Resources

- A large, transparent plastic, rectangular tank with a close-fitting lid that includes air vents
- Twigs and soil
- Food plants of the butterfly species you are hatching:
  - Large white butterfly – plants from the cabbage family
  - Peacock butterfly – common nettle
  - Red admiral butterfly – common nettle.

www.ukbutterflies.co.uk/foodplants.php is a good source of information.

Introducing the activity

With butterflies there is only one way to get this activity started and that is to read *The Very Hungry Caterpillar* by Eric Carle (2002, Puffin). Share the story with the children and enjoy the simple but effective illustrations.

Make a circle of string on the carpet and choose four children to represent the egg, caterpillar, pupa and adult of the butterfly. Ask the children to stand on the string to form a circle and ask the rest of the class to check that they are in the right places.

Conducting the activity

- Place your plastic tank on a firm surface such as a worktop in your classroom so it is at a height where children can look through the sides.
- Lay soil on the bottom of the tank and arrange a few twigs so they are leaning against the side – this is where the pupa will attach itself.
- Take the children out to search for eggs. They will need to wear gloves if searching for peacock and red admiral eggs on the underside of nettle leaves.
- In your school vegetable garden, grow a few cabbage plants to attract large white butterflies – if you don't have a school vegetable garden then grow some cabbages in pots specially to attract butterflies.
- Pick a few leaves and transfer them to your tank.
- Over the days that follow, watch to see when the eggs hatch into caterpillars and when the caterpillars construct their pupae.

- Record all this information on a chart kept next to the plastic tank.

Health and safety

You are using a plastic tank here for health and safety reasons rather than a glass one. The real issue is the safety of the butterfly. As soon as the pupa is ready to open, take the lid off the tank. Once the adult butterfly emerges you will have just a short while to marvel at its beauty before you open a window and allow it to escape into the wide world when it is ready.

Follow-up activities

The traditional activity that goes with butterflies is to paint symmetrical butterflies. I like to do straw-blown coloured ink blots on white paper and then fold the paper to produce a symmetrical image. Cut out the shape of a butterfly once the ink is dry.

Teaching points

Draw up a rota of monitors to check on and record the progress of your developing butterflies.

14. Life cycles – frogs

Why study the life cycle of frogs?

Collecting frogspawn and watching the eggs turn into tadpoles and then into froglets is one of the great disasters of school wildlife study throughout the history of our education system. Countless millions of frogs have failed to make it to adulthood because of the poor collecting techniques of overly enthusiastic teachers and children. Keeping tadpoles is, however, a valid activity if carried out with due care and consideration.

Ethical frog farming

There are two stages to keeping frogs: the frogspawn/tadpole stage and the froglet stage. You can keep your frogspawn and tadpoles in a tank of water initially but as soon as they have legs, move them to a large and more suitable tank with access to land. If you cannot provide this then return them to the pond where you found them. Create a vivarium to house your developing froglets. A vivarium is a glass or plastic tank like an aquarium, but in this case used for studying reptiles and amphibians. A thoughtfully created vivarium is the most humane way to keep froglets in school. This gives your children the pleasure of seeing the growth and development of froglets close up while allowing the froglets a reasonable degree of comfort. Go to *www.froglife.org* for further advice.

Learning objectives

While life cycles (Science: Life processes) is a key concept to study through this activity, the powerful message is care and respect for other living things. This comes in the PSHE curriculum for KS1 children and PSED for EYFS children. You will be doing your children and our native wildlife a great service if you really encourage empathy towards the needs of your frogs.

Resources

The frogspawn/tadpole stage

- A 9 to 10-litre transparent plastic tank with a vented lid
- Water
- A bag of washed gravel
- Pond plants.

The froglet stage

A very large, rectangular glass tank with a lid – 60cm by 50cm by 50cm would be about the right dimensions. You can pick these up on eBay or Freecycle, or you might be able to get an unwanted tank with an appeal in your school newsletter. If you are serious about keeping froglets then this is what you will need. And I would urge you not to keep froglets unless you are going to do it properly.

You will also need:

- A small plastic washing-up bowl
- A wheelbarrow load of soil
- Some rocks about the size of grapefruits
- A handful of pond plants.

Introducing the activity

Children will be very excited about collecting frogspawn and keeping frogs in school. Harness this enthusiasm to a discussion of the needs of tadpoles and how we can take care of them before you do any practical work.

Collecting your frogspawn

Resist the temptation to collect lots of frogspawn. Collect half a jam jar full of fresh new frogspawn – the egg will still be a clear black dot without any growth visible and each dot will be inside firm, round pieces of jelly. The ideal ratio is three to five tadpoles per litre of water. In your 9 to 10-litre tank you really don't want more than 50 tadpoles swimming around. There are about 300 to 400 eggs in a clump of spawn laid by a single female. Collect your frogspawn from a garden pond rather than the wild to reduce your impact on the frog population. There will almost certainly be parents at the school who have a garden pond teeming with frogspawn every February or March. Put a request in the school newsletter, but make it clear you really don't want a bucketful.

Place your clump of frogspawn in the tank of water and watch it develop.

Conducting the activity – vivarium

- Place the small washing-up bowl in the corner of your vivarium.
- Surround the bowl with soil right up to the lip.
- Fill the bowl with water from the tap one week before you are ready to introduce your maturing tadpoles – tap water needs a week to lose its chlorine content and make it suitable for tadpoles to live in.
- Place rocks and twigs on the soil.
- Place pond plants in the water and at the same time introduce the tadpoles.

Health and safety

It is important not to put your froglets in a different pond when you are ready to return them. There is a disease called redleg that affects frogs and you don't want to be responsible for helping it spread. There is no evidence that redleg can spread to humans or pets.

Follow-up activities

Appoint monitors to check regularly on the wellbeing of the developing froglets. Record their progress on a chart with labelled diagrams and written notes.

The day you release your froglets back into their original pond needs to be seen as a special day by the children. You are doing the right thing by returning them to the natural world and you can celebrate this level of responsibility to reinforce it as a behaviour.

Teaching points

Gently take a tadpole out of the water on a plastic teaspoon and study it under a magnifying glass before returning it to the water.

15. Making mini habitats for minibeasts

What are mini habitats?

There is a variety of ways in which you can make your school grounds, however barren they may appear to be, more attractive to minibeasts. Mini habitats are the homes of minibeasts. Habitat is just a posh Latin word for 'home'!

Why make mini habitats?

Providing your local wildlife with a home is a caring thing to do, which will engender a sense of responsibility and respect in your children. Making mini habitats also means that whenever you want to study minibeasts you know just where to go to find them.

Learning objectives

There is a certain level of construction skill involved in making some of these mini habitats. Link this work in with your design and technology curriculum for KS1 children. For EYFS children there is the opportunity to use different materials in creative development.

Resources

- Logs (a dozen or so – about 10cm in diameter and about 30 to 40cm long)
- Rocks (a wheelbarrow load)
- Paving slab (one)
- Bricks (a wheelbarrow load)
- Bamboo canes (three each measuring one metre long)
- Terracotta plant pots (two or three)
- Thin plastic piping (a couple of metres).

Introducing the activity

This is a good activity to do when you are engaged in studying homes. Talk with your children about what makes a home and how they could make homes to benefit wildlife.

Conducting the activity

Log and rock piles

In an unused corner of the school field pile up a load of old logs. Next to them pile up a load of rocks. Minibeasts will move in and after a while you can compare the bugs and beasties that live in the log pile with those that live in the rock pile.

Paving slabs

Simply lay a paving slab on the grass and leave it alone for six months. When you go back to it you will find all sorts of little tunnels and earth works where burrowing minibeasts have been making homes. Have a quick look and then carefully replace the paving slab so they can get on with their lives.

Bumblebee nest

Partly fill a terracotta plant pot with soft material such as sawdust and hay. Bury the pot upside down in the ground. Place four stones on the surface of the ground beside the pot and use these to support a piece of slate over the pot to keep water out. The bumblebee will crawl under the slate and get into the pot through the drainage hole in its bottom.

Solitary bees

Hollow stems are the place single bees head for. Cut some hollow bamboo cane into lengths about 25cm long. You will need about 10 or 12 of these. Bind them together with some elastic bands and attach underneath a windowsill.

Mining bees

In the spring, in a corner of the school field where no one really goes, dig a trench about 30cm wide, 30cm deep and 100cm long. It will need to get some sun, but doesn't need to be in full sun. If you are lucky, mining bees will move in and you will be able to watch them coming and going. The last time I did this it was by accident. I had dug a new pond and before I could line it the mining bees had moved in and made their little tunnels. There were loads of them and I had to wait until the autumn before I could line and fill my pond.

Health and safety

Take care when moving rocks and logs. Place your bee habitat in a secluded place and advise your children to only view it from a distance of more than five metres to avoid annoying the bees.

Follow-up activities

Watch the habitats you have constructed to see who visits and when. Keep a record of the different wildlife you are able to attract at different times of year.

Teaching points

Give older children a diagram rather than verbal instructions and see if they can construct one of these habitats themselves without your help.

1. Piece of slate
2. Four supporting stones
3. Terracotta pot
4. Sawdust and hay

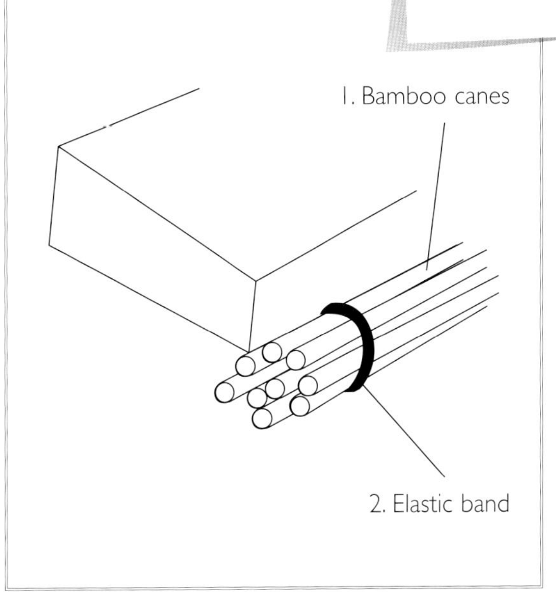

16. Make a moth trap

Why make a moth trap?

Butterflies tend to get most of the attention as they come out during the day. Much more exciting is to discover what is flying around your school after you've all gone home.

Learning objectives

This is a construction activity and so can support your design and technology curriculum in KS1. It is also about discovering aspects of nature that children are unfamiliar with so it covers science themes to do with the diversity of life. EYFS children will be finding out about, and identifying, features of living things.

Resources

- A plastic bucket
- A few egg boxes
- An old conical lampshade
- A small but bright torch with long-lasting batteries
- Masking tape
- An identification guide to British moths.

Introducing the activity

Show the children pictures of some common butterflies and see if they can name any. They might know the red admiral or peacock, and some might know the brimstone or the large white if you are lucky. Ask if anyone can name a moth. Probably not (can you?). Do the children know anything about moths? Tell them that tomorrow morning you will show them a large variety of moths and then get to work on making your moth trap.

Conducting the activity

Cut the lids off three or four egg boxes and place the egg trays topsy-turvy in the bottom of the plastic bucket.

Turn the conical lampshade upside down and place in the mouth of the bucket so it forms a funnel.

Explain to the children that the torch will attract moths. They will land on the lamp shade and slide into the bucket. Because they can't get out they will settle down among the egg boxes and will be there for them to see in the morning.

Tape the torch to the inside of the conical lampshade with the masking tape and turn it on before you go home.

The next morning take the bucket into a shady place and remove the lampshade and torch so that you can gently take out the egg boxes and see the moths you have trapped.

The moths will be a little disorientated. Some will fly away straight away. Some may drop to the ground and stay there or settle on a nearby wall or fence. Leave them alone and they will sort themselves out and go on their way.

Health and safety

I deliberately use a torch for this activity rather than an electric light, which is what a lepidopterist (someone who studies moths) would use. Using an ordinary battery powered torch makes this activity safe for children.

Follow-up activities

Next time you do artwork on symmetry make it about moths and not butterflies.

Year 2 children could follow up this activity by designing an improved moth trap and seeing if they can catch more moths.

Teaching points

Ask children why moths are not brightly coloured like butterflies and see what reasons they come up with.

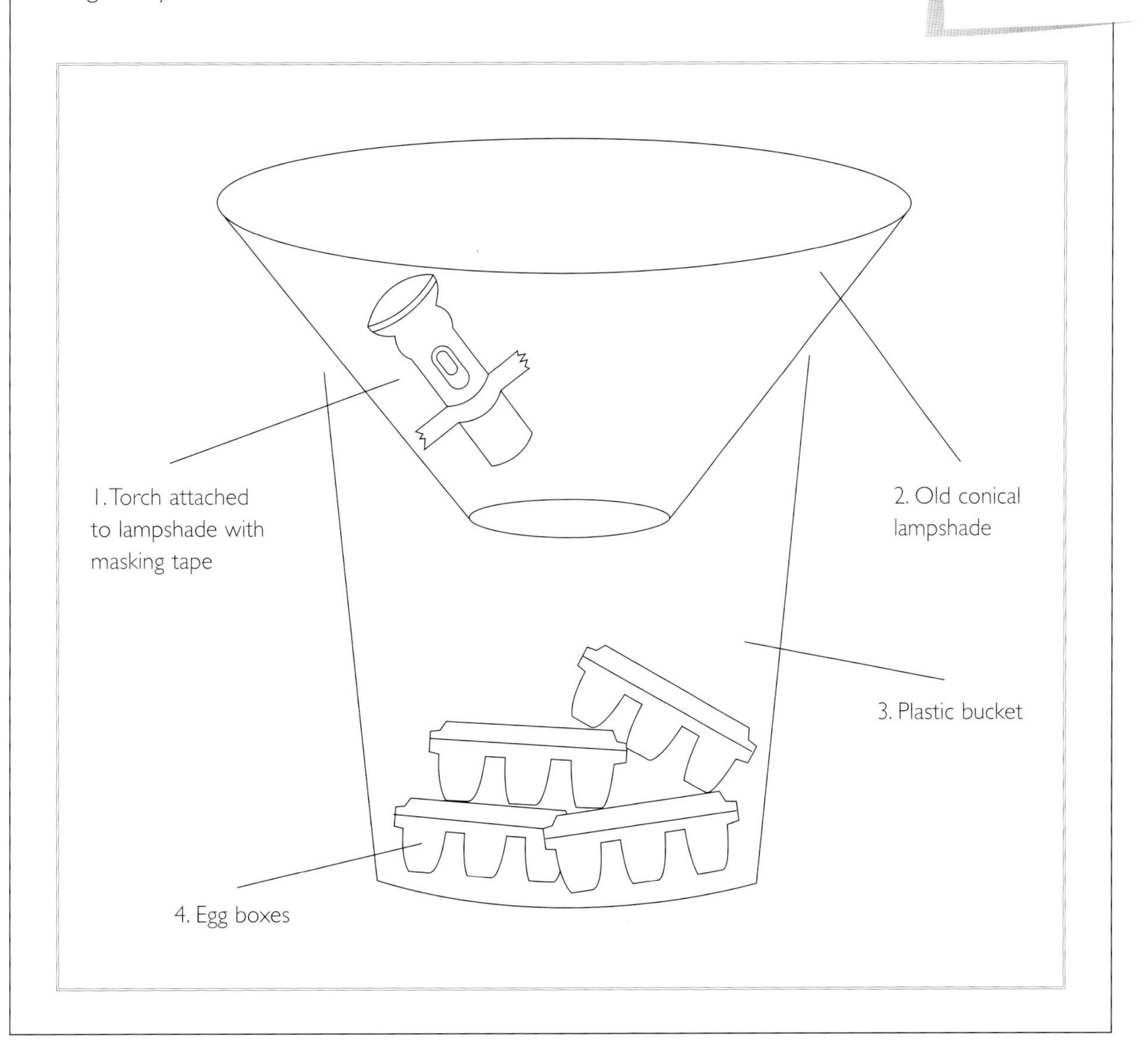

17. Ant town

What is an ant town?

The correct term is 'formicarium' and it is simply an artificial habitat that you create for ants to live and work in so that you can study them.

Why make an ant town?

We are used to treating ants as a nuisance and killing them in all sorts of mean ways – poison and boiling water. Actually, ants are a fascinating and useful animal in the natural world. There are about 14,000 species of ants in the world. Studying the work of ants is another opportunity to marvel at the wonders of nature.

Learning objectives

Ants work as a team. Bees are another example of an insect that does this. A single ant is chemically programmed by pheromones released by the queen to work non-stop for the good of its colony. We might not want our children to grow up to be slavishly antlike in their commitment to our society but a little lesson in teamwork and cooperation once in a while never did any harm. This will support PSHE work with your KS1 children and PSED with EYFS. There are also design and technology opportunities.

Resources

- A piece of plywood 30cm square for the base board
- Six strips of wood about 2.5cm wide by 2.5cm deep. One of these strips needs to be 28cm long, another two pieces at 24cm long and three pieces at 10cm long
- Plasticine
- A length of clear plastic tubing 30cm long
- A sheet of hard clear plastic 28cm square
- Plaster of Paris
- Well-drained soil from the garden
- A jam jar with a lid
- A piece of heavy dark cloth to cover the formicarium
- Woodworking saw, hammer and nails
- Hand trowel
- Balls of cotton wool
- Weak sugar solution
- Sticky tape.

Introducing the activity

Explain to the children what a formicarium is and then get down to the fun of building one. The best way to do this is to have all the materials to hand and then either you or your teaching assistant spends a morning making it with groups of four children at a time. Make sure that everyone contributes to a part of the construction process so that they have a stake in the colony. Follow the instructions below.

Conducting the activity

1. Nail five lengths of wood to the base board – the long one at the back, the two medium sized ones along the sides and two of the shorter pieces at the front so they leave a doorway.
2. Place the third short piece just inside the doorway, but don't nail it down.

3. Pass the connecting tube through the doorway and mould it into place with Plasticine.
4. Mould Plasticine to form a network of tunnels and chambers that butt up against the loose block of wood.
5. Mix and pour in the plaster of Paris and leave to set.
6. Turn out the plaster mould by removing the Plasticine and the loose length of wood.
7. Fill the tunnels with soil.
8. Place the glass on top as a sliding cover. Cover with the dark and heavy cloth to keep out the light.
9. Introduce the ants.

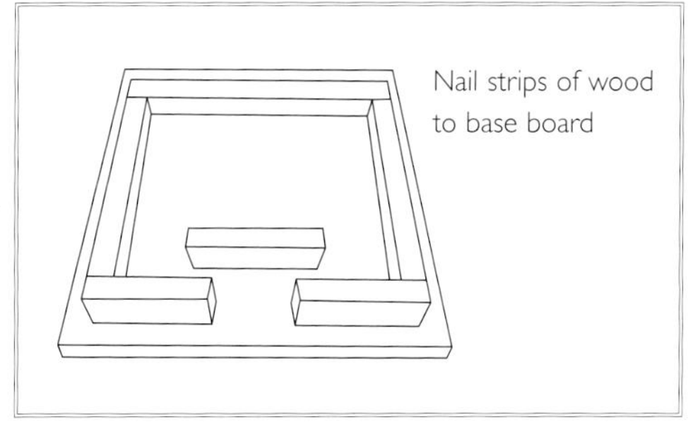

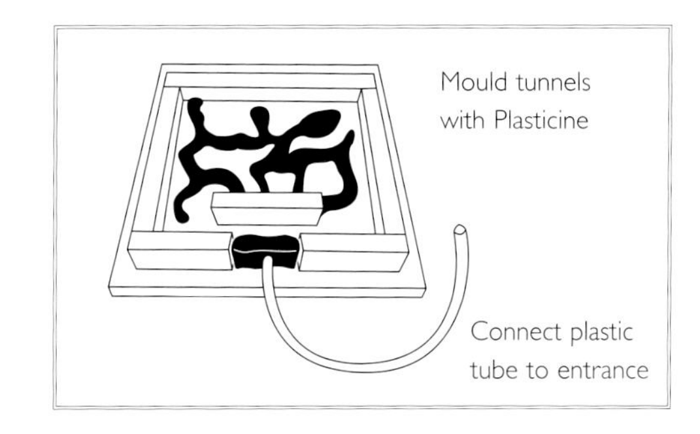

Introducing ants to your ant town

You will need to dig up some ants from the school grounds with a hand trowel. Try to get an egg-laying queen if you can. Place the ants in a jam jar with some balls of cotton wool soaked in weak sugar solution (ant food). Make a hole in the lid of the jam jar. Poke the plastic tubing through and secure with tape.

Place the whole formicarium and jam jar in a warm place out of direct sunlight and let the ants get on with making themselves at home.

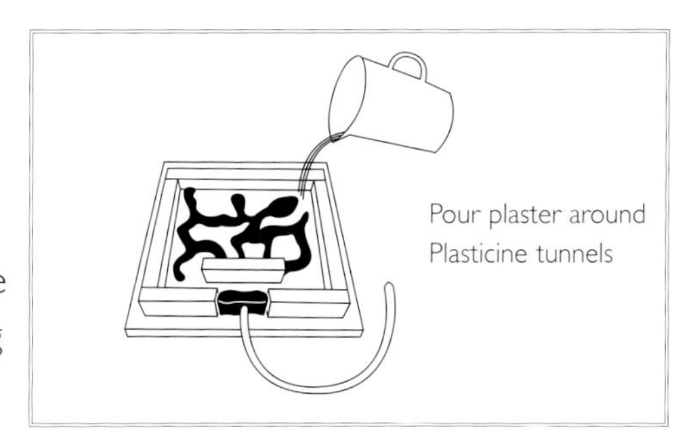

Health and safety

This is a construction activity, which is why the children are working in groups of four with an adult supervisor. Be careful with the tools. Teach the children how to use them safely.

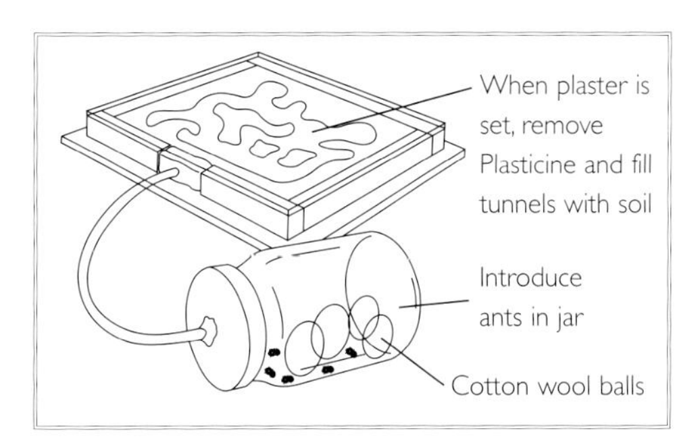

Follow-up activities

You can do some ethical experiments with your ant town once the ants have settled in. Take a very fine paint brush and dab a tiny spot of red paint on the back of one of the ants. Every half an hour lift the cloth and see where the marked ant is. You can track its movements throughout the day and see what it gets up to.

Teaching points
How do ants communicate? Watch to see what happens when two ants meet.

18. Build a bird box

Why build a bird box?

Birds need somewhere safe to nest and raise their young. The modern human-dominated world they live in can make this tricky. Providing artificial nesting places in the form of bird boxes is another way in which we can take responsibility for supporting wildlife.

Learning objectives

This is a construction activity that involves using woodworking tools. Link this activity with the design and technology curriculum.

Resources

- A length of timber plank rough cut and untreated 15cm wide by 1.5cm deep and 150cm long
- A woodworking saw
- Hammer or screwdriver
- Galvanised nails or screws
- A drill with a bit 0.5cm wide and a bit 2.5cm wide
- A strip of rubber 15cm long by 10cm wide.

Introducing the activity

Talk to children about homes and list the basic requirements of a human home: solid walls and a good roof to protect us from rain and wind, warmth, water supply, a toilet, somewhere to relax, a place to cook and eat and somewhere to sleep.

Discuss the needs a bird would have and in particular talk about the needs of different kinds of birds. Encourage the children to see that a blue tit will require a different home from a barn owl.

Explain to the children some of the difficulties birds are experiencing with finding safe places to nest and rear their young – hedgerows are dug up and old barns are turned into houses.

Tell the children they are going to do something to help birds.

Conducting the activity

This construction activity is for you or your teaching assistant to do with groups of four children at a time. It will take a whole morning.

1. Cut out the wood panels for your bird box using the shapes and dimensions given in the diagram.
2. Drill an entrance hole using the 2.5cm drill bit. This is the size of hole for a blue tit, which this box is designed for.
3. The entrance hole needs to be at least 12.5cm above the floor of the box to stop the young birds falling out.
4. Drill half a dozen evenly spaced drainage holes 0.5cm wide in the base.
5. Assemble the box following the diagram attaching the components with screws or nails.
6. Attach the roof with the rubber strip as a hinge so it can be lifted up.

7. Attach your completed bird box with nails or screws to a fence post in a sheltered place out of direct sunlight but visible from a classroom window.

Health and safety

This is a construction activity. Instil in children a careful approach to the use of tools and construction equipment.

Follow-up activities

A really exciting thing to do would be to put a digital video camera inside your bird box and link it up to the computer in the classroom so the children can watch the baby birds developing. These are available commercially for well over a hundred pounds – maybe a keen technologically-minded teacher or parent could do something for you.

Teaching points

Let the children do as much of the work as they can in building the nesting box.

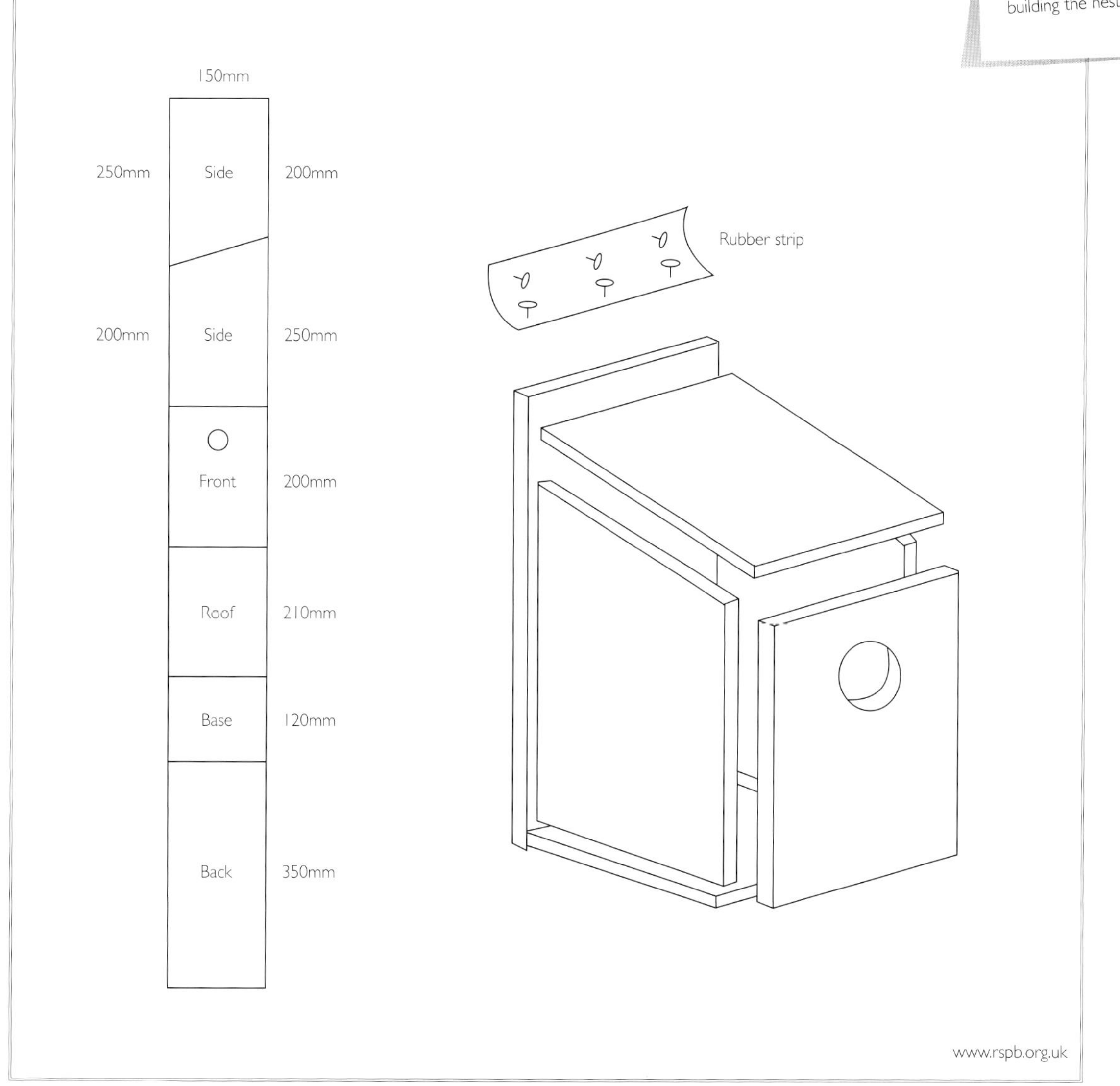

19. Rock pooling and beachcombing

Why go rock pooling and beachcombing?

These activities, by definition, need to be carried out at the seaside. Many schools try to take their children to the seaside while they are in EYFS or KS1. Rock pooling provides another insight into the diversity of the natural world.

Learning objectives

Observation skills once again come to the fore here. Encourage children to really look. EYFS children are using the sense of sight and KS1 children are developing their scientific observational skills. Some things in a rock pool that look like plants may suddenly make quick movements and reveal themselves to be animals. Patience and careful looking can be rewarded.

Resources

- Nets
- Collecting bowls, pots and tubs
- A large transparent plastic tank
- Magnifying glasses
- Identification guides.

Introducing the activity

For some of your children this may be the first time they have been to the seaside. Just take a little time to marvel at the rolling waves and the long-distance views out to the horizon.

Gather the children together on the beach and explain the safety aspects of rock pooling and beachcombing. Then set off and find a rock pool to explore or walk along the shoreline for your beachcombing.

Your local authority will have guidance on ratios of adults to children for school trips, but with young children the more adults you can take the better. For a trip to the seaside a ratio of one adult to two children is not extravagant: one in each hand is a good safety policy.

Conducting the activity

Rock pooling

Go rock pooling at low tide. Spend a little time just peering into the pool to see what is happening before you dip in with nets to catch any crustaceans that might be there.

Crabs are the most fun animals to catch at the seaside. Crab lines that can be bought from seaside shops include hooks and these are not a good idea for children or crabs. Use the little nets that come with some washing powder tablets. Place a piece of raw bacon in the net, tie it to a piece of string and drop it into a likely looking nook or cranny in the rock pool to see if you can catch a crab. Lift the net out every few minutes to see if you have a crab and if you do, drop it into your clear plastic tank for closer observation.

Place some seaweed in your tank and watch to see what emerges from it.

Once you have had a good look at the contents of the rock pool, gently pour the water from your tank back into the pool. And say thank you and goodbye to all those amazing animals you have just met.

Beachcombing

Simply walk slowly along the shoreline looking closely to see if anything interesting has been washed up. You will find all sorts of shells, some exotic and from far away across the world. You may find pieces of driftwood worn down by the sea; the same goes for fragments of old bricks and Victorian glass which have been worn smooth by the action of over 100 years of waves. If you are lucky you will find crab skeletons or shark egg cases (mermaids' purses).

Anything that is obviously not living (wood, brick, smooth glass or an empty shell, etc) can be bagged and taken back to school.

Health and safety

Go rock pooling when the tide is at its lowest and make certain you know the time of the next high tide so that you can be off the beach before the waves come rolling in. Information about the tides is available from the local tourist information office or online at *www.bbc.co.uk/weather/coast/tides.*

Wear appropriate footwear, ie non-slip, thick soles. Ensure that there is appropriate adult supervision, and that everyone is warned about the slipperiness of the rock pools.

Return all living things to the place where you found them.

Follow-up activities

In the sand on the beach, try making sculptures of the animals you caught in the rock pool.

Back at school you can use your beachcombing finds to create imaginative collages of wild and wonderful sea monsters.

Teaching points

Explain to children that animals belong to different groups and that crabs are known as crustaceans.

Theme: Science

Science: Introduction

Something has changed in the world of science teaching over the last 10 years. I see a lot more worksheets and a lot more drumming information into children through labelled diagrams. Surely true learning in science can *only* be gained through practical (and fun) experimental work?

This culture has come about purely through preparing children for SAT tests. Children don't need to be able to do experimental work to sit a written test – they just need to know what would happen if they *had* done the experiment. What a boring way to learn! It is time for a revolution in science teaching! The activities in this section will fire children's imagination about the possibilities of science. Science is about attitude as well as methodology. From the earliest age encourage children's natural desire to know how things work and why things happen. Take everyday opportunities such as cooking and playing with toy cars to discuss the scientific principles of our world.

Learning objectives

Specific learning objectives are given for each activity. Here is an overview list of learning objectives for science activities in general.

Early Years Foundation Stage

Personal, social and emotional development

- Be confident to try new activities, initiate ideas and speak in a familiar group.
- Work as part of a group or class, taking turns and sharing fairly.

Communication, language and literacy

- Interact with others, negotiating plans and activities and taking turns in conversations.
- Sustain attentive listening, responding to what they have heard with relevant comments, questions and actions.
- Extend their vocabulary, exploring the meanings and sounds of new words.
- Use talk to organise, sequence and clarify thinking, ideas, feelings and events.
- Attempt writing for different purposes.

Problem solving, reasoning and numeracy

- Count reliably up to 10 everyday objects.
- Use language such as 'more' and 'less' to compare two numbers.
- Use developing mathematical ideas and methods to solve practical problems.
- Use language such as 'greater', 'smaller', 'heavier' or 'lighter' to compare quantities.

Knowledge and understanding of the world

- Investigate objects and materials by using all of their senses as appropriate.
- Find out about, and identify, some features of living things, objects and events they have observed.
- Look closely at similarities, differences, patterns and change.
- Ask questions about why things happen and how things work.

Physical development

- Use a range of small and large equipment.
- Handle tools safely and with increasing control.

Creative development

- Respond in a variety of ways to what they see, hear, smell, touch and feel.

Key Stage 1
Science

Sc3 Materials and their properties
Knowledge, skills and understanding
Grouping materials

1. Pupils should be taught to:

a. use their senses to explore and recognise the similarities and differences between materials
b. sort objects into groups on the basis of simple material properties (for example, roughness, hardness, shininess, ability to float, transparency and whether they are magnetic or non-magnetic)
c. recognise and name common types of material (for example, metal, plastic, wood, paper, rock) and recognise that some of them are found naturally
d. find out about the uses of a variety of materials (for example, glass, wood, wool) and how these are chosen for specific uses on the basis of their simple properties.

Changing materials

1. Pupils should be taught to:

a. find out how the shapes of objects made from some materials can be changed by some processes, including squashing, bending, twisting and stretching
b. explore and describe the way some everyday materials (for example, water, chocolate, bread, clay) change when they are heated or cooled.

Sc4 Physical processes
Knowledge, skills and understanding
Forces and motion

2. Pupils should be taught:

a. to find out about, and describe the movement of, familiar things (for example, cars going faster, slowing down, changing direction)
b. that both pushes and pulls are examples of forces
c. to recognise that when things speed up, slow down or change direction, there is a cause (for example, a push or a pull).

Light and sound

3. Pupils should be taught:

Light and dark

a. to identify different light sources, including the sun
b. that darkness is the absence of light.

Making and detecting sounds

a. that there are many kinds of sound and sources of sound

b. that sounds travel away from sources, getting fainter as they do so, and that they are heard when they enter the ear.

Literacy links

Writing up practical science work

There is a certain methodology associated with scientific work, which I feel is important to establish from a young age. That doesn't mean that five and six-year-olds need to write a thesis every time they do some practical work! Discuss the practical work you do and scribe for the children under the following headings:

- What is the title of our experiment?
- What do we think will happen?
- What equipment did we use?
- What did we do?
- What happened?
- Were we right?
- What did we learn?

You might not do all of these with every experiment and certainly some activities you should just do for fun. But it does help to establish a good scientific approach to your science work and it will help to encourage writing for a purpose.

Hotseat a famous scientist

KS1 children are familiar with the historical characters of Samuel Pepys, Florence Nightingale and Mary Seacole. Why not introduce them to some historical characters associated with scientific discoveries. Sir Isaac Newton could explain some simple physics.

Hotseating involves going into role as a character and answering questions. The easiest way I have found to do this with scientific characters is to discuss with children beforehand some questions they would like to have answered by the visitor. I then do my research and answer their questions as if I were the character. I like to do this sort of work in costume, but there is no reason why you shouldn't do it without the added drama.

Health and safety

One of the reasons that practical science teaching has declined in schools is that it is seen as a risky business. It needn't be. Do practical work with younger children in small groups with teacher or TA support. While you are engaged on a task, ask the children what they see as the safety issues. Ask them for their ideas on keeping safe during these activities and teach them clear safety procedures.

1. The night sky

Why study the night sky?

This may sound like an activity that couldn't be carried out during school time, but in December and January it is dark at 5pm so it is perfectly possible to study the night sky with young children as a one-off after-school activity. For children to see Venus, Mars, Jupiter, Saturn and the moon is fascinating. To pick out the shapes of the constellations is exciting. Study the night sky simply to capture children's imagination about the possibilities of science.

Learning objectives

The Earth and space doesn't come into the KS1 science curriculum or the EYFS curriculum guidance, but that is not a reason for missing out on the excitement. There is also the pattern-forming aspect of spotting constellations and this links in with maths work on shape.

Resources

- Warm clothing
- Binoculars and a telescope if you can borrow some
- Star charts available from bookshops or online
- A magnetic compass
- Torches with red tissue paper over the lens.

Introducing the activity

Keep an eye on your local newspaper. Many of these have a monthly column written by a local astronomy enthusiast. The column will tell you which planets are visible that month and where to look for them. It will also tell you of any significant constellations to look out for.

The internet is also a source of useful information when planning your stargazing evening. Visit the Royal Astronomical Society website at *www.ras.org.uk* and click on 'Education' for a wealth of information.

Conducting the activity

If you can invite a local astronomy enthusiast to come along, that would be great.

Go out onto the school field before dark and set up a table with all your equipment.

Bring the children out onto the field and spend some time adjusting to the dark. The human eye contains a lens, which is adjusted to light levels by muscles and these muscles need a bit of a workout. Get the children to look at the silhouettes of buildings and trees in the near and middle distance. Spend some time just looking around at the sky. It takes about 20 minutes for eyes to become fully adjusted – children will notice that they can then spot more stars.

Do your stargazing on an evening when the moon is three or four days new. Check your diary – most of them list new moon dates. At this stage the moon is just a thin crescent like a toenail clipping in the western sky and its light will not dazzle other stars and planets too much. You can always go out at the time of a full moon as well to show children the difference.

Venus and Jupiter are bright planets and easily spotted, so if these are in the sky at the time of your visit, seek them out. Venus is closer to the sun than Earth, so is only visible in the west just after sunset or the east just before sunrise. Jupiter can be in different places depending on its cycle. Look at Jupiter through a pair of binoculars and you may be lucky enough to see four of its brightest moons as tiny dots alongside the planet. You will need a telescope to see the rings of Saturn.

Use your magnetic compass to find north. Turn your attention to the northern sky and find the Great Bear or Plough (the constellation that looks like a saucepan). Follow the line of the two stars opposite the handle and find the North Star. Carry your gaze on past the North Star and you will see a wonky W-shaped constellation. This is Cassiopeia. The constellations around the North Star are always above the horizon and visible all year round.

Turn to the south. The constellations you can see here will change during the year. Use your star chart to identify them. This is where the red-covered torch comes in. You can illuminate your star chart without the need for a bright light, which would make your eyes adjust again.

Health and safety

Make sure children know why they must never look directly at the sun.

Follow-up activities

Read the children's tales from Greek mythology, which tell the stories of the heroes and heroines, gods and goddesses who gave their names to the constellations.

Sketch out the patterns of the constellations with dots on large graph paper and then draw the shape of the animal or person the constellation is named after lightly over the top.

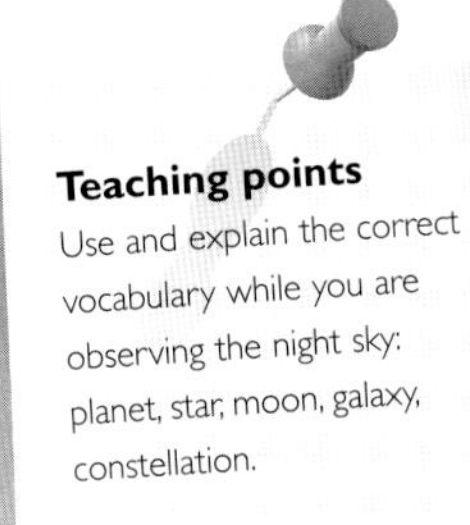

2. Make a sundial

What is a sundial?

A sundial is an ancient tool for measuring the passage of the sun through the sky and dividing that passage up into the 12 daylight hours. The Romans had 12 hours of day and 12 hours of night and those hours were different lengths depending on the time of year.

Why make a sundial?

Making a sundial and plotting the passage and length of a shadow over the course of a day is a good way to demonstrate the passage of time. It will also lead into discussions about the Earth turning and moving around the sun.

Learning objectives

Link this activity in with maths work on time. Make your marks on the sundial at regular intervals of an hour and get your children into the habit of reading the analogue time off your classroom clock.

Resources

- A piece of chalk
- A hand drill
- A square of flat wood about 30cm by 30cm
- Ruler and pencil
- A 15cm-long piece of dowelling
- A piece of Plasticine
- Wood glue
- A magnetic compass.

Introducing the activity

Talk about the structure of a child's day in sequence: get up, get dressed, have breakfast, walk to school, etc.

Use a large clock face to review your children's learning on time. With Reception age children this will simply be that the big hand is on the 12 and the little hand is on the 10 so it is ten o'clock and that is the time we have our fruit. With Year 2 some will be well versed in quarter to and quarter past.

Ask children how people told the time before there were clocks. Some may have heard of a sundial.

Conducting the activity

A simple sundial

At nine o'clock in the morning, choose a child and get them to stand on a spot on the playground you have marked with a cross. Draw around their shadow with chalk. At 10am and 11am and so on throughout the day do the same thing with the same child. Children will notice that the child's shadow gets shorter as midday approaches and longer as the afternoon progresses and it moves throughout the day.

Make a portable sundial

- Draw a line with a ruler right across the middle of the flat piece of wood.
- Make a small hole through the flat piece of wood on the line and about 3cm in from one edge.

- Push the dowelling through and glue in place.
- Put a knob of Plasticine on the end of the dowelling to protect eyes.
- Use your magnetic compass to aline your piece of wood so that the line you have drawn is pointing north/south with the dowelling at the southern end.
- Throughout the day mark on the wood with a pen the line of the dowelling's shadow at each hour. Write the number of the hour at the end of the line.
- You've made your own clock!

Tell the time with your portable sundial

- You can take your sundial away and put it out again on another day. As long as you line it up north/south it will be accurate.
- At eleven o'clock in the morning the shadow of the dowelling should line up with the eleven o'clock line on your sundial. Bingo! You're telling the time in the same way ancient people did.

Health and safety

The Plasticine on the end of the dowelling is there to stop children getting a poke in the eye. Children should be fully supervised when using a hand drill.

Follow-up activities

Other ancient clocks you could make include sand timers, water clocks and candle clocks. Some of my Reception children loved checking the class sand timers to see if they really did measure a minute or five minutes. I left a stopwatch on the investigation table with the sand timers and it kept them actively learning for ages.

Teaching points

Explain to the children that the sun doesn't go around the Earth – it just looks like that because the Earth is spinning around..

A simple water clock can be made by poking a very small hole in the bottom of a yogurt pot and filling the pot with water. Time how long the water all takes to drip out. Children might like to design and make their own improved versions.

Investigate candle clocks by measuring a tall thin candle. Burn the candle for one hour and measure how much shorter it is. Burn the candle for another hour and measure then another hour and measure. If you use the same type of candle and mark the measurements on it in pen you can use it as a moderately accurate clock.

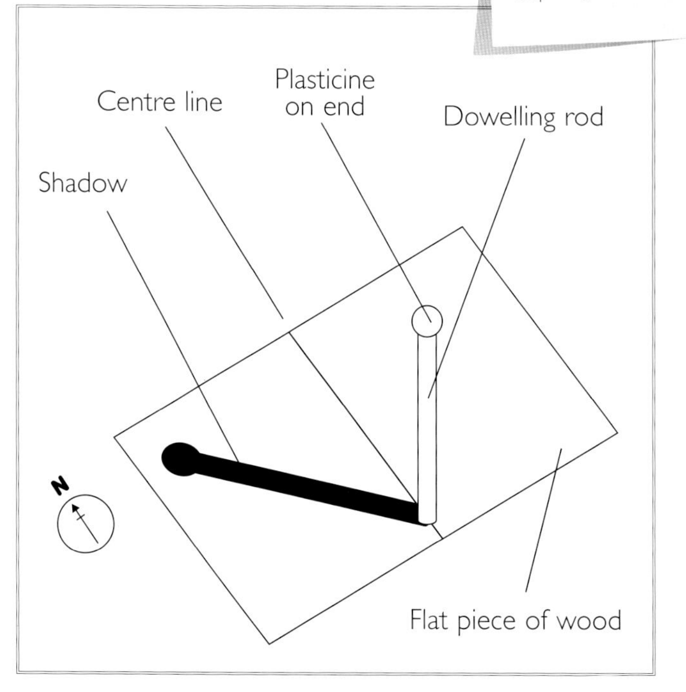

3. Weather – recording, predicting and enjoying

Why study the weather?

The weather is another big area of learning that has effectively been left out of the National Curriculum and QCA schemes of work. Yet, it is a national obsession. If we expect our children to grow up to be able to discuss the weather along with the rest of us then we had better teach them what it is all about!

Learning objectives

There are links here with the geography curriculum. You can bring in some design and technology by constructing the apparatus to measure the weather. EYFS children are gaining an insight into the passage of time through studying the weather over the course of the seasons.

Resources

Resources for constructing simple weather measuring equipment are easily obtainable. Individual requirements are given for each activity.

Introducing the activity

Most Reception classrooms have a weather board where the children can record the daily weather through the use of symbols. This is a good staring point and can certainly be built on in years one and two with increased accuracy of recording particular aspects of the weather. Get your children into the habit of describing the weather. Take a look at the BBC online forecast for the weekend on a Friday and discuss with the children how the outlook will affect any plans their families may have made.

Conducting the activity

Recording the weather

Temperature: A simple maximum/minimum thermometer can be purchased for just a few pounds from a DIY store (although I find farmers' suppliers are cheapest for all sorts of outdoors stuff). Hang the thermometer in a sheltered spot on a wall in your outdoor classroom. It will tell you the warmest temperature in the last 24 hours and the coolest. Check and record every day to build up a table of data for converting into graphs. You reset the thermometer each day with a magnet and then leave it for another 24 hours. These records are very useful to gardeners as are soil thermometers, which you might also like to use.

Wind speed: Wind speed is measured on the Beaufort Scale, devised by Francis Beaufort in 1805. You don't need any fancy wind-o-meter to measure the wind. You look at the movement of things like smoke, leaves on trees, washing on a line, flags, roof tiles, etc and ascribe a number from 1 to 12 according to the intensity of the wind. If you search for 'Beaufort Scale' on the internet you will find several meteorological sites with details of the scale.

Rainfall: Measuring the rainfall accurately with a rain gauge depends on the gauge having a flat bottom and the mouth of the funnel being the same size as the bottom of the container. You can't just cut a lemonade bottle in half and turn it upside down as the bottom of the bottle is rounded and this will give an inaccurate measurement. Dig around in your science cupboard and find a flat-bottomed plastic beaker and a plastic funnel the same width as the beaker. Place the funnel in the mouth of the beaker and leave outside in an open area. Check for rainwater every day at the same time and measure the depth of rainwater in centimetres with a ruler. Record on a chart. At the end of each month add up your total rainfall and do the same at the end of the year.

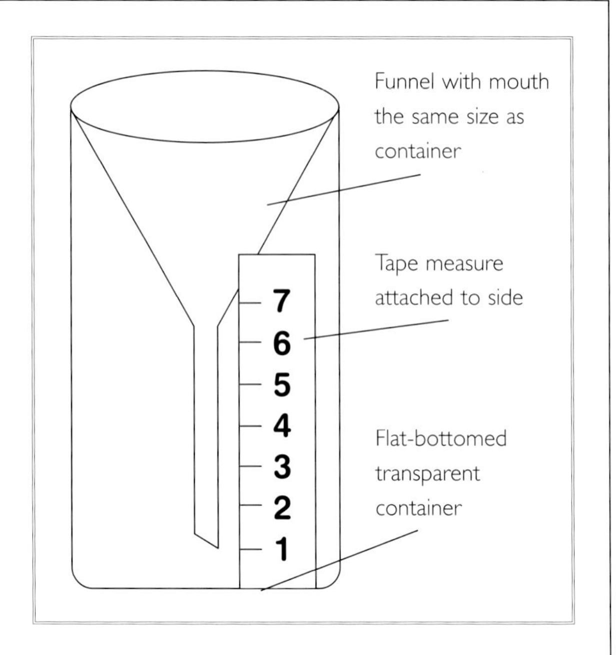

Sunshine and cloud: Meteorologists record the number of sun hours in a day using a Campbell-Stokes sunshine recorder, which burns a ray on a piece of card when the sun is out. A simple way for children to measure sunshine is simply to record every hour on the hour what fraction of the sky is covered in cloud: 1 (the whole sky), ¾, ½ or ¼. Cloud cover is measured in 'oktas' by weather forecasters and each 'okta' is an eighth of the sky.

Predicting the weather

Old wives tales: Test them out and see if they are true:

- Red sky at night, shepherds' delight.
- Red sky at morning, shepherd's warning.
- Rain before seven, fine before eleven.
- (The moon's halo) Near ring, far rain. Far ring, near rain.
- If cows are lying down rain is expected.

Modern ways: There will almost certainly be someone in your local area who measures the weather using quite sophisticated equipment and has some sort of input on local radio. Invite an amateur meteorologist into school to show the children how they can make simple predictions based on the readings they are getting from their own weather equipment.

Enjoying the weather

Make sure children have appropriate clothing.

Puddle jumping: We all tend to run for cover when it rains, but it rains so much in this country we may as well get out there and enjoy it.

Kite flying: A direct link to your weather studies is to make and fly your own kites. There are instructions on kite making in this book in the section on design and technology (p171).

Cloud watching: If you lie on your back on the grass on a pleasant spring day and look up at the sky you can see faces, animals, ships, monsters and all manner of other formations in the cloud shapes and point them out to your friends.

Seaside: Take your children for a day trip to the seaside to really experience the restorative powers of our great British weather.

Snow: If snow falls, try to keep your school open and have the most fun day the children will have in their entire school life by building an igloo.

Health and safety

Weather can be dangerous. By all means take your children out to enjoy splashing about in puddles in light rain, but please don't take them out if storms threaten.

Follow-up activities

Even quite young children will have heard about climate change and they will be aware of extreme weather from news reports on the television. We can take some of the fear out of these things by taking practical action to do something about them. If your school is working towards an Eco-Schools award then find some practical aspects of this that your children can undertake to do their bit to limit the extent of climate change. If there is a global weather-related disaster on the news you might organise a cake sale to raise money to buy tents for refugees. The world is a troubled place, but we all feel better about it if we do something practical.

Teaching points
Create an ICT link by investing in wireless weather measuring devices and gathering weather statistics on your classroom computer.

4. Make a magnetic compass

Why make a magnetic compass?

Magnetic compasses have allowed navigators to explore the seven seas and fly to the moon and back. Magnetic compasses are cheap to buy, but making one offers you the opportunity to discuss magnetism with children as you are making it.

Learning objectives

This is a good activity to get EYFS children extending their vocabulary and exploring the meanings and sounds of new words (CLL). KS1 children will benefit from discussing forces and motion and will also be able to increase their understanding of the properties of materials.

Resources

- Sewing needle
- Bar magnet
- Small bowl of water
- Cork from a wine bottle
- Serrated knife.

Introducing the activity

Lay out a table with different metal objects and a selection of magnets. Let children spend time playing and discovering for themselves. Show them how to move a paperclip around on a piece of paper by placing a magnet underneath it. Pull model cars across the table with the force of magnetism. Have fun!

Tell your children that the Earth is like a great big magnet and that right at the centre of the Earth there is a huge ball of solid metal. Show them a magnetic compass and tell them that in our part of the world the needle will always point to magnetic north. Does anyone know where it would point if they were in Australia?

Conducting the activity

- Cut a disk about 5mm thick off the cork.
- Rub the bar magnet along the needle several times in one direction – from the eye to the point. This is important as rubbing up and down will not align the polarity of the metal needle and it is this polarity that will make it point north.
- Push the needle through the side of the cork so that it comes out the other side and there is an approximately equal length of needle on each side of the cork.
- Place the cork gently in the bowl of water and watch the point of the needle turn to indicate north.

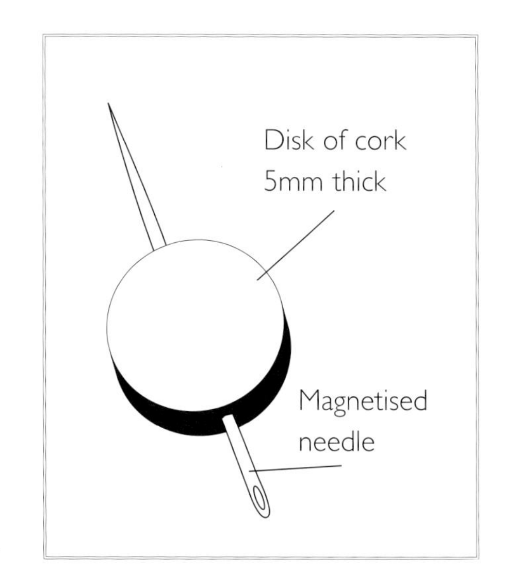

- Check the accuracy of your compass with a 'real' magnetic compass.
- Place the bar magnet next to the bowl of water and move it around the bowl – the needle should follow.

Health and safety

You do the cutting of the cork for the children and push the needle through the cork.

Follow-up activities

Use your magnetic compass on a simple orienteering exercise. Give children a list of instructions such as: Walk five paces to the north, turn west and walk 10 paces, then turn north (and so on). See how accurately they are able to do this. You could even link this in with the making of treasure maps. Follow the instructions accurately to find the buried treasure.

Teaching points

The magnetic compass is another invention we have the Ancient Chinese to thank for..

5. Make your own paper

Why make paper?

As well as dealing with the production of a familiar and common material, this activity will reinforce the message of recycling. We are so used to paper as an everyday item, we don't often stop to think about the processes behind it.

Learning objectives

This activity will help EYFS children to investigate objects and materials by using all of their senses as appropriate. They are also trying out a new and unfamiliar activity and working as a group. KS1 children will have the chance to group materials and investigate the processes involved in changing materials.

Resources

- Old newspapers
- A blender
- A wire coathanger
- An old pair of tights
- Plastic bucket
- Plastic washing-up bowl – rectangular
- PVA glue
- Old wooden spoon
- Two sheets of cloth a little bigger than your finished paper
- Rolling pin.

Introducing the activity

Start by focusing on recycling. If you already have a classroom paper recycling scheme in your school talk with the children about why they think this is important. Talk about where paper comes from and why we recycle paper – to save trees, reduce landfill and reduce the amount of energy and water that is used in paper production.

If you have no paper recycling scheme in your school, now would be a good time to start one and your class could initiate it. They could take their proposal to the school council to add an extra dimension to this activity.

Conducting the activity

- Tear the newspaper up into small pieces and soak in a bowl of water for at least 30 minutes.
- Bend the wire coathanger into a square frame and stretch one leg of the old tights over the frame.
- Put the paper and water in a blender and whizz it up until you have a soupy mixture.
- Half fill your washing-up bowl with warm water and add two tablespoons of PVA glue – this will prevent the finished paper from soaking up too much ink.
- Pour your soupy mixture into the bowl of warm water and give it a good stir.

- Slide your frame to the bottom of the bowl and gently lift it up. Counting slowly to 20 as you lift gives you about the right timing. Hold the frame above the water for about a minute to let the water drain.
- Use your fingers to push gently on the paper to squeeze out more water.
- Lay a piece of cloth on a flat surface and turn your frame over to allow the paper to drop onto the cloth.
- Cover the paper with another piece of cloth.
- Use a rolling pin to press more water out of your sandwich of home-made paper and cloth.
- Remove the top cloth and leave the paper to dry overnight.
- Your home-made paper is now ready to write on.

Health and safety

There are no real health and safety issues with this activity – just make sure you give the blender a good wash out afterwards!

Follow-up activities

Try making paper of different colours by using natural dyes such as red onion skin, beetroot or even grass blended in with your mixture. You can also add scraps of different coloured paper to the mix.

You can give your finished paper a marbled effect by half filling a bowl with water and dribbling some oil-based inks across the surface (don't let children with nut allergies do this as the inks are often nut-based) and then lay your paper briefly on the surface before removing and drying.

Teaching points

Many of our commonly used items have their origins in Ancient China. Paper made from wood pulp is just one of them.

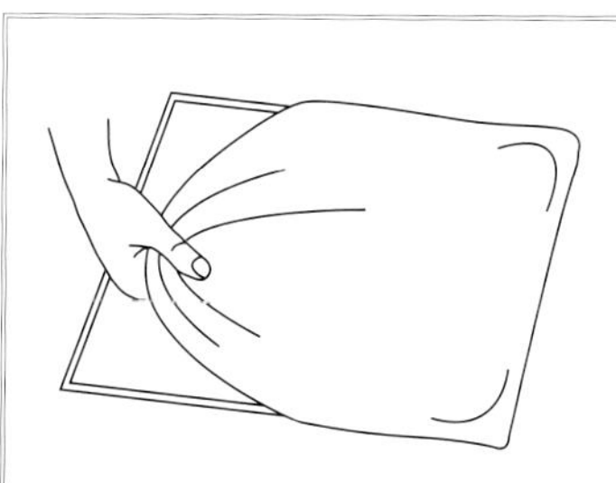

Stretch a pair of old tights over a coathanger frame.

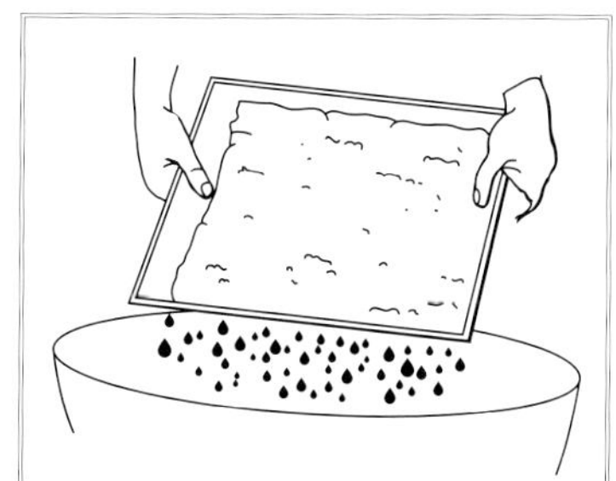

Slide frame to bottom of bowl of paper mix and remove slowly.

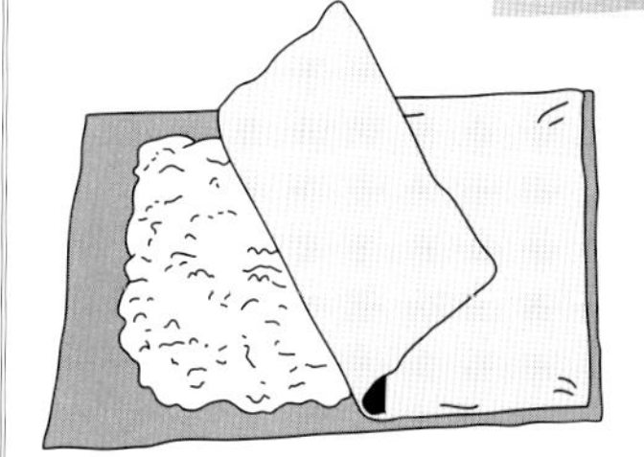

Build up sandwiches of wet paper between pieces of cloth.

6. Build an erupting volcano

Why build an erupting volcano?

We don't have active volcanoes in this country any longer so making your own model one, which really erupts, is a good way to demonstrate to children what they look like.

Learning objectives

While this may appear to be a construction activity, the core principles are based on chemistry. The bicarbonate of soda gives off carbon dioxide when it comes into contact with a mixture of water and vinegar. The washing-up liquid makes foaming bubbles from the gas and the food colouring adds realistic colour to the erupting lava. KS1 children are working on materials and EYFS children are using their senses and also constructing a model using tools.

Resources

For the volcano

- A 500ml yoghurt pot
- A 500ml plastic drink bottle
- Masking tape
- A square of plywood 90cm by 90cm
- Chicken wire
- Tacks
- Lots of newspaper
- Wallpaper paste
- Rock-coloured paint – greens, greys and browns.

For the eruption

- Protective goggles
- 60ml of water
- A teaspoon of bicarbonate of soda
- 60ml of vinegar
- A few drops of red food colouring
- A few drops of washing-up liquid
- A small square of tissue paper
- A long, thin stick.

Introducing the activity

Take a look at the May 1980 eruption of Mount St Helens, USA, on the internet – it's pretty impressive! Discuss with children what happens when a volcano erupts: great clouds of smoke rise into the air, rock and ash are hurled out and great rivers of lava run down the side of the volcano. Be sure to reassure them that we no longer have volcanoes in the British Isles. Tell the children they are going to make a model of an erupting volcano and show them the materials you will use.

Conducting the activity

Make the volcano

- Tape the yogurt pot upside down in the middle of the square of plywood.
- Tape the plastic drinks bottle to the top of the yoghurt pot and remove the lid.
- The top of the bottle will be the crater of the volcano.
- Build a volcano-shaped cone out of chicken wire around the yoghurt pot and drinks bottle.
- Scrunch up some newspaper into balls and pack out the inside of the cone before fixing it to the plywood with tacks.
- Mix up the wallpaper paste and use it to stick strips of newspaper over the chicken wire cone.
- Build up at least four layers of this papier mâché and leave for a couple of days to dry thoroughly.

- Paint your volcano with greens, greys and browns so it looks like a mountain.
- Add model trees and patches of grass on the lower slopes for effect. Improvise boulders from small stones.

A volcanic eruption

- Gather the ingredients for the eruption.
- Put on your protective goggles.
- Pour the water, washing-up liquid, food colouring and vinegar into the plastic bottle at the centre of your volcano and stir it with a long, thin stick.
- Wrap the bicarbonate of soda in the small square of tissue paper and poke it through the neck of the bottle.
- Stand back and watch the eruption as the bicarbonate of soda reacts with the vinegar.

Health and safety

This is one activity where eye protection is necessary. When you are ready to erupt the volcano, do it out on the playground. Keep the children at least five metres back, under the supervision of your teaching assistant. You wear the protective goggles to demonstrate good practice and you initiate the eruption. The children can observe from a distance.

Follow-up activities

See what other natural phenomena your children can make – an earthquake, a flowing river or a tornado. All these things are possible, but I'm not going to tell you how!

Teaching points
Real lava is molten rock that comes pouring out from the inside of the Earth.

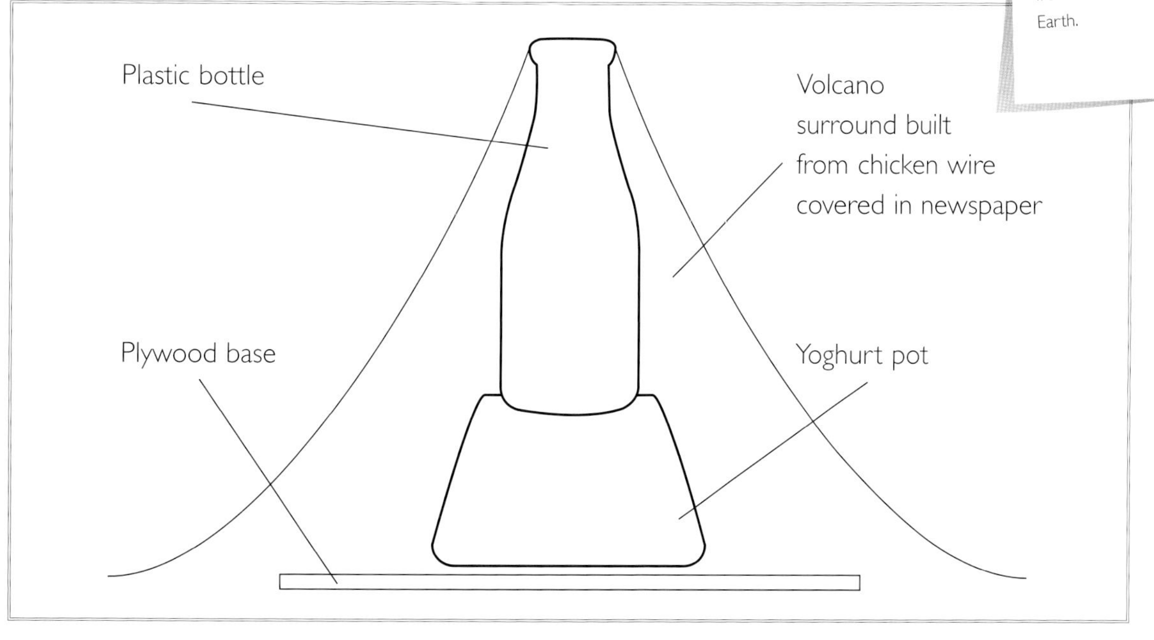

7. Make an electromagnet

What is an electromagnet?

An electromagnet is a bar or rod of metal that becomes magnetic when a small electrical charge is fed through it.

Why make an electromagnet?

The interesting thing about electromagnets is that they are different from the ordinary magnets we are all used to. This novelty value instantly makes the construction of one a good reason for doing it – the learning from this activity will add to children's knowledge of ordinary magnets.

Learning objectives

We are in the realm of grouping materials for KS1 children. In the EYFS, children are finding out about and identifying some features of objects and will also ask questions about why things happen and how things work.

Resources

- A nail 7.5cm long
- 90cm of low-voltage insulated copper wire (from a DIY store)
- A new D battery (1.5V)
- Masking tape
- A sharp knife
- Paperclips.

Introducing the activity

This activity will fit in with ongoing work on grouping materials. Present your children with a range of common objects and ask them which they think will be attracted to magnets and which will not. Test the objects with a magnet to find out. Question the children about their understanding of magnets. Physical processes also come into this so you can take the opportunity to refresh learning on pushes and pulls. Magnetism is a pulling force.

Conducting the activity

1. Wrap the copper wire around the nail leaving 20cm of wire free at each end.
2. Keep the coils on the nail close, but don't overlap them. The more coils you have the more powerful the magnet.
3. Use your sharp knife (adult assistance) to remove 3cm of the plastic coating from each end of the wire.
4. Attach the exposed metal ends of wire to each terminal of the battery with masking tape.
5. Once both ends of the wire are attached to the battery your electromagnet will be live
6. Use it to try to pick up paperclips.
7. Remove one end of the wire from the battery and see what happens to the paperclip.

This simple electromagnet is stronger than the magnetic force of the Earth. You can prove this by placing a magnetic compass on a table about 1 metre away from the magnet and see what happens to the needle of the compass as it is moved closer to your electromagnet. It will be pulled towards your magnet and away from the North Pole.

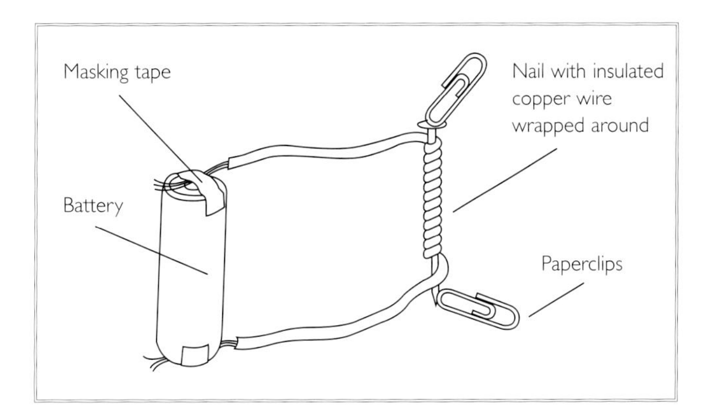

Health and safety

Children will need assistance with the cutting aspects of this activity. The electrical current is not strong so there is no danger from this, but take the opportunity to reinforce general safety around electricity.

Follow-up activities

In modern life, electromagnets are used in everyday items such as doorbells and computer hard drives. Link your work on electromagnets in with a design and technology project on wheeled vehicles to see if children can come up with ways of harnessing the magnetism they have created.

Teaching points

Magnetism occurs naturally in rocks. Magnetism can be used to magnetise metal and this is how ordinary household magnets are made..

8. Make a pinhole camera

What is a pinhole camera?

This is the very earliest camera and involves the light from an image being projected through a small hole and onto a screen.

Why make a pinhole camera?

This activity will illustrate the fact that light travels and that images can be captured.

Learning objectives

EYFS children will ask questions about why things happen and how things work as they do this activity (KUW). KS1 children are working on the light and dark aspect of the physical processes section of the science curriculum. There are design and technology skills in here too; these are limited to the actual construction techniques, but it offers good practice in following a plan.

Resources

- Pringles can
- Ruler
- Knife
- Needle
- White tissue paper
- Scissors
- Masking tape
- Aluminium foil.

Introducing the activity

View digital images on the electronic whiteboard of your class engaged in fun activities. Ask the children how they think these images have been captured. Talk about how much photography has changed in recent times. Even if you are a young teacher you will still be able to remember having to send your snaps off for processing.

Conducting the activity

Making the camera

- Take the plastic lid off the Pringles can and put to one side.
- Mark a line all around the can 5cm up from the metal bottom and cut so you now have a long hollow tube and a short tube with a metal base.
- Use the needle to make a small hole in the middle of the metal base.
- Cut a disk of white tissue paper and glue inside the Pringles can lid.
- Put the plastic lid on the shorter piece of tube.
- Place the longer piece of tube on top and tape all the pieces together.
- Wrap a double thickness of foil all the way around the outside of the Pringles can and tape securely into place – this will keep light out (leave the ends unblocked!).

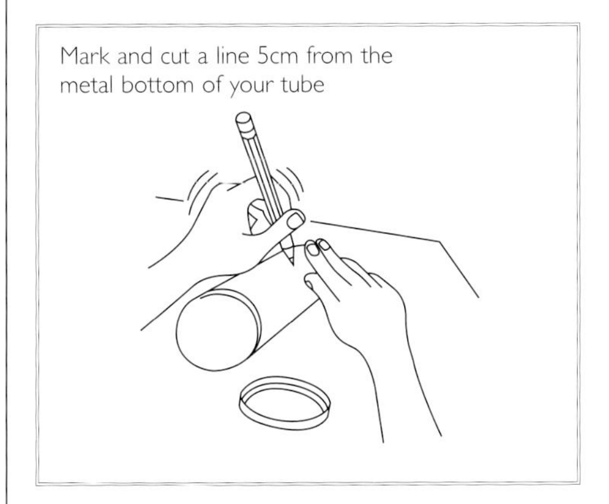

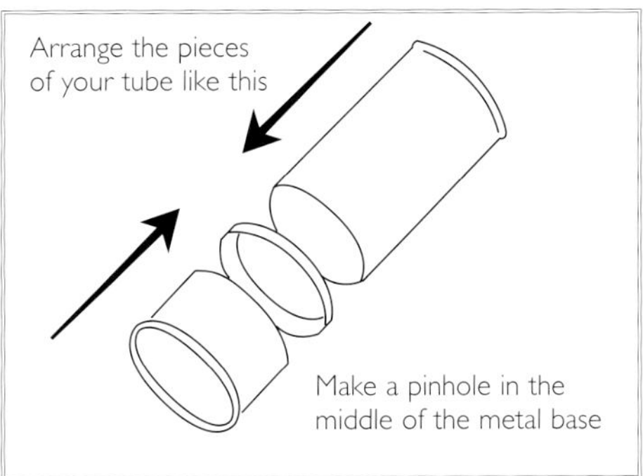

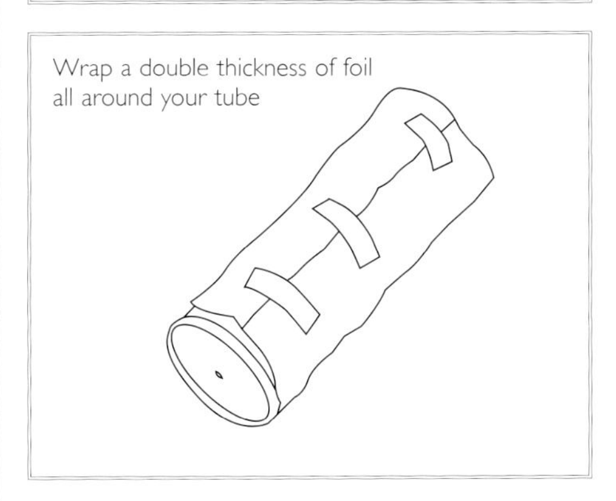

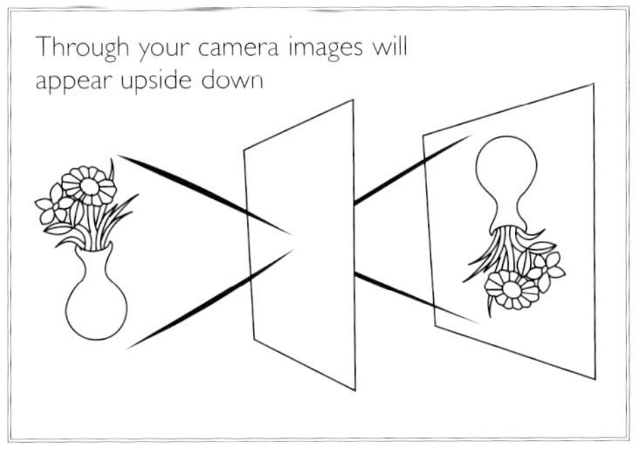

Using the camera

- Go outside on a sunny day.
- Point the closed end of your pinhole camera at a well lit and colourful object such as a spread of flowers.
- Look through the open end of the camera – cup your hands around the opening to try to keep out as much light as possible or cover your head with a dark cloth like old-fashioned photographers did.
- You should be able to see an image of the object on the white tissue paper screen – but it will be upside down!

Health and safety

The normal health and safety guidance for simple construction tasks applies to this activity. Be careful with scissors and take the opportunity to teach children to use tools appropriately. Remind children that they must never look directly at the sun.

Follow-up activities

If you want to take this activity to its logical conclusion you can make a pinhole camera out of a shoebox and place a piece of photographic paper inside to capture the image. Providing you exclude all light from the box there should be a useable image on the paper that a chemist will be able to process for you. Visit *http://tinyurl.com/kodac-pinhole* to find out more. For World Pinhole Photography Day see *www.pinholeday.org*.

Teaching points

The real name for a pinhole camera is a 'camera obscura' – which is Latin for 'dark chamber'.

9. Make a periscope

What is a periscope?

A periscope is a simple spying device that allows you to see over walls and around corners. The most well known use is in submarines, but tanks also use them.

Why make a periscope?

The way in which light is directed by the mirrors of a periscope is a practical demonstration of how light travels. Making a periscope will also allow children to have all sorts of fun spying on one another.

Learning objectives

EYFS children will ask questions about why things happen and how things work as they do this activity (KUW). KS1 children can cover the whole of the light and dark aspect of the physical processes section of the science curriculum with this one activity. There are design and technology skills in here too, though these are limited to the actual construction techniques.

Resources

- A large sheet of thick card measuring 70cm by 50cm
- Two square mirrors, 10cm by 10cm
- Insulating or duct tape
- Scissors
- Sharp knife
- Torches.

Introducing the activity

Turn the lights off in the classroom and close the blinds. Tape paper over the door. Do everything you can to make it really dark. Give children a mirror and torch to play with and ask them to bounce the light beams from the torch off the mirror. Give them some specific targets to aim their light beam at: 'Who can make their light beam hit the calendar? See if you can aim at the book corner.'

After a bit of fun, collect the resources and return the classroom to normality. Discuss with your children different sources of light and ask them to describe different uses people make of light. Once they are warmed up to the theme, announce that the most important use of light for us is simply that it allows us to see. Light bounces off objects and into our eyes so that we can see them.

Have a periscope made up and show the children how you can see what they are up to even though you are hiding behind the bookcase. They will love this! Then tell them they are going to make their own periscope and they will be really excited.

Conducting the activity

- Cut out the thick card according to the dimensions shown on the net diagram below – you may need to adapt these slightly if your mirrors are not exactly 10cm by 10cm.
- Fold along the lines as shown.

- Secure the tabs that hold the cardboard tube together at the sides but leave the ends open.
- Tape the top and bottom mirrors in place at an angle of 45 degrees.
- Check that they work as they should before securing the top and bottom cardboard flaps.
- To make the periscope last longer wrap tape around the whole structure.
- Take your periscope outside and peer over some fences and around some walls.

Health and safety

There is some cutting associated with this activity and some of that will need to be done with a sharp knife by an adult. When using the periscope remind children that they must never look directly at the sun.

Follow-up activities

Shine a light into the bottom of the periscope and ask children to predict where on the classroom wall it will shine.

Set up some problem-solving activities where children play a stalking game around the school field using the periscopes to find out where their 'enemy' is without being detected.

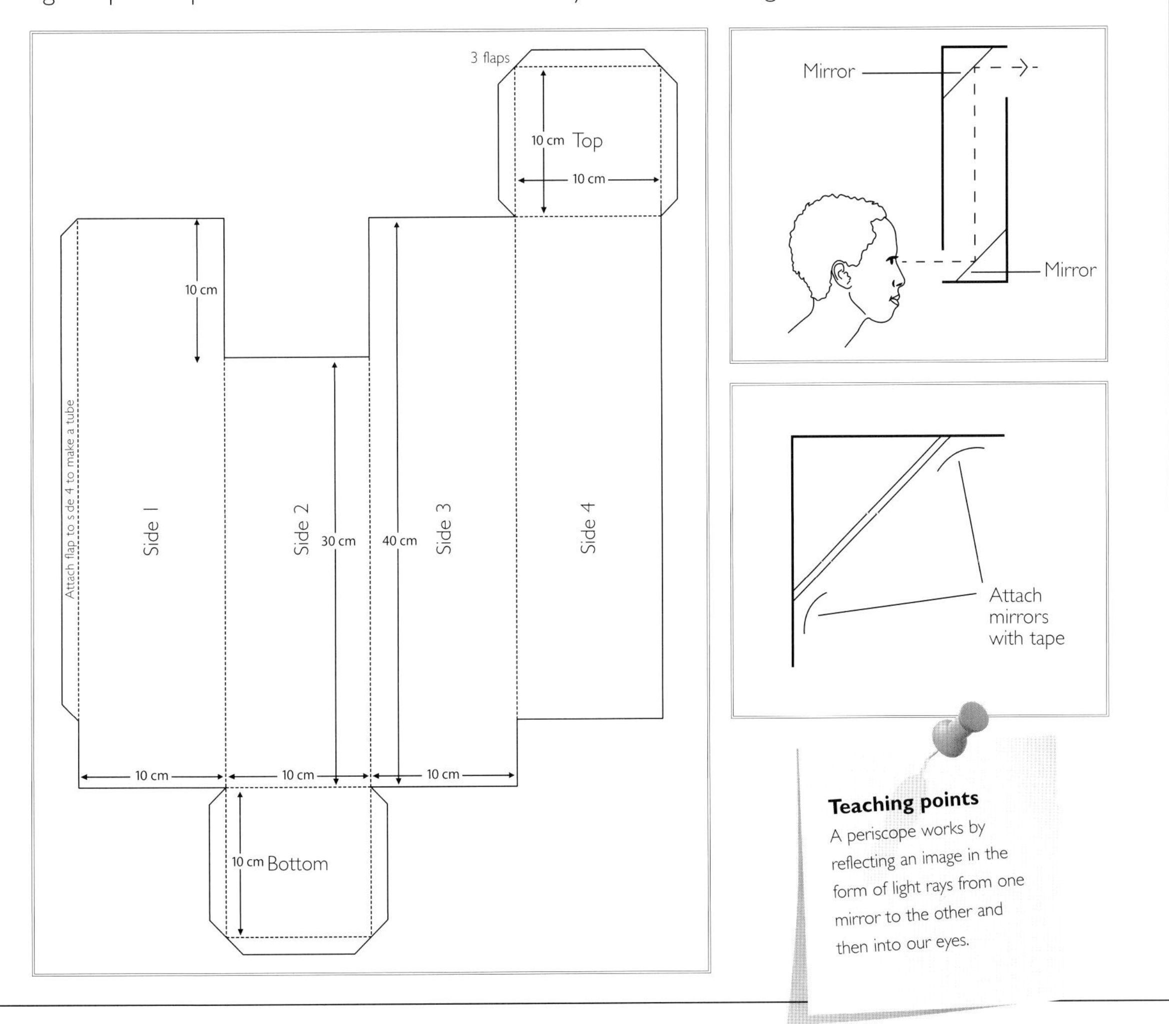

Theme: Art

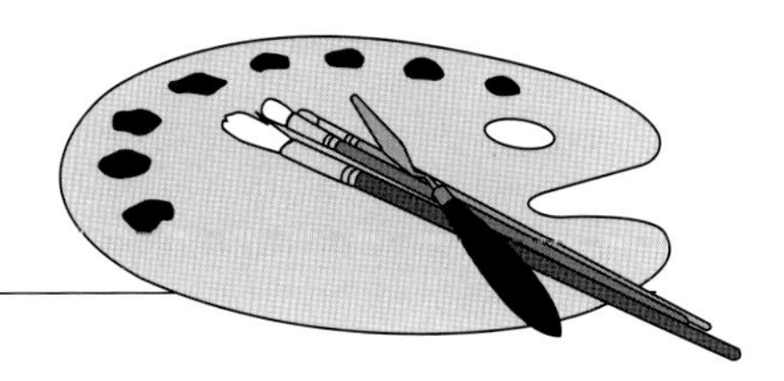

Art: Introduction

Adventurous art involves going out and doing artistic things with the natural world. This might be in your outdoor classroom, on your school field, in a local park or nature reserve or further afield on a day trip. Children use their senses to explore and gain inspiration from the natural world. They experiment with materials to create their own art. This gives them a greater understanding of the world around them as well as the opportunity to develop their own artistic styles.

Learning objectives

Here is an overview list of learning objectives for art activities in general.

Early Years Foundation Stage

Personal, social and emotional development

- Be confident to try new activities, initiate ideas and speak in a familiar group.

Communication, language and literacy

- Interact with others, negotiating plans and activities and taking turns in conversations.
- Use talk to organise, sequence and clarify thinking, ideas, feelings and events.

Problem solving, reasoning and numeracy

- Use language such as 'greater', 'smaller', 'heavier' or 'lighter' to compare quantities.
- Talk about, recognise and recreate simple patterns.
- Use everyday words to describe position.

Knowledge and understanding of the world

- Investigate objects and materials by using all of their senses as appropriate.
- Build and construct with a wide range of objects, selecting appropriate resources and adapting their work where necessary.

Creative development

- Express and communicate their ideas, thoughts and feelings by using a widening range of materials.

Key Stage 1

We are focused on the art curriculum. Here are some relevant extracts from the National Curriculum. The important thing is to follow the process: *ideas* followed by *making and doing* followed by *evaluating and developing* the work. Knowledge and understanding come about through the discussions you have with the children as you work on an adventurous art activity together.

Knowledge, skills and understanding

Exploring and developing ideas

1. Pupils should be taught to:

a. record from first-hand observation, experience and imagination, and explore ideas

b. ask and answer questions about the starting points for their work, and develop their ideas.

Investigating and making art, craft and design

2. Pupils should be taught to:

a. investigate the possibilities of a range of materials and processes
b. try out tools and techniques and apply these to materials and processes, including drawing
c. represent observations, ideas and feelings, and design and make images and artefacts.

Evaluating and developing work

3. Pupils should be taught to:

a. review what they and others have done and say what they think and feel about it
b. identify what they might change in their current work or develop in their future work.

Knowledge and understanding

4. Pupils should be taught about:

a. visual and tactile elements, including colour, pattern and texture, line and tone, shape, form and space
b. materials and processes used in making art, craft and design.

Breadth of study

5. During the key stage, pupils should be taught the Knowledge, skills and understanding through:

a. exploring a range of starting points for practical work
b. working on their own, and collaborating with others, on projects in two and three dimensions and on different scales
c. using a range of materials and processes
d. investigating different kinds of art, craft and design.

Health and safety

Art activities, even adventurous ones, are relatively safe. Give the children specific guidance on what they can and cannot use when searching for art materials. Specific health and safety guidance is given for each activity.

Literacy links

Interview an artist

Artists are everywhere! A call to the local adult education centre or a visit to a local arts centre will give you contact details for local artists who are inspired by nature. Invite an artist into school to share their work and answer children's questions about technique. Some artists will provide master classes for schools at a modest fee. The literacy link here is the learning children gain through asking pertinent questions, listening to the answers and incorporating those answers into their own future work.

Artwork accompaniment

In art galleries or at outdoor art installations there is often a short piece of text accompanying the work. This may give the context within which the artwork was produced or the artist's thoughts on the development of the piece. Children really don't like being told to write about it after doing a piece of practical work! Why not record their thoughts and feelings about their artwork instead? You can do this with an MP3 player for visitors to listen to as they tour your exhibition.

1. A living willow dome

What is a living willow dome?

This is a structure made out of living willow trees. It will grow and change with the seasons.

Why make a living willow dome?

A living willow dome can be used as a den or as a space for storytelling or for circle time.

Learning objectives

This activity lends itself particularly to interacting with others (CLL), describing position and recreating simple patterns (PSRN) in the EYFS curriculum. There is also a design and technology focus. Weaving materials together is an ancient way of making them join. For thousands of years people have woven baskets out of grasses and reeds and people have been living in woven structures for that long too. There are history opportunities here – explore houses and homes through the ages.

Resources

- Bundles of living willow saplings (you will need 32 willow saplings)
- Garden twine – biodegradable
- Sticks as markers
- A garden dibber
- Compost
- Watering can.

Introducing the activity

If you are able to take the children to a local wildlife reserve, country park or community farm where there are some willow structures to see this will give them lots of ideas to get started. If this is not possible, go to *www.thewillowbank.co.uk* or *www.englishwillowbaskets.co.uk* to view photos of structures made from living willow.

You will need to order your living willow saplings in advance. Both these companies offer mail order and will be happy to discuss your needs and offer advice.

This activity will take some years to come to fruition, but children will love to revisit it as they move up through the school.

Conducting the activity

Planting (first year)

1. When your willow bundles arrive, stand them upright with the roots in large tubs of water to prevent them drying out and dying.
2. Mark out a circle of three metres diameter. Place a peg in the middle of your site and tie a length of string to it. One and a half metres along the string tie a sharp stick and use this to draw a circle with a diameter of three metres in the turf – like you would with a compass.
3. Around this circle place a marker stick every 30cm. Leave a 60cm gap for the entrance.

4. At each marker stick make a hole with a dibber about 30cm deep. Fill these with compost and water to prepare them for taking the living willow plant.
5. Place a living willow sapling in each hole and firm the ground around each one.
6. Leave your willow saplings to settle into their new home.

Shaping (second year)

Unless you are able to buy very long saplings initially your trees will need a year to settle in and grow to a height of about three metres before you shape your dome.

7. Bend each alternate willow sapling to meet the one opposite and tie these with biodegradable string to form a series of arches that create a basic dome shape. Ideally you want four of these arches made up of eight willow saplings.
8. The other willow saplings (the ones between those you have already bent to shape) are then woven diagonally through the stems that make up the arches.
9. Take the willow saplings on either side of the entrance and bend them over to join and create a low arch here.

Health and safety

Work at this project in groups of six with an adult to avoid collisions when weaving. Have a set place on your work site where you keep tools when they are not in use so that no one trips over them.

Follow-up activities

Don't content yourself with a storytelling and meeting dome – go on to make willow sculptures such as dinosaurs or a leaping deer. The possibilities are as big as the children's imaginations.

If you have a local arts centre, why not work on a joint project with them in your local community. Many of these centres are able to provide sculptors or other artists who work with living materials.

Teaching points

Willow is one of our most energetic trees. Pull off a single side stem and put it in a jam jar of water to show children how quickly it puts out new roots.

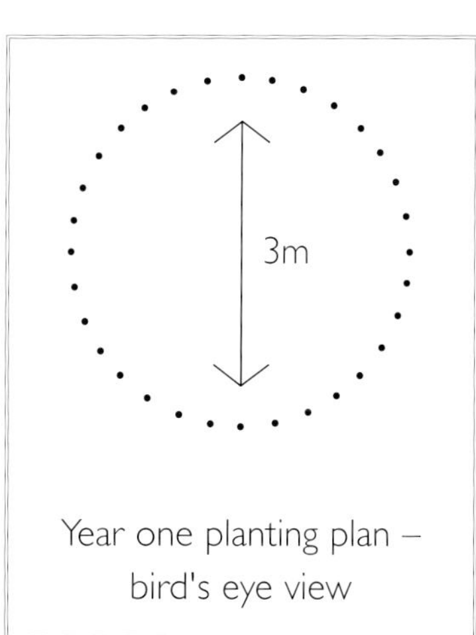

Year one planting plan – bird's eye view

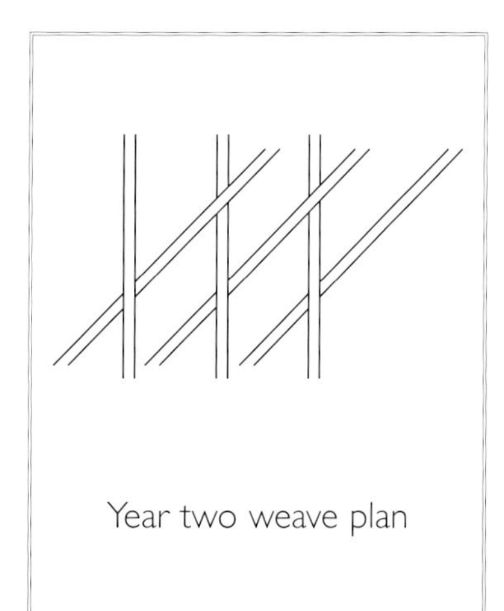

Year two weave plan

Finished dome pattern

2. Found art

What is found art?

Found art is made out of natural (or sometimes unnatural) things that you find when out and about exploring. If you want some examples look at the sculptures of Andy Goldsworthy (*see www.goldsworthy.cc.gla.ac.uk*).

Why create found art?

Creating found art is a great way into story making and story writing. Some of the best found art I have seen children make is when we have been on a beach or in the forest and they have simply been invited to create a character.

Learning objectives

In the EYFS this activity allows children to express and communicate their ideas, thoughts and feelings by using a widening range of materials. This activity covers exploring and developing ideas and investigating and making art, craft and design in the KS1 art curriculum.

Resources

- Whatever you find while on a walk along a beach, through a forest, along a river bank, up a big hill or through your local park.

Introducing the activity

One way of introducing this activity is to gather up all the garden debris you find in your outdoor classroom while you are having a tidy up. This might include dead flower heads, random pieces of bark or stone, fallen leaves, broken flower pots and the odd crisp packet. Lay these out on a table and begin to play around with them on a large piece of sugar paper. Ask the children if they can see what you are making as you begin to shape a troll's face out of bark or a delicate fairy out of leaf skeletons.

Conducting the activity

Take the children out to a place where there is likely to be plenty of natural debris. Where you go will affect what you are able to make. Here are some ideas to get you going.

In a forest: Select twigs and tie them together with pieces of ivy to create the framework for a character. Use moss and leaves for the hair and rolled pieces of mud or small stones to create eyes.

At the seaside: Use seaweed and driftwood, shells and stones to make your characters. Have a go at sand sculpting. Build a large heap of sand and then set to work shaping it into a sea serpent or some other character with your hands. Add shells and stones and so on for decoration.

At the park: Talk to the parks department of your local authority to let them know you are coming and they may provide a park keeper to accompany you as you search. The park keeper will know the best place to look for the most interesting stuff.

In the town: Even in urban areas there is natural debris that you can use for your found art. After a blowy autumn night take a walk along any street and you will find leaves and twigs, bits of moss or seed cases from sycamore trees.

Think about where you place your character. He or she may be peering round a tree or even hanging from a branch. Give your character a name and a story.

Health and safety

Just be careful what the children are picking up. Give them an introductory talk before sending them off to find materials.

Follow-up activities

Another way of looking at the natural world is to look for the faces that emerge when you peer at the bark of a tree. Look for knots in the bark and find two together for the eyes (unless this is a three- or one-eyed character). Look for swirls in the bark that form the mouth or jutting out stumps of twigs that could be arms. Close-up digital photography allows you to take these images back to school with you. Give these tree folk names and build stories around them.

Teaching points
If you are working entirely with natural materials you can let your natural sculpture disintegrate over time back into the soil.

3. Make an Iron Age pot

Why make an Iron Age pot?

We don't tend to deal with specific historical periods during EYFS and KS1, but there is no real reason why we shouldn't mention specific times every once in a while. The particular interest about Iron Age pot making is that this is the period before the potters' wheel was introduced to Britain. Here we are dealing with the making of thumb pots and coil pots.

Learning objectives

The art side of this activity deals with the creative process and also covers the detailed pattern making once the pot is constructed. There is also a design and technology element to this activity, which involves the construction of the pot shape and the rigidity of the clay you are using once it is dried and fired. EYFS children will be expressing their own ideas through the use of a different material (CD).

Resources

- Clay – either buy it in bags or dig it up for yourselves (much more fun!)
- Squares of plywood 30cm by 30cm to work on
- A pot of water for dipping fingers in while working with clay
- Thin sticks for mark making and patterning on finished pots.

Introducing the activity

Digging for clay

The most fun way to introduce this activity is to dig your own clay. If you live in a clay area simply dig a hole in the school field and remove some of the clay from about 30cm below the surface. Even in areas that are not rich in clay some sub-soils can be made workable. Talk to the ceramics teacher at your local secondary school or visit a local potter for advice. It will be worth the effort – children love getting muddy!

Conducting the activity

Work with groups of six children and model for them the different pot-making techniques.

Making a thumb pot

1. Take a lump of clay a little smaller than a tennis ball and shape it into a sphere.
2. Press your thumb hard into the middle and keep it there.
3. Shape the pot by pressing with your fingers on the outside and your thumb in the inside until the clay is about 0.5cm thick.
4. Make the bottom of your pot flat so that it will stand up.
5. Wet your fingers a little and smooth the inside and outside surfaces of your pot.

Making a coil pot

1. Make your clay into small balls about the size of a golf ball.
2. Roll these out into long thin sausages abut 0.5cm thick.

3. Use one or two of your clay sausages to coil into a spiral to form the base of your pot.
4. Now add coils and gradually build up the sides of your pot.
5. Smooth the clay sausages with just a little water on the end of your finger to create a 'slip'. This is like clay glue and will help to bond the sausages as you build your pot upwards.
6. Once you are happy with the size of your pot you can leave it as a coiled pattern or you can smooth the coils into one another to create a smooth finished pot.

Decorating your pots

Use the same techniques that Iron Age people used to create patterns on their pots. Press your fingernail into the clay. Scratch the surface with the end of a twig. Press small stones or shells into the surface and remove them to leave the impression.

Drying and firing

- Once you have finished smoothing and patterning your pot leave it to dry for a few days. Some commercial clay only needs to be air dried.
- You might like to try firing your pot in the embers of an open fire like our ancestors did. For advice on making a safe open fire see the woodcraft section of this book (p119).

Health and safety

The only health and safety consideration is if you choose to fire your pots on an open fire. Follow the advice in the woodcraft section (p119).

Follow-up activities

You could choose to pursue the Iron Age theme and paint your pots using natural paints made from ground-up rocks and minerals. There are several companies supplying these on the internet.

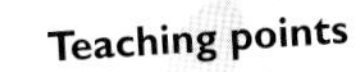

Teaching points

Look at some clay under a microscope to see the tiny particles of ground-up rock from which clay is formed.

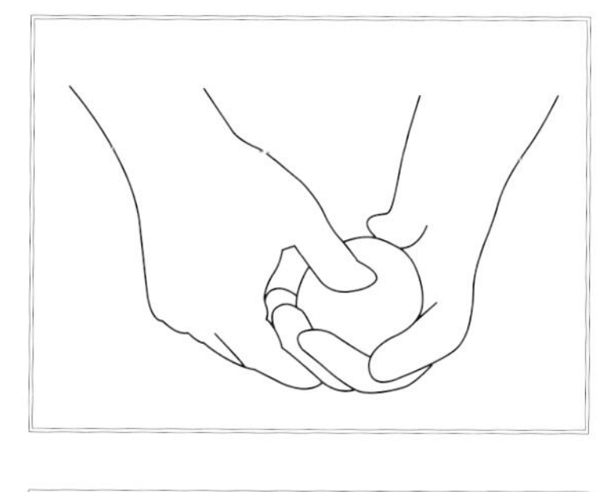

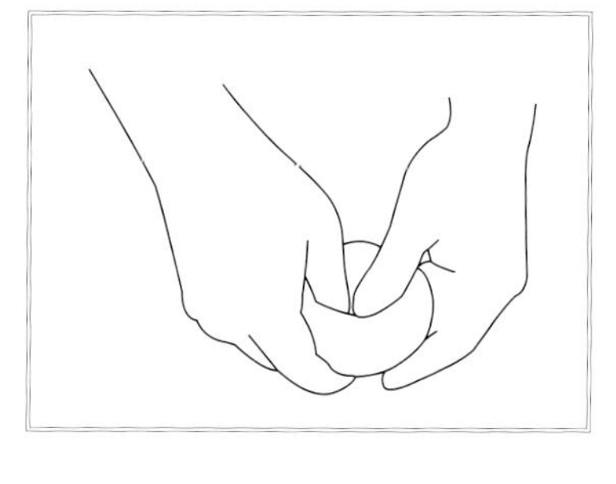

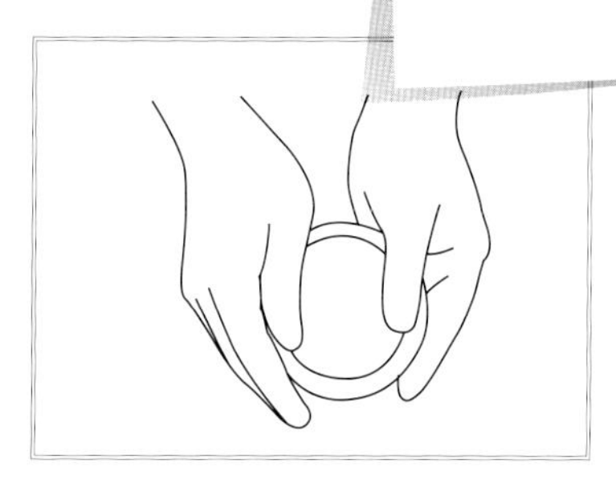

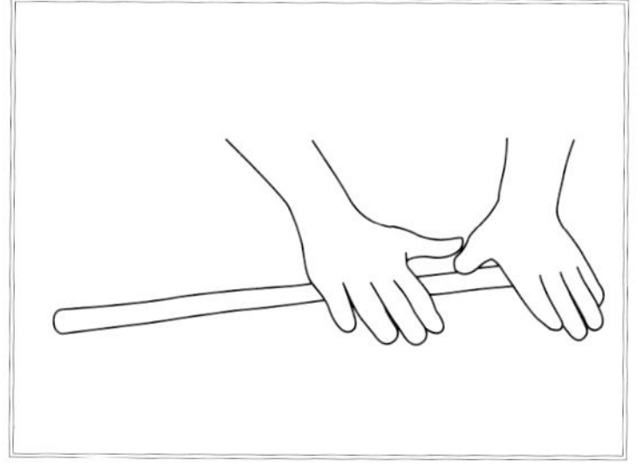

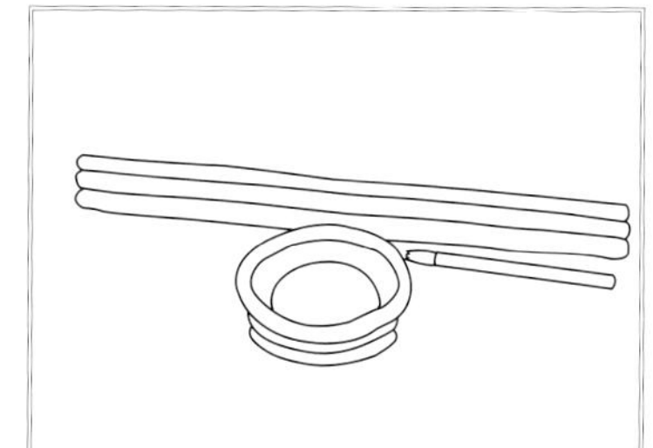

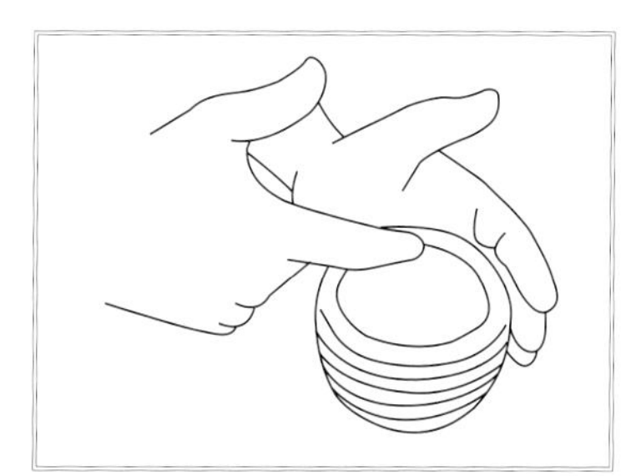

4. Natural dyes

What are natural dyes?

These are natural materials, such as berries, leaves and roots, which are treated in a particular way so as to extract their colour.

Why use natural dyes?

There was a time when every child would have done natural dyeing at some point during their time in primary school. It is a great way in to work on colour as it shows children one source of colourings for our clothing and paints. We are so used to buying our clothes ready-made and ready-coloured – it will come as quite a surprise to children that in some parts of the world people shear sheep, knit with the wool and dye their own clothes.

Learning objectives

All children will gain a greater understanding of colour from this activity. KS1 children can review the process and try to improve their dyes. For EYFS children this is an opportunity to test responses to a new and unusual activity as well as see who can cooperate in group tasks.

Resources

- Natural materials for dyeing – blackberries, elderberries, etc
- Water
- Powdered alum – from a chemists
- Pestle and mortar
- Large old saucepan – stainless steel is best
- Sieve
- Large plastic bowls or buckets
- Laundry tongs
- Large metal spoon
- Scraps of plain cotton or natural wool.

Introducing the activity

Take out of a carrier bag several clothing items – one at a time. Ask the children to name the colours of the clothing. Include some that are not simply red, yellow or green in order to extend colour vocabulary. Talk about materials and their sources – cotton, wool, silk and man-made materials such as polyester. Get children to look in the labels of their sweatshirts to see what they are made from.

Talk about how we get clothes of different colours. Do children know? Most clothes dyes are now made by extracting chemicals from oil. In the olden days, cotton and wool were dyed using natural materials.

Bring out some of the natural materials you have brought in to use as dyestuffs and ask the children what colours they think will come from each natural material. Make a note of their responses so you can return to it after you have dyed some material.

Conducting the activity

1. Lay out an art table and work with small groups.
2. Crush the berries with a pestle and mortar and add to the saucepan.
3. Cover with water and add powdered alum.
4. Simmer until lots of juice colour has come out.
5. Remove the pan from the heat and leave the mixture to cool before sieving the dye into a large plastic bowl.
6. Place your cotton or wool in the bowl with the coloured water and leave to soak.
7. If you want a light colour, leave the material in for less time – for a darker colour, leave longer. Experiment with different times – an hour, two hours, an afternoon or overnight – and see what results you come up with. It really does depend on the materials you are using.
8. Take your material out of the liquid and dry on a drying rack.

Health and safety

Even though you are using natural materials for this activity there are still health and safety issues. Children should wear rubber gloves to protect their hands from dyestuffs and an apron to protect their clothing. Because you are heating the liquid you also need to be aware of health and safety around the cooker.

Follow-up activities

Display strips of coloured material alongside samples of the natural materials you used to make the dye. Put these in a booklet so you have your own colour charts.

Teaching points

The main original source of indigo dye was the indigo plant. It is grown mainly in southeastern Asia and has clusters of pink or purple flowers. It is where the colour for denim jeans originally came from – some are still coloured this way.

Theme: Woodcraft

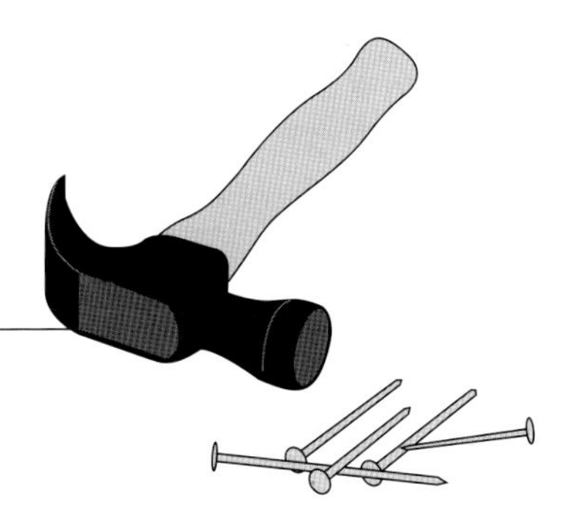

Woodcraft: Introduction

Cooking on open fires and making dens has become quite popular with children through television programmes about survival techniques. It is just a shame that so many children don't get the opportunity to go out into the woods and actually try out these things! There is a whole movement called Forest Schools that is aiming to bring children into contact with the natural world through the excitement of woodcraft skills. They can be contacted via *www.forestschools.com*

The scouting and guiding movements have always been at the forefront of this sort of thing. Developing links with your local scout and guide leaders would overcome some of the resourcing and skill difficulties of doing these activities.

Woodcraft skills bring a sense of adventure into school life and your school doesn't have to be in the heart of the countryside to practise them. Dens can be built in your school grounds using scrap materials from local industrial estates. The local park can be the place where your children lay and follow trails. Cooking on an open fire is perfectly safe as long as you take sensible precautions, and bags of firewood can be bought from your local petrol station. What woodcraft skills will give your children is a real enthusiasm and excitement for learning about their world.

Learning objectives

Specific learning objectives are given for each activity. Here is an overview list of learning objectives for woodcraft activities in general.

Early Years Foundation Stage

Personal, social and emotional development

- Be confident to try new activities, initiate ideas and speak in a familiar group.
- Respond to significant experiences, showing a range of feelings when appropriate.
- Work as part of a group or class, taking turns and sharing fairly.

Communication, language and literacy

- Interact with others, negotiating plans and activities and taking turns in conversations.
- Extend their vocabulary, exploring the meanings and sounds of new words.
- Use talk to organise, sequence and clarify thinking, ideas, feelings and events.

Problem solving, reasoning and numeracy

- Use everyday words to describe position.
- Use developing mathematical ideas and methods to solve practical problems.

Knowledge and understanding of the world

- Investigate objects and materials by using all of their senses as appropriate.
- Ask questions about why things happen and how things work.
- Build and construct a wide range of objects, selecting appropriate resources and adapting their work where necessary.
- Select the tools and techniques they need to shape, assemble and join materials they are using.
- Make short-term future plans.

Physical development

- Use a range of small and large equipment.

Creative development

- Respond in a variety of ways to what they see, hear, smell, touch and feel.
- Express and communicate their ideas, thoughts and feelings by using a widening range of materials.

Key Stage 1

Geography

Knowledge, skills and understanding

Geographical enquiry and skills

1. In undertaking geographical enquiry, pupils should be taught to:

a. ask geographical questions

c. express their own views about people, places and environments

d. communicate in different ways.

2. In developing geographical skills, pupils should be taught to:

a. use geographical vocabulary

b. use fieldwork skills

c. use globes, maps and plans at a range of scales

e. make maps and plans.

Knowledge and understanding of places

3. Pupils should be taught to:

a. identify and describe what places are like

b. identify and describe where places are.

Knowledge and understanding of patterns and processes

4. Pupils should be taught to:

a. make observations about where things are located and about other features in the environment.

Design and technology

Knowledge, skills and understanding

Developing, planning and communicating ideas

1. Pupils should be taught to:

a. generate ideas by drawing on their own and other people's experiences

b. develop ideas by shaping materials and putting together components

c. talk about their ideas

d. plan by suggesting what to do next as their ideas develop

e. communicate their ideas using a variety of methods, including drawing and making models.

Working with tools, equipment, materials and components to make quality products

2. Pupils should be taught to:

a. select tools, techniques and materials for making their product from a range suggested by the teacher

b. explore the sensory qualities of materials
c. measure, mark out, cut and shape a range of materials
d. assemble, join and combine materials and components
e. use simple finishing techniques to improve the appearance of their product, using a range of equipment
f. follow safe procedures for food safety and hygiene.

Evaluating processes and products

3. Pupils should be taught to:
a. talk about their ideas, saying what they like and dislike
b. identify what they could have done differently or how they could improve their work in the future.

Knowledge and understanding of materials and components

4. Pupils should be taught:
a. about the working characteristics of materials.

Breadth of study

5. During the key stage, pupils should be taught the Knowledge, skills and understanding through:
b. focused practical tasks that develop a range of techniques, skills, processes and knowledge
c. design and make assignments using a range of materials, including food.

Health and safety

The reason we don't do much woodcraft in schools is because of health and safety issues: fires, saws, ropes and sticks – it's all very daunting! But children need these experiences if they are to grow up with a sense of proportion about risk and an ability to measure and respond to risk appropriately. Play your part in unwrapping children from their cotton wool prison. Just do it with a high degree of preparation and planning so that you are taking risk into account and responding to it.

Literacy links

Story making

If you use several of these activities together you have the ingredients for a very exciting story about an explorer surviving in the wild. His or her adventures can be developed through role-play during a hall session and the practical activities in this section can provide the inspiration for written material. Using maps and satellite images *(www.google.com/maps)* from around the world allows you to send your explorer off anywhere you like – the Amazon rainforest or the Arctic tundra.

Labelled diagrams

There is a lot of making and doing involved in these activities. If children are fully engaged in a practical activity they don't even realise they are practising their writing skills when it comes to labelling diagrams or giving written instructions.

1. Cooking on a campfire

Why cook on a campfire?

When I first taught Reception, we cooked jacket potatoes on a campfire in November. We sat around a picnic table with the parents and ate the potatoes with lashings of butter. It was great! It can also be completely safe as long as you take sensible precautions. What the children get out of it is a sense of achievement at having produced food for themselves without a gas or electric cooker. They get to feel what it must have been like for our ancestors long ago.

Learning objectives

I like to link this activity with art. While the children are waiting for their turn to cut firewood or riddle the fire they can sit and draw with charcoal and chalk what the fire looks like. Poetry comes into this as well and some children will enjoy jotting down their thoughts while gazing at the crackling embers. There is also a good deal of science, which tends to just flow as children talk about what is happening to the fire and the potatoes.

Resources

- Rocks or bricks
- Logs and kindling – you can buy these from a petrol station forecourt
- Matches
- Newspaper
- A long metal poker
- Several big buckets of water.

Introducing the activity

Have all the resources laid out and take the children outside to get cooking as soon as registration is finished. It will take the whole morning to get the fire ready and cook the potatoes, so you don't really have time for an introduction – except to make the safety rules absolutely clear from the outset.

Conducting the activity

Preparation

- Set out your rocks or bricks in a circle about 75cm across to create a fire pit.
- Place a semicircle of chairs, at least five metres away from the fire, for children to sit on.

Making the fire

- Scrunch up sheets of newspaper and place them in the centre of the fire pit.
- Build a pyramid of kindling wood around the newspaper.
- Light the newspaper in several places.
- Invite one child at a time to come out and place logs on the fire or to riddle the fire with the poker.
- The fire will need to burn for about an hour to an hour and a half before it is ready for cooking .
- When you have a bed of glowing red embers it is ready.

Cooking potatoes

- Have a table set out with a washing-up bowl full of water, your spuds, a fork and tin foil.
- Each child can wash, prick and wrap their own potato in foil.
- One child at a time can drop their potato in the fire with you right next to them.
- Poke the potatoes around every 10 minutes with the poker to make sure they don't burn.
- A potato about the size of an adult fist will take just over an hour to cook.
- Lay out a table with knives, forks and plates and a bowl of butter.
- When your potatoes are ready take them out of the embers using thick gardening gloves and let them cool for a few minutes before unwrapping and eating.

Health and safety

Have only one child at a time cutting firewood or putting wood on the fire and make sure you are right next to them. Your adult assistant can manage the children who are sitting drawing or writing. Beware windy weather and smoke in eyes.

Follow-up activities

Children will want to do this again and another good thing to cook is chestnuts at Christmas. To do this get a large metal biscuit tin and punch some holes in the bottom with a nail. Make a slit in the skin of each chestnut and put them in the tin with the lid on. Place the tin in the embers of the fire and give the tin a rattle every now and then (wear thick gardening gloves for this). Check inside every 10 minutes to see if the chestnuts have finished roasting. They will have slightly burned skins when they are ready. Let them cool a little before peeling and eating. Yum!

You can also toast marshmallows on long, thin sticks or make up a simple stiff paste of flour and water and plait it around sticks to make a simple bread.

Teaching points

Not everyone has an electric or gas cooker. In many parts of the world people cook on open fires.

2. Build a shelter

Why build a shelter?

Adventurers and explorers need to be able to improvise a shelter they can sleep in from the natural materials they find on their journey. Children will develop their skills of improvisation through this activity. They will also develop teamwork and cooperation.

Learning objectives

This is a design and technology activity and will help get EYFS children started on construction, selecting appropriate resources and adapting their work where necessary. They will have to select the tools and techniques they need to shape, assemble and join the materials they are using. KS1 children can use the full range of design and technology skills – idea, design, make, evaluate and improve.

Resources

Natural shelter

- Branches and twigs from the woodland floor
- Bracken
- Ivy
- Leaves
- Mud.

Recycled shelter

- Reclaimed pallet wood from a local factory
- Old rope
- Discarded cardboard boxes
- Old plastic sheet
- String
- Elastic bands
- Hammer and nails
- Wood saw.

Introducing the activity

Discuss with children the basic needs that we all have: the need for shelter, food, warmth and clean water. Talk about explorers and adventurers. If there has been an example in the news recently look at television news reports online or read newspaper reports. There is usually someone adventuring somewhere in the world. Talk about each of the basic human needs and how the children think an explorer would meet these. Some children will have knowledge of survival techniques they have picked up from watching television programmes or from camping trips.

Conducting the activity

Principles of building a shelter

The first thing to do is to construct a framework. Then cover in overlapping materials to keep the rain out. Build your shelter against a tree for additional support.

Natural shelter

Carry out this activity in the woods or an overgrown part of the local park. Organise the children into groups of four with an adult assigned to each group. Give the groups a time limit and send them off to forage for materials and build a shelter. Build the framework with branches leaning together to form a triangular structure tied with ivy.

The simplest natural structure is to lean branches up all around a tree trunk to create a cone. Weave twigs and leaves of bracken in between the branches.

Recycled shelter

In preparation for this activity you will need to visit a local factory and gather unwanted timber. You could mention your project in a school newsletter as parents may be able to help out with this.

Gather together your resources and have children working in groups of four with an adult so that construction and safety skills can be taught and reinforced. Once the timber framework is constructed you can cover it with old cardboard and a large old plastic sheet. Don't be too worried what it looks like – being waterproof is more important than attractiveness!

Sleeping out

I have built shelters with older children and we have slept in them. You probably wouldn't want to do this with Reception and KS1. But, if you are an adventurous teacher and you have an adventurous colleague who will accompany you then you could test out the children's shelters by sleeping in them for the night and giving the children feedback the next morning.

Health and safety

Make sure any recycled timber you used is free from toxic chemicals, nails and screws. Remind children about the safe and appropriate use of rope and string. Children should be fully supervised when using a wood saw. Gloves should be worn as a precaution when working with ivy – some ornamental ivy may cause irritation.

Follow-up activities

Many children around the world live in makeshift shelters in shanty towns. Explore the reasons why this is so and come up with ways in which your class can raise some money to help provide medicines, clean water and education for these children.

Link this activity with your Eco-Schools bid by emphasising the use of recycled materials as educational resources.

3. Leave a trail

What is a trail?

A trail is a series of signs made from natural materials purposefully left to indicate a route that should be followed. It is a classic woodcraft activity derived from the techniques of Native Americans and other indigenous peoples around the world.

Why leave a trail?

This activity is a great way to help children really immerse themselves in the natural world as the trail can be laid through all sorts of interesting places. It is also a good way of developing children's appreciation of the way that we use signs and symbols to give messages to other people.

Learning objectives

In the EYFS curriculum, this is a CLL activity as it teaches children about the use of signs and symbols to communicate information, although it does not specifically meet any of the CLL criteria. In KS1, use this activity to enhance children's geographical vocabulary as well as their understanding of signs and symbols.

Resources

The resources you use for this activity will be those you find while out in the countryside or at your local park: sticks, stones, fir cones, blades of grass and so on.

Introducing the activity

Look at some common symbols that children will be familiar with from their everyday life. Commercial signs and symbols from shops and branded goods are one form. Road signs are another. Religious symbols, such as the cross of Christianity or the crescent moon and star of Islam, will be familiar through RE work. Use some easy ones first to get the children warmed up (crossroads or men at work road signs) and then introduce some where they have to think (slippery road or no overtaking).

Discuss the importance of signs in our lives and why it is important that they are easy to understand. Signs can warn us about dangers as well as giving us useful information. Explain to the children that you are going to use signs to lay a trail.

Conducting the activity

Photocopy the signs on the next page and give a copy each to trail layers and trail followers. Send the trail layers off to lay their trail. Tell children to copy the trail signs on the photocopy making their own signs out of sticks, stones, grass and so on. Send an adult with them to ensure the signs laid are clear and also that the trail is not too long. Signs should be left at about every 20 paces. Once the trail layers have finished their task the trail followers can try to follow their signs.

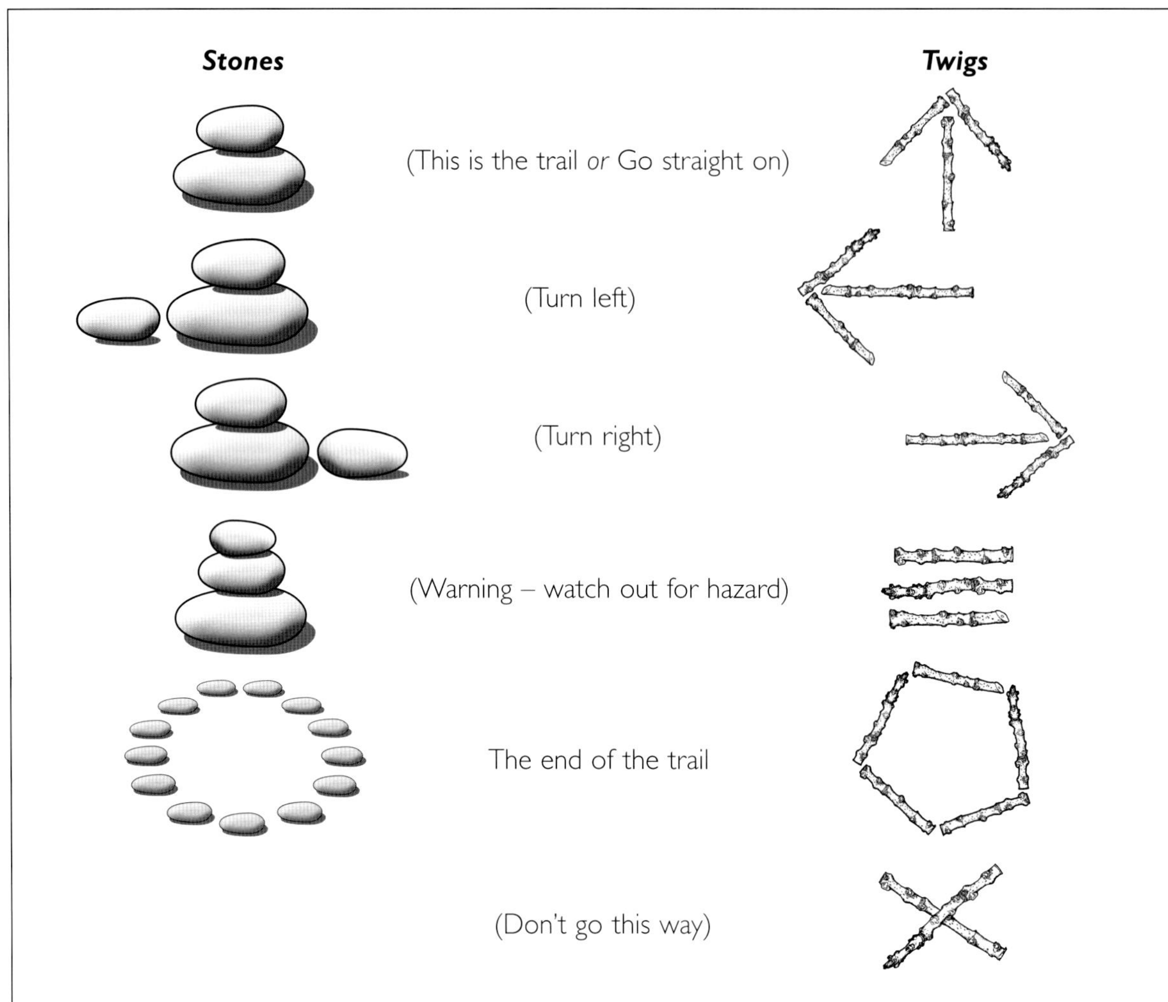

Once the children have returned from their trail, sit in a large circle and share the experience. Sit children in pairs with someone from a different group who followed a different trail. Encourage children to use geographical language to describe their route: we went up the hill and turned left, then we went through the thicket and down into the valley and across the stream.

Health and safety

You need to check over the area where the children are going to lay their trail to ensure there are no hazards.

Follow-up activities

This activity can lead into map making (see the next activity) and can also be used in story mapping. Use the 'Found art' activity in the art section of this book (p108) to create a character and imagine that character on a journey along the trail.

See what signs children come up with to give more complex messages.

Use chalk to lay a trail around the school grounds or in town.

Teaching points
Remind children not to use parts of living plants or trees for trail signs, only twigs and stones and so on that they find on the ground.

4. Making and reading maps

Why make and read maps?

One of the key skills of being an adventurer or explorer is being able to read a map.

Learning objectives

We are in the realm of the geography curriculum here. Making and using maps is part of the development of geographical skills in KS1.

Resources

- Small world play resources
- Clipboards, paper and pencils
- Different types of maps.

Introducing the activity

Talk with your children about a recent long journey that you have taken. Describe your route and how long it took you. Tell them the distance. Talk about journeys the children have been on. How did their parents know the way – was it somewhere they had been before? If not, how did they know what route to take? Many people have SatNav now, but some will have used road maps.

Get out some different maps and take a look at them. Use Google Maps to find your school and then switch from a map view to a satellite view. The children will be very excited if they spot their own house and see their car on the driveway.

Conducting the activity

It is important to teach map work as a progression of skills.

Reception

Small world play with play mats depicting roads, villages, towns, farms, shopping centres and so on, together with model cars, buildings and people, is the way into map work for Reception children. Road play mats with model buildings, people and vehicles are particularly useful as they allow children to move back and forth from the bird's eye view (by standing up) and the sideways or ant's eye view (by lying down). Stories such as *We're Going on a Bear Hunt* by Michael Rosen (1996, Walker Books) are excellent for introducing in a visual way the idea of going on a journey. Develop the bird's eye view approach further by helping children to create a plan of the classroom using cut out rectangles of paper to represent tables, chairs and other furniture.

Year 1

Children can produce their own map from memory of their route to school or you can take them out on slightly longer walks around the local area than you would with foundation stage children. Each child can produce a drawing map of their route to school and add key features as face-on two-dimensional drawings (a more accurate representation of the bird's eye view of buildings and other features such as trees will develop later). Walk around your local area with printed outline maps of just the roads and paths and get the children to draw features on the map.

Giving and following directions is another great way to develop fledgling map work skills. Give children the opportunity to guide visitors around the school. Vocabulary is essential. Develop a strong vocabulary of map work through giving directions: turn left, turn right, straight ahead, just past the post office, up the hill, round the corner. Start to use symbols to represent features.

Year 2

Introduce a basic key – an emphasis on colour in early work on symbols and keys helps to embed the learning. Take the children out in the local area to follow basic road plans. Ensure they know the names and locations of roads in their community.

Introduce coordinates – there is a strong link to numeracy here. Use a letter/number grid to start with where columns are identified by a letter and rows are identified by a number so that each square on the grid can be identified by a letter/number, such as B6.

It is time also for some detailed work on scale. Floor robots can be a useful way into this. Programme the robot to run a course involving some right and left turns and use a scale to represent the distance travelled. On grid paper use one square to represent one unit of distance and draw the route of the floor robot.

Health and safety

The normal considerations apply if you are taking children out of school. One way to get an understanding of a bird's eye view is to stand on a chair and look down on a model farm or town. Make sure someone is holding the child's hand while they are on the chair.

Follow-up activities

A good way to finish Key Stage 1 is with children drawing their own detailed plan of the school buildings and grounds from a bird's eye view and using simple coloured symbols and a coloured key. Stick with a scale of 1 centimetre equals one pace for now. Make it a class project and put the finished map on display.

Teaching points

When writing stories, ask children to draw a story map to show the journey of the story and the key characters.

5. Tying knots

Why tie knots?

Tying knots will help with many of the other activities in this book: den building, making structures to grow French beans up, big construction and so on.

Learning objectives

This activity will help particularly with the development of fine motor skills and hand/eye coordination.

Resources

- String
- Rope
- Bamboo canes
- Illustrations of knots (*www.animatedknots.com*).

Introducing the activity

Tying knots is an unfamiliar activity for many children (and for many adults). Practise with the knots yourself before teaching the children. This activity requires minimal introduction – just get on and tie the knots and make sure you have enough string and rope for every child.

Conducting the activity

Tying knots is best learned through looking at diagrams and practising. Put the illustrations from *www.animatedknots.com* up on your smart board, give the children a piece of string each and follow the animations.

Reef knot

This is the basis of a shoe-tying bow, but in the full reef knot we pull the bow tight. This is the first knot to learn.

Bowline

This is the way to produce a reasonably secure loop at the end of a rope.

Clove hitch

This is the knot to use in construction work when you want to attach a lashing to a pole.

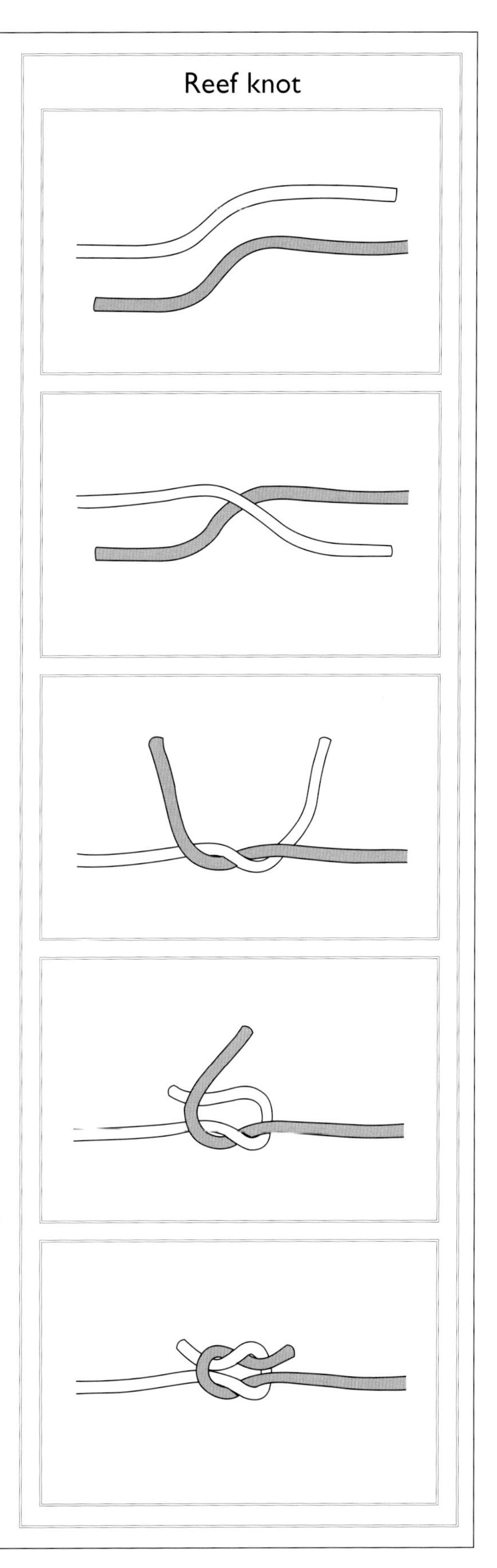

Health and safety

Watch out for trip hazards when using string and ropes and tell children they must never put string or rope around their necks.

Follow-up activities

Practise using knots in everyday situations such as tying shoelaces, wrapping parcels with paper and string and tying ties.

Teaching points

Rope has been used for thousands of years. The ropes used to drag blocks to build the pyramids were probably made from waterweed fibres. Ropes used to build Stonehenge may have been made from leather.

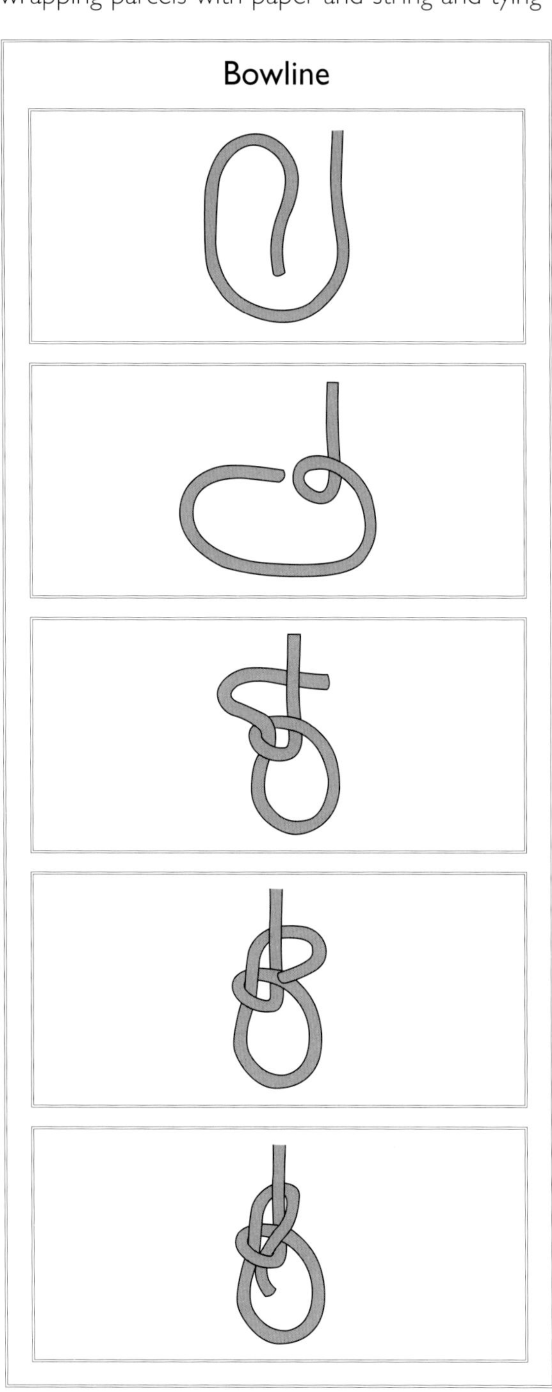

6. Build a rope bridge

Why build a rope bridge?

Building a rope bridge in your outdoor classroom not only gives children the opportunity to undertake a construction activity, it also provides a new piece of play equipment! Schools spend a lot of money on play equipment, but some of it, like the rope bridge, is really quite straightforward to build yourselves. This activity is in the woodcraft section because you might like to try building a rope bridge across a local muddy ditch using real trees as your uprights instead of poles.

Learning objectives

This is a construction activity where you do the planning and the children help do the work. What the children get from it is learning the kind of construction techniques real builders use.

Resources

- Four round wooden poles measuring 125cm long and with a diameter of 20cm
- Two round wooden poles measuring 50cm long and with a diameter of 7.5cm
- New rope – three pieces each measuring four metres long and with a diameter of 2.5cm
- Wooden battens to support poles while concrete sets
- Hardcore – broken bricks and stones – one bucketful per post
- Four sacks of fast-setting concrete mix
- Spade
- Watering can
- Large sheet of wood to mix concrete on
- Drill and 2.5cm bit.

Introducing the activity

This is a very exciting project and you will simply want to tell the children what you are going to do and then get on with it.

Conducting the activity

Preparation

- Purchase all your materials in advance.
- Lay out your materials and tools next to your work site – use a grassed area.

Placing the wooden poles

- Mark the positions of the four wooden poles on the ground.
- Dig a hole for each point measuring 40cm by 40cm by 50cm deep.
- Place a 5cm layer of hardcore in the bottom of each hole and tamp it down firmly with the end of one of the poles.
- Place a wooden pole in the hole, add some more hardcore around it and tamp down firmly.
- Support the post in a vertical position by nailing two or three thin battens of timber to it as diagonal struts.
- Mix up your fast-setting concrete according to the instructions on the sack.

- Pour concrete around the pole up to about five cm from the surface.
- Double check that the pole is upright.
- Once the concrete has set fill the remainder of the hole with earth.
- Repeat these procedures for each of the four poles.
- Between each pair of upright poles hammer in the smaller wooden stakes so that about 15cm is sticking out of the ground.

Attaching the rope

- Drill a hole right through each pole about 5cm from the top.
- Run your rope through two opposite posts and tie a knot in each end.
- Run rope through the other two posts and tie knots.
- Your handrails are now in place.
- Attach the final piece of rope to the smaller poles by tying it around the poles so that it is about 10cm off the ground.
- This is the piece the children walk along.

Commissioning your rope bridge

Double check that everything is firm and secure before allowing children to use the rope bridge.

Health and safety

This is an adult-style construction task and needs to be undertaken by two adults working with groups of four children at a time to ensure correct use of tools and material. You might like to get an experienced parent in to help with this one.

Teaching points

Concrete is made from a mixture of clay, ground-up limestone and chalk and has been used in many construction tasks since the Romans invented it.

Follow-up activities

Build on the success of this project by asking the children what other play equipment they might make for themselves.

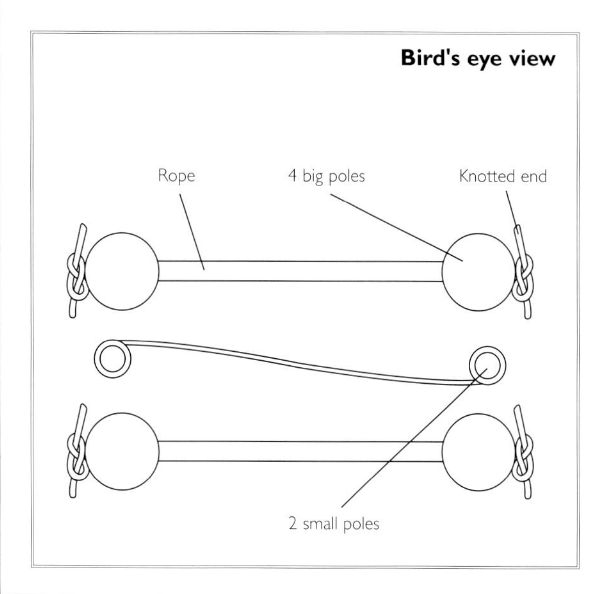

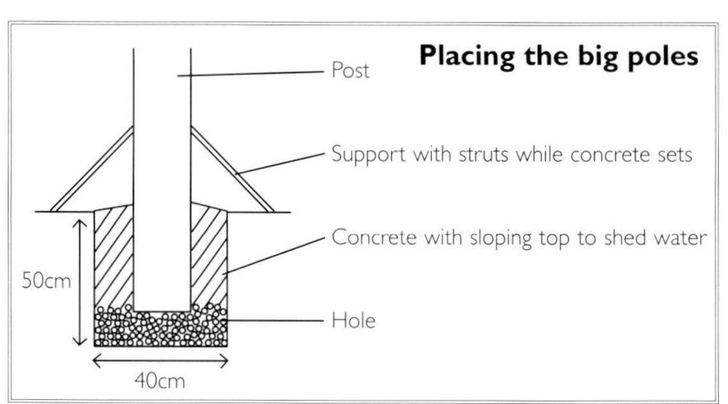

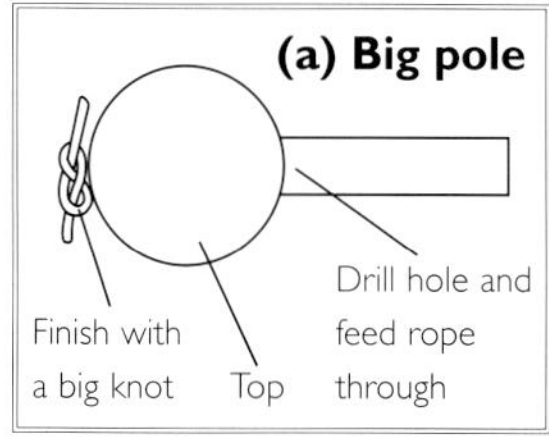

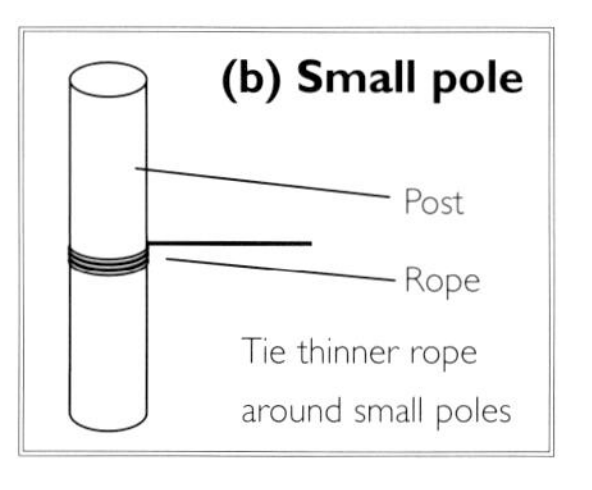

7. Finding north and telling the time by the sun

Why find north and tell the time by the sun?

Telling the time by the sun is useful if you are adventuring without a watch. Knowing the location of north is particularly important if you are trying to navigate. We can all make an educated guess at telling the time and finding north if we have some basic information about how the world works.

Learning objectives

This activity brings in some maths work on direction, position and simple angles. For EYFS children, it will help develop the concept of time in terms of dividing up the day according to the movement of the sun in the sky.

Resources

- A directional compass (to check your accuracy)
- A stick one metre long
- A lump of Plasticine
- A watch with hands (to check your accuracy).

Introducing the activity

Play the compass game in the school hall. Before the children come in, find out for yourself where north is with a directional compass. When the children come in, point to and name the wall that is north. Then point and name the south, east and west walls. The children start in the middle and when you shout out a direction they run to that wall. After a few attempts to orientate themselves call again and the last child to the wall is out. Keep going until you are left with the person with the fastest sense of direction. You can add NE, SE, NW and NE with Year 2 children.

Once the children have dressed after PE, take them out onto the playground and ask if any of them know where north is. Then conduct the following activity.

Conducting the activity

Finding north without a compass

You need to do this on a sunny day:

1. Place a stick one metre long upright in the ground.
2. Make a mark at the very tip of the shadow cast by the stick and number it 1.
3. Twenty minutes later, make a second mark and number it 2.
4. Stand with your left foot on the first mark and your right foot on the second mark and look straight ahead.
5. You are looking north and behind you is south. East is to your right and west is to your left.

Telling the time without a watch

If you know where north and south are, you can practise telling the time using your shadow. By practising with a watch to begin with, you will come to know where the shadow lies at certain times of the day and will then be able to estimate reasonably accurately without the watch, just using the sun.

1. Stand facing north.
2. If your shadow is to your left, it is the morning and if it is to your right, it is the afternoon – but that isn't a high degree of accuracy!
3. See where your shadow is at 9am and at 12 midday and it is possible to roughly work out 10.30am as it will be half way.
4. With practise you can get a rough idea of where your shadow is at any hour between 9am and 3pm in the winter and 4am and 8pm in the summer.

Health and safety

Put a piece of Plasticine on the top of your pointy stick to prevent eye-related accidents. Remind children that they must *never* look at the sun.

Follow-up activities

Make up your own mnemonic for remembering the NESW order: Never Eat Shredded Wheat is how I always remember it, but Shredded Wheat is actually quite healthy so Naughty Elephants Squirt Water might be a better one for children to learn.

Teaching points

The sun does not move around the Earth. It only looks like it does. The Earth turns around once every 24 hours.

8. Codes and signals

Why send signals?

If you are an adventurous explorer there will come a time when you want to send a secret message to other members of your expedition. There are several ways you can do this, and as well as being exciting, they will help children with the structure of the alphabet.

Learning objectives

Codes are a good way of developing alphabet and number skills as well as a general agility of mind. They can be used by EYFS children once they have a basic grasp of the alphabet. KS1 children can practise using signals quickly to enhance alphabetical dexterity.

Resources

- A4 paper and coloured pencils for making flags
- Simple electrical circuit with a buzzer and switch for Morse Code
- Lemons and red cabbage for invisible ink messages.

Introducing the activity

Write the letters of the alphabet in capitals on your whiteboard in a coloured marker. Under each letter write the alphabet backwards in a different colour. A is now Z, L is now O and V is now E. Write your name in code and see if the children can work it out. Give them an A4 whiteboard and they can write simple messages for their partner to decode.

Explain that codes and signals have important uses such as in emergencies at sea and in signalling messages between units of an army at war. Signals have been used throughout history to send warnings. When the Spanish Armada sailed to attack Britain, the whole country was warned by a chain of bonfires burning on the tops of hills and mountains.

Conducting the activity

Flags

In 1800 Sir Home Popham devised a simple flag code for ships to use to send messages to each other while at sea. His system was known as the Telegraphic Signals of Marine Vocabulary. This system used only ten flags to spell out the letters of the alphabet by numbering the flags zero to nine. The thirteenth letter of the alphabet (M) could be made with flags one and three held up together. See Popham's flags for yourself at *http://flagspot.net/flags/xf~psf.html*. Make and colour the flags on A4 paper and send messages across the school field.

Morse code

This code was created by Samuel FB Morse in the early 1840s to send messages electronically along telegraph wires. Construct a simple circuit with a buzzer and a switch and send messages across the classroom with dots and dashes just like the Victorians did.

Invisible ink

Write an invisible message using lemon juice and a feather as a quill. Reveal the message with red cabbage juice spray. Cut up a red cabbage and cover with water in a saucepan. Boil until you have a dark purple liquid. Strain the juice into a spray bottle. Spray the cabbage juice over the message and the lemon juice will slowly reveal itself.

Health and safety

Hold A4 paper flags up rather that attach them to sticks and wave them around as this reduces risk to eyes. Mind children don't get lemon juice in their eyes when extracting it.

Follow-up activities

If you want to be really adventurous you might like to try sending smoke messages. Light a small fire and add some wet grass. Two adults can hold a blanket about a metre above the fire and pull it away to release a cloud of smoke, then return the blanket to gather another cloud. Devise your own code for sending messages. Different numbers of smoke clouds have different meanings.

Morse Code Alphabet

The International Morse code characters are:

A .-	N -.	0 -----
B -...	O ---	1 .----
C -.-.	P .--.	2 ..---
D -..	Q --.-	3 ...--
E .	R .-.	4 ....-
F ..-.	S ...	5 .....
G --.	T -	6 -....
H	U ..-	7 --...
I ..	V ...-	8 ---..
J .---	W .--	9 ----.
K -.-	X -..-	Fullstop .-.-.-
L .-..	Y -.--	Comma --..--
M --	Z --..	

Teaching points

Modern ships are equipped with radar and radios, but if something goes wrong they still carry flags and smoke rockets if they need to send an emergency signal.

9. Hiking

What is hiking?

Hiking is basically walking, but 'hiking' sounds more exciting! Hiking is what adventurers and explorers do. It is a good way to get out into the world to see what is going on.

Why go on a hike?

We are always hearing how unfit today's children are. Well, walking is a very simple exercise that most of us can do and it brings great fitness benefits if done regularly.

Learning objectives

This activity is particularly suited to the physical development curriculum in EYFS and the physical education curriculum in KS1. EYFS children are recognising the importance of keeping healthy and KS1 children are learning how important it is to be active.

Resources

- A pair of trainers
- Warm clothing
- A waterproof jacket and hat
- A small knapsack
- A packed lunch
- Local maps.

Introducing the activity

Get out some local maps and look for interesting places for a hike. Even in the city there are cycle tracks along disused railway lines and canal towpaths. Write to parents and tell them what you are going to do and invite them along for the hike and picnic. Part of the learning from this activity comes from effective preparation; children need to be wearing suitable clothing and as a class you need to have planned your route.

Conducting the activity

This activity simply involves going for a walk. If you add a bit of structure to it you can increase the benefits. For example, why not make it school policy that in Reception the children are taken on a one-mile walk three times a year? In Year 1 increase it to two miles and to three miles in Year 2.

Use other activities from this book to enhance the experience of your hike.

Health and safety

Walk the route yourself first to check out any likely hazards and find safe places to cross roads. Take plenty of adults with you.

Teaching points

Teach children to take their pulse and measure it while strolling gently and while walking up a hill to see the difference physical exercise makes to our bodies.

Follow-up activities

Draw a map of your hike. If you do several of these you can make a simple photocopied booklet of local walks to sell to parents.

Organise a whole-school walk to an interesting local place and have a day of activities at your destination.

Theme: Role-play

Role-play: Introduction

Learning through imaginative play is so important to the development of young minds and young bodies. Children play naturally and need very little encouragement. Giving a structured framework and theme to their play is a good way of focusing children on developing a wider range of skills. Your input will mean that the same children don't just play princesses or superhero games all the time.

Role-play is a fantastic vehicle for exploring all manner of complexities that affect our lives and influence our development as individuals and members of a society. We can explore conflict through role-play and learn to deal with it. Role-play will allow you to give your children opportunities to safely explore threatening situations such as traffic accidents, fires and hospitals. Learning about these situations through play and working with adults they trust can help prepare children for the realities of life, which they may experience at some point as they grow up.

Role-play is also great for learning about history. The past is a colourful place and exploring it through costumed play really brings it to life.

Learning objectives

Specific learning objectives are given for each activity. Here is an overview list of learning objectives for role-play activities in general.

Early Years Foundation Stage

Personal, social and emotional development

- Be confident to try new activities, initiate ideas and speak in a familiar group.
- Respond to significant experiences, showing a range of feelings when appropriate.
- Work as part of a group or class, taking turns and sharing fairly, understanding that there need to be agreed values and codes of behaviour for groups of people.
- Consider the consequences of their words and actions for themselves and others.
- Select and use activities and resources independently..

Communication, language and literacy

- Interact with others, negotiating plans and activities and taking turns in conversations.
- Extend their vocabulary, exploring the meanings and sounds of new words.
- Use talk to organise, sequence and clarify thinking, ideas, feelings and events.

Problem solving, reasoning and numeracy

- Count reliably up to 10 everyday objects.
- In practical activities and discussion, begin to use the vocabulary involved in adding and subtracting.
- Use language such as 'more' and 'less' to compare two numbers.
- Use everyday words to describe position.
- Use developing mathematical ideas and methods to solve practical problems.

Knowledge and understanding of the world

- Build and construct a wide range of objects, selecting appropriate resources and adapting their work where necessary.

- Select the tools and techniques they need to shape, assemble and join materials they are using.
- Make short-term future plans.

Physical development

- Use a range of small and large equipment.

Creative development

- Respond in a variety of ways to what they see, hear, smell, touch and feel.
- Express and communicate their ideas, thoughts and feelings by using a widening range of materials.

Key Stage 1

Focus on the PSHE curriculum when engaged in role-play.

PSHE

Knowledge, skills and understanding

Developing confidence and responsibility and making the most of their abilities

1. Pupils should be taught:

a. to recognise what they like and dislike, what is fair and unfair, and what is right and wrong
b. to share their opinions on things that matter to them and explain their views
c. to recognise, name and deal with their feelings in a positive way
d. to think about themselves, learn from their experiences and recognise what they are good at
e. how to set simple goals.

Preparing to play an active role as citizens

2. Pupils should be taught:

a. to take part in discussions with one other person and the whole class
b. to take part in a simple debate about topical issues
c. to recognise choices they can make, and recognise the difference between right and wrong
d. to agree and follow rules for their group and classroom, and understand how rules help them
e. to realise that people and other living things have needs, and that they have responsibilities to meet them
f. that they belong to various groups and communities, such as family and school
g. what improves and harms their local, natural and built environments and about some of the ways people look after them
h. to contribute to the life of the class and school
i. to realise that money comes from different sources and can be used for different purposes.

Developing a healthy, safer lifestyle

3. Pupils should be taught:

a. how to make simple choices that improve their health and wellbeing
b. to maintain personal hygiene
c. how some diseases spread and can be controlled
d. about the process of growing from young to old and how people's needs change
e. the names of the main parts of the body

f. that all household products, including medicines, can be harmful if not used properly
g. rules for, and ways of, keeping safe, including basic road safety, and about people who can help them to stay safe.

Developing good relationships and respecting the differences between people
4. Pupils should be taught:
a. to recognise how their behaviour affects other people
b. to listen to other people, and play and work cooperatively
c. to identify and respect the differences and similarities between people
d. that family and friends should care for each other
e. that there are different types of teasing and bullying, that bullying is wrong, and how to get help to deal with bullying.

Breadth of opportunities
5. During the key stage, pupils should be taught the Knowledge, skills and understanding through opportunities to:
a. take and share responsibility
b. feel positive about themselves
c. take part in discussions
d. make real choices, meet and talk with people
e. develop relationships through work and play
f. consider social and moral dilemmas that they come across in everyday life
g. ask for help.

Literacy links

Non-fiction research

The activities in this section will inspire children to want to find out more about the theme they have been exploring. Take them to the school library and find books on that theme. Reception year children are able to select books by picture clues and you can then read with them and discuss the information they can get from pictures. Older children can pose questions they want to find answers to and then seek those answers using contents and index pages. Children might like to go on to make their own non-fiction books on the subject they have been learning about.

Diary writing

Many of these activities lend themselves to the writing skill of recount. Children, however, don't always like being asked to write about something they have just enjoyed doing! The way round this is to incorporate the writing into the role-play. Provide a desk within the role-play if you can and writing materials. Writing journals and diaries is a particularly good way to help develop an understanding of history.

Health and safety

Role-play is generally quite safe, providing you plan carefully the equipment you give children to play with. One or two of these activities have more health and safety issues and details are given.

1. Knights and castles

Why role-play knights and castles?

Knights and castles are not to be found in the National Curriculum, but they are a popular theme – especially with boys. Role-playing knights and castles will provide boys with the boisterous play they need to develop their gross motor skills and will also allow their social skills to develop. My experience tells me that girls soon join in too and get just as much fun and learning out of this activity as the boys.

Learning objectives

In terms of meeting criteria, this activity focuses on social skills. EYFS children will learn about agreed values and codes of behaviour as well as considering the consequences of their actions (PSED). KS1 children can focus on developing relationships (PSHE).

Resources

Jousting

- Two space hoppers
- Two foam insulating pipes measuring one metre long
- A plastic knight's helmet and plastic shield.

Swordplay

- Two plastic shields
- Two plastic swords
- Two plastic knights' helmets.

Castle building

- Lots of big sheets of cardboard
- Masking tape
- Paints.

Introducing the activity

When I have done this activity I have simply asked the children to bring in anything from home that they would like to share on the theme of knights and castles. I have been inundated with role-play costumes of princesses and knights, pop-up books showing the structure of a castle, family photos of visits to historical re-enactments and other memorabilia. We have then spent time sharing and discussing the theme. I have then scribed a mind map as the children made suggestions about what they would like to do to explore this theme further. The activities below come from this list.

Conducting the activity

Jousting

Two children are the knights and they each sit astride a space hopper with a foam lance facing each other about five metres apart. The children hop towards each other and aim to knock their opponent off their hopper. The thing is that they both want to win! We found that introducing a plastic knight's helmet and shield helped. The person who wears the armour has to allow him/herself to be knocked off the space hopper. It seemed to work. Children will learn to take turns if you provide a blackboard where they can add their name to the list of jousters.

Swordplay

We found that doing this in slow motion and concentrating on the actual movements helped to prevent it from just becoming a fight.

Castle building

Working with small groups of children at a time, build a large cardboard castle with authentic looking crenellations and turrets, a drawbridge and arrow slits in the walls. Paint your castle in greys and browns. Children can then role-play sieges and attacks and they will learn a lot about life in medieval times from this. When we did this the girls decided they wanted a whole morning of princess play in the castle.

Health and safety

Using foam pipes as lances makes this a safe activity. When jousting, play on a grassed area so that tumbles do not hurt.

Follow-up activities

This activity lends itself well to painting and drawing to capture the action.

Put on a knights and castles day where children come to school in costume and enjoy medieval food, games, dances and stories.

Link this activity in with design and technology by making working models of medieval siege engines and catapults.

Teaching points

Early castles were made of wood and later replaced with stone to make them stronger.

2. Garden centre

Why role-play a garden centre?

Creating a garden centre in your classroom (or even better, outside) will give your children experience of running their own shop. Associated with this are many literacy and numeracy opportunities as well as links with any gardening projects you are engaged in.

Learning objectives

Both KS1 and EYFS children can develop their shape, space and measure skills through the construction of the garden centre and their number skills through running a shop. On the literacy side of things there are order forms to complete and catalogues to make. This is very much about writing with a purpose.

Resources

- A space for constructing your garden centre – about two metres by two metres is sufficient
- Trellis
- String
- Plant pots
- Seed catalogues and order forms
- Gardening posters
- Toy till, plastic money, notes and debit cards
- Telephone
- Computer terminal – if you wish to make your shop really fancy
- Clipboard, paper and pen.

Introducing the activity

When we constructed our garden centre we invited the manager of a local DIY store in to talk to the children about what it is like to fulfil this role. You could visit a local garden centre to get ideas for your project. Plan with children what your garden centre will look like on a large sheet of paper. Cut out pictures of the different things they want to include and stick them on the plan.

Conducting the activity

Constructing the garden centre

If you have a play hut in your outdoor classroom, that makes an excellent focus for construction of a garden centre. If not, then improvise by constructing a framework of trellis and decorating with posters, paper flowers, etc. Provide a desk and chair and place the telephone, order forms and so on there. We linked our garden centre in with our outside cars and children delivered orders of flowers. Children can make order forms and catalogues to include in the garden centre.

Playing in the garden centre

- Allocate time slots for small groups of children to play in the garden centre.
- Model the kind of tasks children can do – planting, taking orders, making up orders, talking on the phone and giving gardening advice.
- Observe your children at play and make notes for assessment purposes.

Health and safety

This is a construction activity so the usual health and safety considerations apply: work in small groups supervised by an adult and be careful with string and scissors. Put plastic balls or yoghurt pots on top of bamboo canes to prevent eye poking.

Follow-up activities

Make paper flowers with wire stems and loops of wire for petals and cover in tissue paper. These make good Mother's Day presents. Spring is generally a good time to do this project so you can link it in with making Mother's Day cards as well.

Make your garden centre even more real by staging a real plant sale. Invite parents to come along after school and buy pots of herb plants the children have grown. Just make sure the adults pay with real money!

Teaching points

Look at merchandising materials from garden centres to help generate ideas for display materials in your garden centre.

3. Emergency ward

Why role-play an emergency ward?

We set up our emergency ward after two of the cars crashed in our outdoor street play area. It gave us the chance to learn about people who help us and find out some more about procedures like x-rays. It was also great fun.

Learning objectives

EYFS children are extending their knowledge and understanding of the world through responding to significant experiences and showing a range of feelings when appropriate. KS1 children can develop their PSHE skills through finding out about how we care for each other and about asking for help.

Resources

- Tables and chairs
- Hospital-related play equipment
- Office role-play equipment for the receptionist
- A4 whiteboards and pens
- Real bandages and plasters.

Introducing the activity

If you get the opportunity to do this activity after a spontaneous event then it does make it that much more meaningful. If you want to include it in ongoing work about people who help us, that also works. Try to use children's real experiences wherever possible. If a child had to go to hospital to have stitches after falling off their bike then incorporate this into your role-play.

Conducting the activity

Setting up your emergency ward

- Lay out your tables and chairs so that you have a waiting room with a receptionist and a consultation room.
- Provide specialist spaces such as an x-ray room and an operating theatre.
- Lay out hospital equipment in the appropriate places.
- If this is an ongoing activity rather than a spontaneous one then you can design and include health posters and leaflets in your emergency ward for authenticity.

Playing in the emergency ward

- Model for the children the different things that would happen in an emergency ward and then allow them to explore and play.
- Lay a whiteboard on a child's chest and draw ribs and a spine on the board to create an authentic looking x-ray.
- Practise bandaging sprained ankles and broken wrists.
- Use lots of appropriate vocabulary.
- After everyone has had a go at role-play in the emergency ward discuss the experience to find out what the children have learned from it.

Health and safety

Health and safety is the focus of the learning in this activity so take the opportunity to discuss with children how we can prevent accidents. Check that individual children aren't allergic to plasters if you include these in the play equipment.

Follow-up activities

Ask a nurse to come into school and demonstrate for the children how wounds are dressed and to discuss keeping safe and promoting good hygiene.

Ask a traffic officer or a fire officer to come in and share tips with the children for keeping safe.

Take the opportunity to check children's understanding of the names of the different parts of their bodies.

Teaching points

Role-play a 999 call so that children are confident about calling for help if they ever need to.

4. Pirate Day

Why stage a Pirate Day?

Pirates are a part of history that does not always feel as if it is in history. Often it feels more like a fantasy story theme, but there were (and still are) pirates and role-play is a fun way of learning about them. This theme also allows you to explore concepts such as right and wrong.

Learning objectives

EYFS children are learning more about their world (KUW) and can develop their CLL skills through extending their vocabulary and exploring the meanings and sounds of new words. KS1 children will be able to debate and discuss right and wrong in the PSHE curriculum.

Resources

General

- Costumes
- Toy weapons
- Treasure.

Explore a pirate ship

- PE apparatus in your school hall.

Map making

- A3 plain paper
- Black ink pens
- A candle
- Cold tea
- Instant coffee granules
- Ribbon.

Introducing the activity

Write to the parents and tell them of your intention to stage a Pirate Day. Ask them to dress their children accordingly and list some basic clothing to help them improvise:

- Three-quarter length trousers
- Belt
- Neckerchief
- A tee shirt
- An eye patch
- Bare feet
- Chin stubble and scars painted on faces with an eyeliner pencil.

One way to start your Pirate Day is to come in yourself dressed as a pirate and recruit the children to your crew. Tell them you have come to retrieve your buried treasure and take them on a trek across the school field to find a treasure chest filled with interesting pirate memorabilia such as a treasure map, a cutlass, a telescope, gold coins and so on.

Conducting the activity

Pirate Day

Once you have enlisted your crew you can have a variety of activities going on in the classroom and groups of children can circulate around them:

- Treasure map making (see below)
- Jewellery making

- Folded paper hat making
- Model ship building
- Design a pirate flag
- Compose and sing a pirate song.

Pirate treasure map

Children can make their own pirate maps in the following way:

- Draw an island in black pen on a sheet of A3 paper.
- Embellish the island with drawings of features such as trees, swamps, rope bridges and caves.
- Give these places interesting names such as Skeleton Swamp.
- Add a large X to show where the treasure is buried.
- Once children are happy with their map they need to burn the edges with a candle to make it look old (with adult assistance).
- Screw up the paper and then flatten it our again.
- Then they paint the map on front and back with cold tea.
- Finally drop a few granules of instant coffee on the map and as these soak into the tea they will add old-looking stains.
- Allow your map to dry and then finish it off with a ribbon and a wax seal.

Pirate ship

Set up your apparatus in the school hall so that climbing frames and ropes, etc, become a passable-looking pirate ship. Pop a Jolly Roger on the top if you wish. Children can explore the pirate ship and practise climbing ropes and walking the plank – but they should do this in their proper PE clothing and not their pirate costumes.

Health and safety

Watch out for the toy weapons and encourage children not to get too carried away with them. Children should wear proper PE clothing when exploring the PE apparatus pirate ship. They will need help with burning the edges of their treasure maps.

Follow-up activities

Story writing follows on well from a Pirate Day and this is best done first thing in the morning of the next day while the children's adventures are still fresh in their memories.

KS1 children could research the theme of pirates and stage a debate to decide whether or not piracy was right. Some pirates were actually given permission to be pirates by the king or queen of their home country.

Teaching points

There really were pirates in the Caribbean. One of them was called Blackbeard. His real name was Edward Teach and he was born in Bristol in 1680.

5. Fire!

Why role-play fire?

This is a historical themed role-play opportunity and it links in with the hugely popular Great Fire of London topic. Role-playing fire-fighting and rebuilding London is a great way to pass on the facts and figures of the fire to children. I have always found children are fascinated by the details of this event.

Learning objectives

Most schools leave this theme until Year 2 and I agree that is the right thing to do. This fits in with aspects of the history curriculum on people and places and using historical evidence.

Resources

- Lots of red, orange and yellow sheets
- Logs and planks
- Buckets
- A yellow football.

Introducing the activity

The very best way to introduce the Great Fire of London is to hotseat Samuel Pepys. Hotseating involves putting a knowledgeable individual in a chair and allowing the children to ask him or her questions. In this case, you are the knowledgeable person. Jot down some key facts about the fire and then sit in the hotseat in character as Samuel Pepys. You don't have to put on a voice, but it is great fun to dress up if you are that way inclined. Once you have told the children a few pieces of information, the questions will come flowing. If there is anything you can't answer, it can become the focus for research.

Conducting the activity

Scene setting

Turn your school hall into a scene from the Great Fire of London:

- Set up PE apparatus and drape fire coloured sheeting over it.
- Lay logs and planks on the ground.
- Close all the curtains and turn off the lights.

Living through the fire

Lead your children in small groups through the scene you have created and tell them the story of the fire:

- 'Here is the baker's shop in Pudding Lane where it started'.
- 'London Bridge is on fire'.
- 'The fire is spreading across the rooftops'.

Give children tasks to mime:

- Passing buckets of water along a line.
- Loading up a cart with their possessions.
- Running from the flames and jumping in the river.
- Blowing up houses with gunpowder.

Make one of the children Samuel Pepys and he or she can act out the things we know he did during the fire:

- Woken in the night by his maid but went back to sleep because he thought the fire was nothing to worry about.
- Going and telling the king that houses needed to be blown up to stop the fire spreading.
- Going out onto the Thames in a boat to observe the fire.
- Burying his best Parmesan cheese (the yellow football) in his garden.
- Moving his possessions out of the city on a cart.

Rebuilding London

You can do this with the whole class:

- Clear away the fire scene so that you have an empty hall to give the feeling of starting afresh.
- Mark out the pattern of roads with lines of skipping ropes or chalk.
- Mime building new houses out of brick and stone.
- For a final, big, teamwork effort, work together to mime rebuilding St Paul's Cathedral.

Health and safety

The children aren't going to be climbing on the PE apparatus, just moving around among it so they don't need to wear their PE kit. Make sure they don't trip over logs and planks.

Follow-up activities

Poetry writing is a great way to capture the experience the children have just had. Mind map a whole range of atmospheric words and turn these into poetic sentences before constructing a class poem.

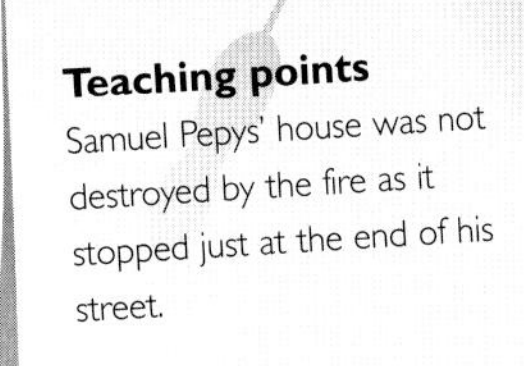

Teaching points

Samuel Pepys' house was not destroyed by the fire as it stopped just at the end of his street.

Theme:
Design and technology

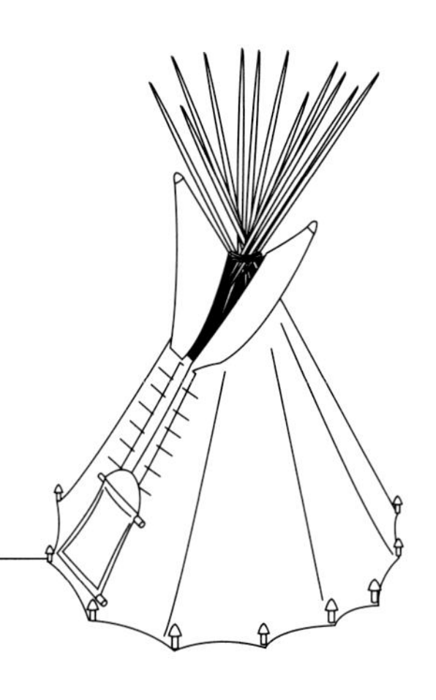

Design and technology: Introduction

I have always found that the best design and technology projects come out of the children's imaginations and allowing them open access to a wide variety of materials. For some time now most D and T in schools has been restricted to following the QCA schemes. While some of their suggestions are good, it does rather limit the vital injection of innovation that brings so much of the fun into realising an imaginative idea.

There is a lot of improvisation in the use of materials that goes into a good D and T activity. Build up a varied store of materials that can be used. Also make sure you have a good selection of tools and that children know how to use them.

The important thing is to follow the D and T process through. Children generate ideas having been inspired in some way. They create their own designs from these ideas. They then make their design and evaluate it before suggesting and making any improvements.

Learning objectives

Specific learning objectives are given for each activity. Here is an overview list of learning objectives for design and technology activities in general.

Early Years Foundation Stage

Personal, social and emotional development

- Be confident to try new activities, initiate ideas and speak in a familiar group.
- Work as part of a group or class, taking turns and sharing fairly.

Communication, language and literacy

- Interact with others, negotiating plans and activities and taking turns in conversations.
- Extend their vocabulary, exploring the meanings and sounds of new words.
- Use talk to organise, sequence and clarify thinking, ideas, feelings and events.
- Use their phonic knowledge to write simple regular words and make phonetically plausible attempts at more complex words.
- Attempt writing for different purposes.

Problem solving, reasoning and numeracy

- Use developing mathematical ideas and methods to solve practical problems.
- Use language such as 'greater', 'smaller', 'heavier' or 'lighter' to compare quantities.
- Use language such as 'circle' or 'bigger' to describe the shape and size of solids and flat shapes.
- Use everyday words to describe position.

Knowledge and understanding of the world

- Investigate objects and materials by using all of their senses as appropriate.
- Ask questions about why things happen and how things work.
- Build and construct with a wide range of objects, selecting appropriate resources and adapting their work where necessary.

- Select the tools and techniques they need to shape, assemble and join materials they are using.
- Find out about and identify the uses of everyday technology.

Physical development

- Use a range of small and large equipment.
- Handle tools safely and with increasing control.

Creative development

- Express and communicate their ideas, thoughts and feelings by using a widening range of materials.

Key Stage 1

Design and technology

Teaching should ensure that knowledge and understanding are applied when developing ideas, planning, making products and evaluating them.

Knowledge, skills and understanding

Developing, planning and communicating ideas

1. Pupils should be taught to:

a. generate ideas by drawing on their own and other people's experiences
b. develop ideas by shaping materials and putting together components
c. talk about their ideas
d. plan by suggesting what to do next as their ideas develop
e. communicate their ideas using a variety of methods, including drawing and making models.

Working with tools, equipment, materials and components to make quality products

2. Pupils should be taught to:

a. select tools, techniques and materials for making their product from a range suggested by the teacher
b. explore the sensory qualities of materials
c. measure, mark out, cut and shape a range of materials
d. assemble, join and combine materials and components
e. use simple finishing techniques to improve the appearance of their product, using a range of equipment
f. follow safe procedures for food safety and hygiene.

Evaluating processes and products

3. Pupils should be taught to:

a. talk about their ideas, saying what they like and dislike
b. identify what they could have done differently or how they could improve their work in the future.

Knowledge and understanding of materials and components

4. Pupils should be taught:

a. about the working characteristics of materials
b. how mechanisms can be used in different ways.

Breadth of study

5. During the key stage, pupils should be taught the Knowledge, skills and understanding through:

a. investigating and evaluating a range of familiar products
b. focused practical tasks that develop a range of techniques, skills, processes and knowledge
c. design and make assignments using a range of materials, including food, items that can be put together to make products, and textiles.

Health and safety

There are several key safety skills that children need to learn as they progress in the development of D and T skills:

Using tools safely – Teach children to use scissors and other cutting tools in a safe way, and how to carry tools and store them away safely.

Hygiene – Every time you cook, instil in children the discipline of washing hands and washing utensils, not eating raw egg and keeping surfaces clean. Good habits will grow out of this regular reinforcement.

Tidying up – This is a health and safety issue because if tools and materials are left lying around they can be a hazard in the classroom; another good habit to develop.

Literacy links

Cookery cards

Writing up recipes provides good handwriting practice for older children. Write up recipes on a card and keep them in a card index for parents to borrow and try at home.

Drawing plans

While drawing is the key part of drawing plans there can be quite a lot of writing involved in labelling plans. Encourage children to make phonetic attempts at unfamiliar words that they want to use in their plan.

Giving instructions

One way to encourage writing linked to D and T is to get one child to write simple instructions for performing a straightforward task, such as measuring and cutting wood to size. Ask another child to follow the instructions and evaluate how effective they were.

1. Big construction

What do we mean by big construction?

For a child there is something special about making a structure that is bigger than they are. It means they can get inside it or look up at it in wonder at what they have achieved. Commercial big construction such as Lego Soft and Quadro bring all sorts of possibilities. So does a pile of cardboard boxes, some cardboard carpet rolls and a load of string.

Why construct big things?

In the EYFS we often give children small construction to help develop their fine motor skills, but as children move into KS1 the activities become more teacher directed with a definite purpose. Sometimes it is worthwhile just letting children have the construction kits out to see what they make of them.

Learning objectives

Avoid the temptation to get children to draw a design first for this activity. Let them explore the construction materials. This will help them to develop skills in communicating ideas about design and construction principles. There is also a lot of speaking going on (but not a lot of listening) and children will find that if they work together, they can achieve so much more. EYFS children are developing the skills of working as part of a group, taking turns and sharing. KS1 children have hopefully developed these skills and can move on to the D and T skills of selecting materials and experimenting with them.

Resources

Commercial big construction:

- Lego Soft Brick
- Quadro (*www.quadroplay.co.uk*).

DIY big construction:

- Cardboard boxes in a variety of sizes
- Cardboard tubes from the inside of carpet rolls
- Lots of string and masking tape
- Bamboo canes.

Introducing the activity

I find it is best to have an actual problem to solve. This gives children a focus for their construction. We had an outdoor classroom that was half grass and half asphalt. The problem was that during heavy weather the grass got muddy and the children brought all the mud into the indoor classroom with them. We discussed the problem and someone (not me) came up with the idea of building a fence out of Quadro. This took all morning and it was a very effective barrier as the children had created it for themselves. Introduce big construction when you have a real problem to solve and start by talking about the problem and how the children are going to solve it.

Conducting the activity

While this may sound like a do-what-you-want activity, you can introduce quite a lot of learning simply through playing with the children as they construct. You can also be a physical construction aid for them: you are able to reach higher than they are and can assist them in building really big structures.

Some challenges and projects I have done with children include an occasion when a ball got stuck on the roof of our classroom and the children decided to make a very long Quadro arm to reach up and pull it down. They then went on to see if they could make a Quadro arm as tall as the school hall. My job was to help them lift the arm up once they had built it along the ground and estimated the height. We have also built a greenhouse frame out of Quadro and covered it in a large sheet of plastic to get our tomatoes off to an early start. With Lego Soft we have practised building bridge arches strong enough to take the weight of a child.

DIY big construction is even more flexible. We have used carpet rolls and a big cardboard box with a child inside to recreate the moving of stones to build Stonehenge. We have also built all manner of tents and dens.

Health and safety

Watch out for bamboo canes and eyes. Use those tennis ball-sized rigid plastic balls with holes in from the PE cupboard to put on the ends of bamboo canes or use big lumps of Plasticine.

Follow-up activities

It is important to keep letting children have these spontaneous construction opportunities. Too often we tell children what to make. As children move from EYFS through KS1 and even into KS2, be on the lookout for any chance to make something big and, most importantly, something with a purpose.

Teaching points

Help children see that constructing in units such as cubes gives strength to their construction. Some shapes are not strong – learn from your mistakes.

2. Junk dragon puppets

What are junk dragon puppets?

This activity came out of a story I made up years ago with my class. The junk dragons are creatures that live on a rubbish dump and eat our waste – one possible solution to our shortage of landfill sites! We made puppets for our story out of waste that the children brought in from home.

Why make junk dragon puppets?

An important point is that we don't need to spend lots of money on commercial construction kits in order to practise our D and T skills. We can make use of our junk to learn. This activity reinforces the message of reuse and recycling of materials.

Learning objectives

This activity will allow EYFS children to build and construct with a wide range of objects, select appropriate resources and adapt their work where necessary. It will also allow them to express and communicate their ideas, thoughts and feelings by using a widening range of materials. KS1 children can use their design skills to draw plans before making, evaluating and improving their design.

Resources

- Lots of clean junk – cereal boxes, toothpaste boxes, bottle lids, matchsticks, lolly sticks, crisp packets and so on
- Attachment materials – glue, string, sticky tape, treasury tags
- Scissors
- Dowelling.

Introducing the activity

Feel free to start this activity with my story about the junk dragons. An egg hatches on a rubbish tip and the delicate little creature starts gathering junk to build a shell to protect itself from the harsh world in which it has emerged. As the junk dragon grows it develops a taste for eating junk. I won't tell you my ending – I'm sure your children will come up with their own.

Conducting the activity

Lay out a table with various pieces of junk and a selection of attachment materials. Children can work in pairs or small groups to select materials and experiment with ways of attaching them. Each pair or group can be given a different type of puppet to create.

Sock puppets

Put out an appeal for parents to send in random single socks and then decorate these with colourful pieces of scrap paper and material to make a simple junk dragon puppet.

Two-handed puppets

Work with a small group of children to teach simple sewing techniques and use scrap material to make a dragon shape that can take two hands – one for the head and one for the body. Decorate with small pieces of junk.

String puppets

This is where larger pieces of junk come in. Connect egg boxes, kitchen paper roll tubes and cereal boxes with string to create your junk dragon and suspend the legs, body and head from pieces of string attached to a cross-frame of dowelling so that you can make the various parts of the dragon move. Decorate your finished puppet with more colourful junk.

Shadow puppets

Suspend a white sheet and illuminate with a torch. Move your puppets around between the sheet and the torch to create a shadow puppet show. The great thing about shadow junk puppets is that the children watching them can guess what junk was used to make the puppet.

Health and safety

Make sure you only use clean junk and don't use bottles that once contained toxic materials such as bleach.

Follow-up activities

Once the children have created their puppets and a story to go with them you are duty bound to put on puppet shows. Film these with your digital video camera. You can also experiment with stop/go animation to produce a short film.

Make music using instruments made out of junk to accompany your production. Record this as a sound track to your film.

Teaching points

'Recycle' is a well-known word now. Introduce 'reuse' as the important stage before recycling, and 'reduce' as the word before that.

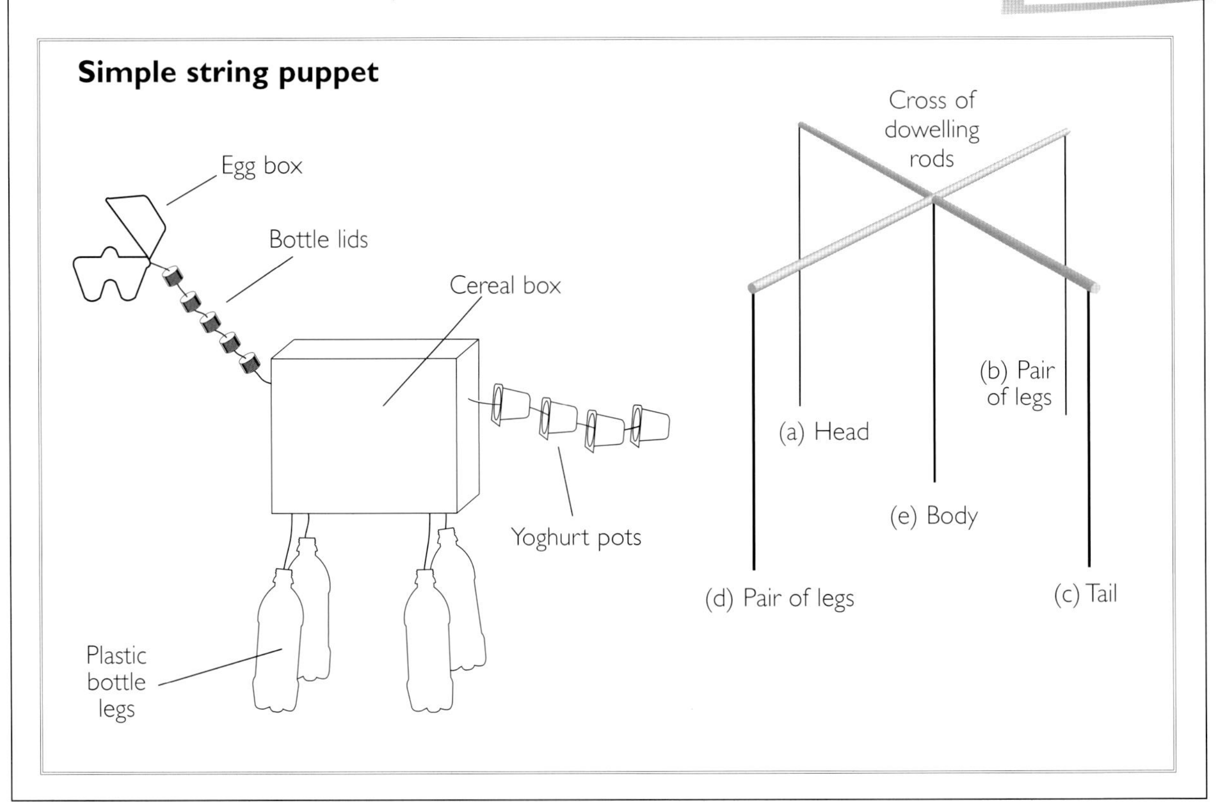

3. Light up a lighthouse

Why light up a lighthouse?

Creating simple lighting circuits is a science activity, but put that lighting circuit to work as the illumination for a model lighthouse and you have a cross-curricular activity. The other great thing about making your own lighthouses is that you can then use them in your small world play seaside for imaginative play.

Learning objectives

EYFS children can ask questions about why things happen and how things work, build and construct, select appropriate resources and tools and find out about and identify the uses of everyday technology. KS1 children can be given this task as a D and T problem-solving exercise and develop the full set of skills.

Resources

Lighthouse

- A hollow cardboard tube about 8cm in diameter and about 25cm long
- An empty transparent yoghurt pot
- Sheets of red paper and white paper
- Plasticine for the base
- Glue
- Sticky tape.

Electrical circuit

- Battery (cell)
- Two lengths of electrical wire with a crocodile clip at each end
- Light bulb and holder.

Introducing the activity

Conducting the activity

Construct the lighthouse

- Cut out strips of white and red paper and glue them alternately up the outside of the cardboard tube.
- Attach the transparent yoghurt pot on top of the lighthouse tower once the electrical circuit is in place.

Construct the electrical circuit

- Screw the bulb into the bulb holder.
- Attach the two pieces of wire to each side of the bulb holder with the crocodile clips.
- Attach the other ends of the wires to the battery (cell) to light up the bulb.
- Attach the electrical circuit inside the lighthouse tower using sticky tape.

Improving your lighthouse

The above is a very simple lighthouse. Stand your lighthouse on a base and decorate with stones to add to the effect. Add a simple switch mechanism so you can turn the light on and off.

Health and safety

You are only using household batteries here, so no worries about electric shocks. Take the opportunity, though, to discuss with children the safety aspects of electricity in their lives.

Follow-up activities

I have seen electric model toys made by children that are linked to a computer programme, which turns the lights on and off in a sequence – so you can make things like traffic lights. Very clever! I've never tried it myself, but if you are a technologically-minded teacher you might like to have a go at computerised lighting circuits.

Teaching points
Practise drawing electrical circuit diagrams from Reception onwards. It does make a big difference to future work on electricity.

If you want to go one step further with the D and T on this project and also keep the link with *The Lighthouse Keeper's Lunch* you can use string and pulleys to rig up a pulley mechanism across the classroom like the lighthouse keeper's wife did in the story.

Another link is to design and make healthy sandwiches to put in the basket that you send across the classroom on the pulley.

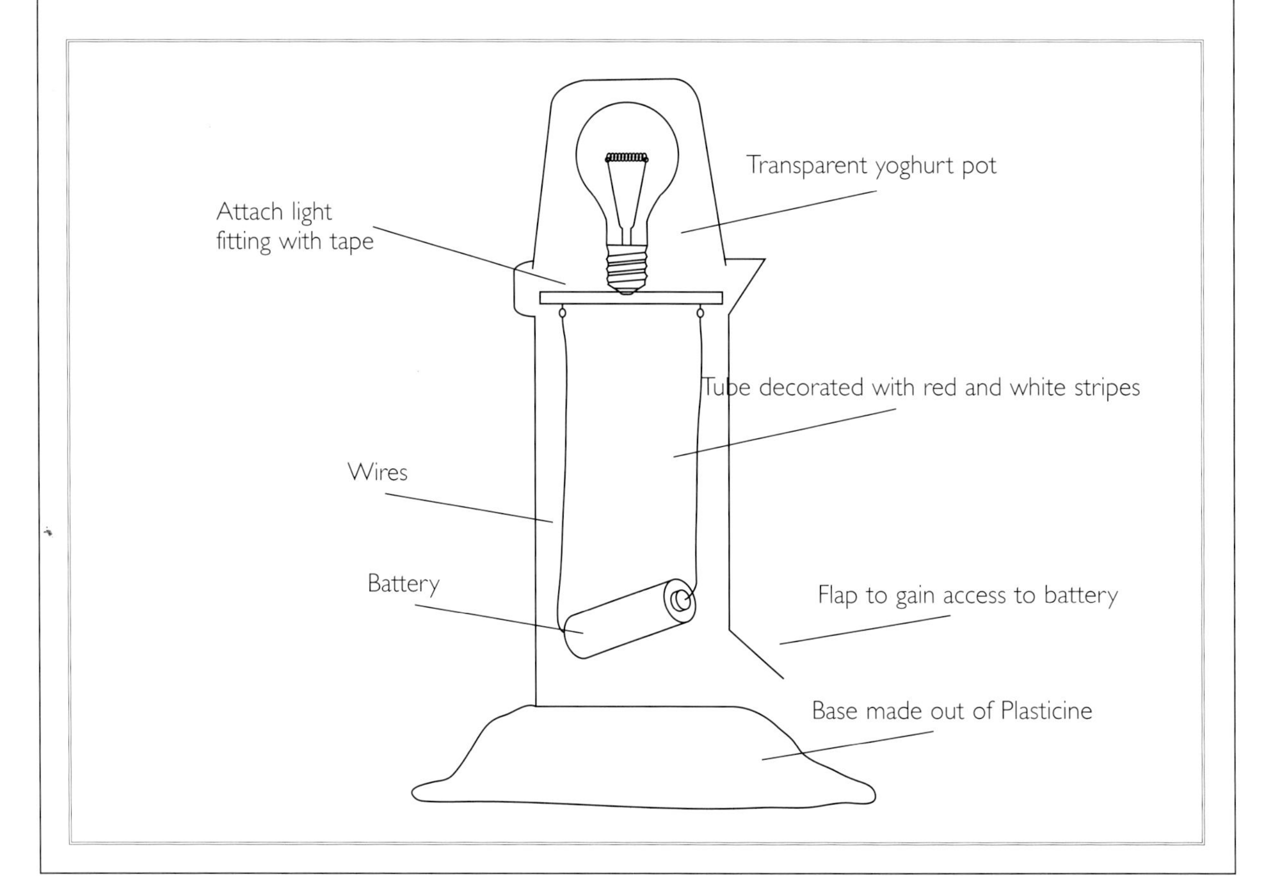

4. Cultural cooking

What is cultural cooking?

There are many cultures around the world, each with their own culinary identity and each with their own favourite ingredients and tastes. We are lucky to live in a culturally diverse country and food is a great way to introduce young children to this diversity.

Why cook culturally?

I like to have a focus when I am cooking with children. There are many festivals belonging to different religious and non-religious traditions. Cooking Chinese moon cakes with children at Chinese New Year gives me the chance to discuss with them the lives of Chinese children. Children are always reluctant to try any new foods at home, but if their teacher offers them something new they usually feel obliged to have a try. Cultural cooking is a good way to broaden children's culinary horizons.

Learning objectives

EYFS children can test their confidence to try out new activities and extend their vocabulary. There are also a lot of counting and measuring opportunities in cooking. KS1 children are applying the full design process – idea, design, make and evaluate – and following safe procedures for food safety and hygiene.

Resources

- The use of a kitchen – preferably child-friendly in size, content and layout, or a mobile kitchen and cooking trolley that can be taken from class to class
- Cooking accessories – aprons, tea towels, dish cloths, etc
- Cleaning materials – washing-up liquid, mild disinfectant spray and cloths
- The necessary ingredients and kitchen equipment are listed under each activity.

Introducing the activity

Depending on the cultural cooking you are doing spend some time talking with the children and showing them images of the culture you are exploring.

Conducting the activity

Chinese moon cakes

These are eaten at Chinese New Year, which takes place at the time of the new moon at the end of January or beginning of February.

Ingredients

- 55g sugar
- 2 free-range egg yolks
- 55g butter.
- 110g all-purpose flour
- 225g strawberry jam

Method

- Preheat the oven to 190°C.
- Blend the butter, sugar and one of the egg yolks and stir.
- Mix in the flour.
- Form the dough into one large ball.

- Wrap the dough in clingfilm and leave in the fridge for half an hour.
- Unwrap the chilled dough and form small balls in the palm of your hand.
- Make a hole with your thumb in the centre of each ball.
- Fill each ball with about half a teaspoon of jam.
- Brush each cake with the other beaten egg yolk and place on a baking sheet.
- Bake for about 20 minutes or just until the moon cakes are golden brown.

Potato latkes

These are a mainstay of the Jewish festival of Hanukkah, which takes place in late November or early December.

Ingredients

- 1kg baking potatoes – peeled and soaked in cold water until needed
- 1 onion – peeled
- 25g plain white flour
- 1 free-range egg – beaten
- Salt and ground white pepper
- Olive or vegetable oil for frying
- Soured cream and apple sauce to serve.

Method

- Grate the potatoes and onion and mix together.
- Put the grated potato and onion into a colander and squeeze out as much of the moisture as you can.
- Mix the potato and onion with the flour, egg, salt and ground white pepper.
- Heat the oil in a frying pan until moderately hot.
- Place a heaped tablespoon of the mixture into the pan and shallow-fry.
- Lower the heat to medium, flatten each latke with the back of a spoon and fry for about five minutes on each side.
- Remove the latkes from the pan and drain on kitchen towel.
- Serve the latkes warm with soured cream and apple sauce.

Whenever I am cooking with children, I always send home a recipe sheet so that families can cook with their children.

Health and safety

This is a cookery activity so take good care with hot things and sharp things and keep reinforcing the hand-washing message.

Follow-up activities

If you have children from different cultures in your class you might like to make a class recipe booklet. You could invite parents into school to share recipes and make traditional dishes for the children to try.

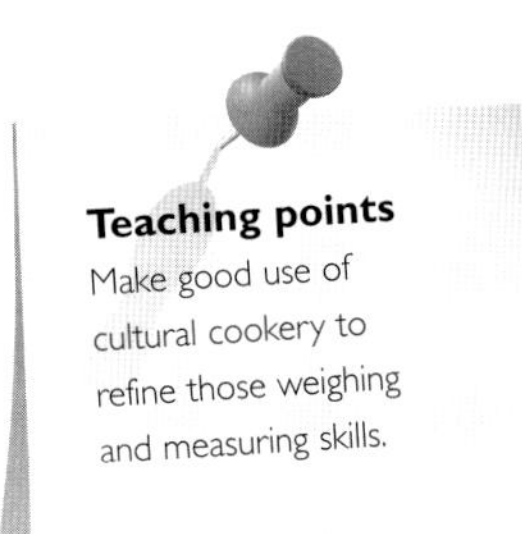

5. Build an igloo

Why build an igloo?

We don't get much snow in most parts of our country, so when we do it is best to make the most of it while it lasts. Some Inuit people who live within the Arctic Circle build these traditional houses out of blocks of ice. Others use snow to insulate their tents and huts, which are made out of whale bone. Either way, a snow house is a cosy habitation and will give children an insight into homes around the world.

Learning objectives

The key learning point is that it is possible to build a self-supporting dome. The dome and arch have been (and still are) very important structures in architecture. As you undertake this design-and-build activity, children will be amazed to see just how strong these structures are and this will bring the benefit of experience to their future D and T projects. EYFS children are interacting with others, negotiating plans and activities and using talk to organise, sequence and clarify thinking, ideas, feelings and events. KS1 children are using a new and unfamiliar material for construction.

Resources

- Lots of snow
- Several plastic storage boxes measuring approximately 35cm deep and 35cm wide by 45cm long
- Hand trowels
- Wellies, warm clothing and gloves.

Introducing the activity

This fits in perfectly with Key Stage 1 work on homes, but you can't always predict when you are going to get snow. If you have already covered homes then review the children's learning. If you haven't already done homes then abandon all other planning and do it now, while the snow lasts!

Discuss with the children what they know about different types of homes. Even within Britain we have lots of different types – three-bed semis, bungalows, terraces, flats, maisonettes and country cottages are just a few of the more common. Some people live in converted chapels or old school buildings and flats can be built in converted mills or factories. Some travelling people live in caravans. Talk about the features of houses and homes – what we all need to make our lives comfortable and easier.

Conducting the activity

Get out in the snow and get making

- Your igloo will be a team effort so stress this from the outset
- One group can dig snow and fill storage boxes.
- Other children can stamp it down to make ice/snow bricks.
- Another group can place them on the igloo and fix them in place with handfuls of snow.

Construction

- Mark out a circle in the snow about two metres across.

- Place a ring of snow blocks on this circle – make your first snow blocks out of the snow within the circle.
- Leave a gap for the door.
- The next circle goes on top of the first and leans slightly in – I have found that making a ledge of snow on the outer edge of the first circle helps tilt the second circle inwards.
- Once the first layer is in place, set two or three children to make the tunnel entrance. This is a bit tricky as you need to interlock the snow blocks of the door with those of the wall and then arch the snow blocks over to form a tunnel once you are on about the fourth layer.
- By the time you have put on five layers of snow blocks you should only have a small hole left in the roof of your igloo.
- Have one person inside lifting snow bricks into place to fill the final hole.
- A tall adult on the outside can lean over and fix blocks into place with snow.

Health and safety

Children aren't going to come to a lot of harm playing in the snow. Do watch out for very cold fingers though. It may be best to have a quarter of the class at a time working on your igloo while the rest are indoors keeping warm. You and your adult assistants can take it in turns to be outside overseeing the construction.

Follow-up activities

You may not feel that you want to sleep in your igloo, but it will make a cosy den for the next few days. Line the floor with a big plastic sheet and cover this with rugs, blankets and cushions. Take children into the igloo in groups for storytelling sessions.

Take photographs of the construction of your igloo and a photograph at the same time every day over the week or so it will take to gradually melt and disintegrate. Put them all together in a slide show and have them running on a laptop outside your classroom door for parents to enjoy.

Teaching points
Check the temperature inside and outside your completed igloo to show that snow is a good insulator.

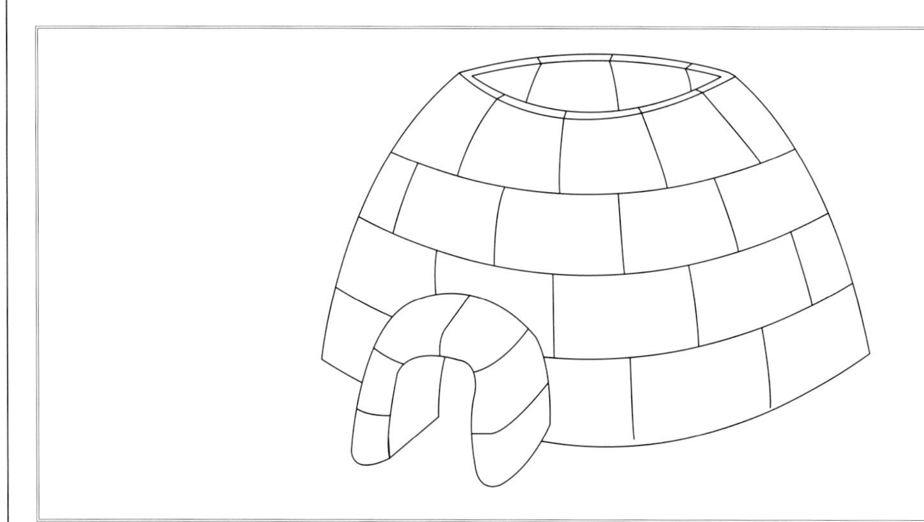

6. Build your own adventure course

Why build your own adventure course?

Schools spend a lot of money on large play equipment for their playgrounds, but it is perfectly possible to build an exciting adventure course on your school field for a fraction of the price. The big advantage of doing it yourself is that the children do the planning and building and they learn from the experience.

Learning objectives

Get EYFS and KS1 children fully involved at all stages of this D and T activity – idea, design, build, evaluate and improve.

Resources

- Old telegraph poles – try your local timber yard
- Rope netting – ask at your local army base
- Old tyres – check the local tyre garage
- Saw for cutting telegraph poles
- Long screws
- Eyelet anchors.

Introducing the activity

Give pairs of children a large sheet of paper and plenty of coloured pens and ask them to design their fantasy adventure course. Get together and compare plans. Identify some items you want to build and make models of them before making the full-size version.

Conducting the activity

Stepping logs

Cut slices 10cm wide off a telegraph pole or large log and lay these on the ground as stepping stones between two activities on your adventure course. There is no need to sink them into the ground as they will sink in a little with the children stepping on them.

Balancing pole

- Saw two pieces (about 50cm each) off the end of a telegraph pole.
- Sink these upright in the ground as supports as described in the rope bridge activity in the woodcraft section of this book (p129).
- Cut right-angled blocks off each end of the telegraph poles.
- Place the cut ends on the uprights and fix into place with long screws.

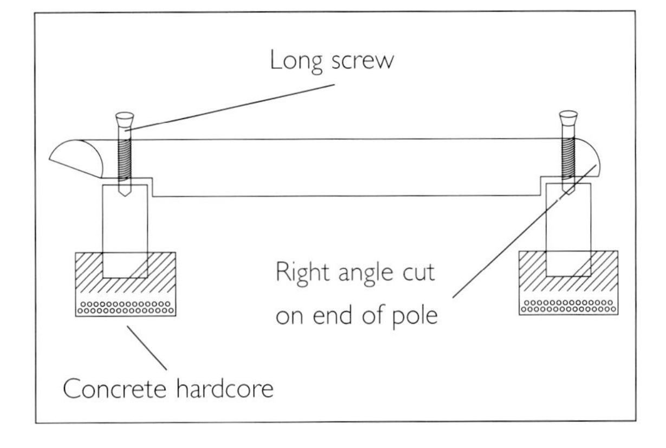

Rope swing

Suspend an old tyre on a length of rope and hang it from a tree branch to produce a rope swing. Mark out a take-off and landing point as part of the course so children have a definite place to aim for in their swinging. Make sure that the area is clear of any other branches or obstacles. See also the rope bridge building activity in the woodcraft section of this book (p129).

Net tunnel and climber

Lay a square of rope netting on the ground and secure the corners with eyelet anchors. Children can crawl under the netting. Another approach is to hang the netting from a low branch of a tree and secure the bottom two corners to the ground as a lower climbing obstacle.

Ditches

Another simple way to add obstacles to your adventure course is to simply dig out some shallow ditches and build mounds of earth.

Tyres

Large tractor tyres can be added to the adventure course for children to walk around the edge or jump in and out of.

Health and safety

This is an area where we have been encouraged to believe that only commercially made and installed equipment is safe for our children. We need to challenge that thinking. Having said that, you must apply a rigorous eye to each item you build and test it out yourself before letting the children on it. These are low pieces of equipment and should be safe on a grassed surface. If you feel you need additional protection, add bark chippings.

Follow-up activities

The great thing about this approach to adventure provision in school is that you can make changes to it. Each year have a design competition for children to come up with new ideas for adventure equipment to build and add to your course. Remove items that have become damaged or are no longer popular.

If you have a local army base, invite some soldiers along to test out your course and interview them afterwards to see how it compares to their own assault courses.

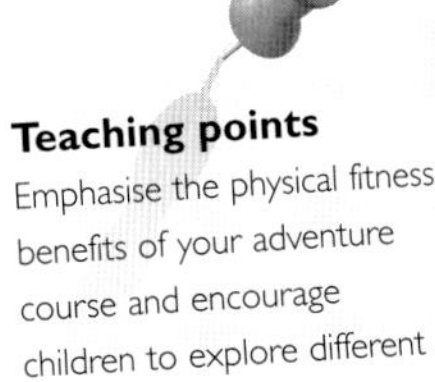

Teaching points

Emphasise the physical fitness benefits of your adventure course and encourage children to explore different ways of using it.

7. Cotton reel car

What is a cotton reel car?

These are a simple little wind-up, self-propelling toy made out of materials that are easy to get hold of. We used to make them when we were kids and race them up and down the street.

Why make cotton reel car?

This is the simplest of wind-up devices and will give children the confidence to move on to more complex techniques and try out ideas for making their own wind-up toys. They can be used in races and will become a favourite playground toy.

Learning objectives

The D and T skill that is being developed here is evaluation and improvement in KS1 as the actual construction is very simple. EYFS children will find lots to talk about during this activity and can develop their working together skills to try to improve the design.

Resources

- Cotton reel
- Pencil
- Elastic band
- Rubber (eraser).

Introducing the activity

Ask children to bring in any examples of wind-up toys they may have at home. Ask your colleagues at school if they have any you might use. Examine the wind-up toys with the children and discuss how they work.

Get out the materials you have gathered to make a cotton reel car and show children just how quick and simple these are to make. Distribute materials and let them make and test their own cotton reel cars.

Conducting the activity

Simple cotton reel car

- Put the elastic band right through the centre of your cotton reel.
- Loop one end around a rubber.
- Put a pencil through the loop at the other end.
- Wind up the elastic band by rotating the pencil.
- Stick a lump of Plasticine on one end of the pencil to provide a counterbalance and stop the pencil flipping over.
- Put your cotton reel car on the ground and watch it go.

A more complex mechanism

Children love to find out how things work. If you can get hold of a broken wind-up clock or watch, which children can take apart, they can see how springs and coils are used instead of elastic bands. Drawing pictures of these mechanisms helps to give children ideas for developing their own designs.

Health and safety

There are no real health and safety issues with the simple activity described here. If you go on to experiment with different kinds of wind-up mechanisms be careful not to overwind the elastic band in case it snaps off and pings someone in the eye.

Follow-up activities

Test your cotton reel cars to see how far and how fast they can go and how you can improve the design.

Try making a model plane with a wind-up propeller using the same basic idea.

Teaching points
The elastic band is storing up energy as you rotate it and when you let go this energy is released and propels the cotton reel car along.

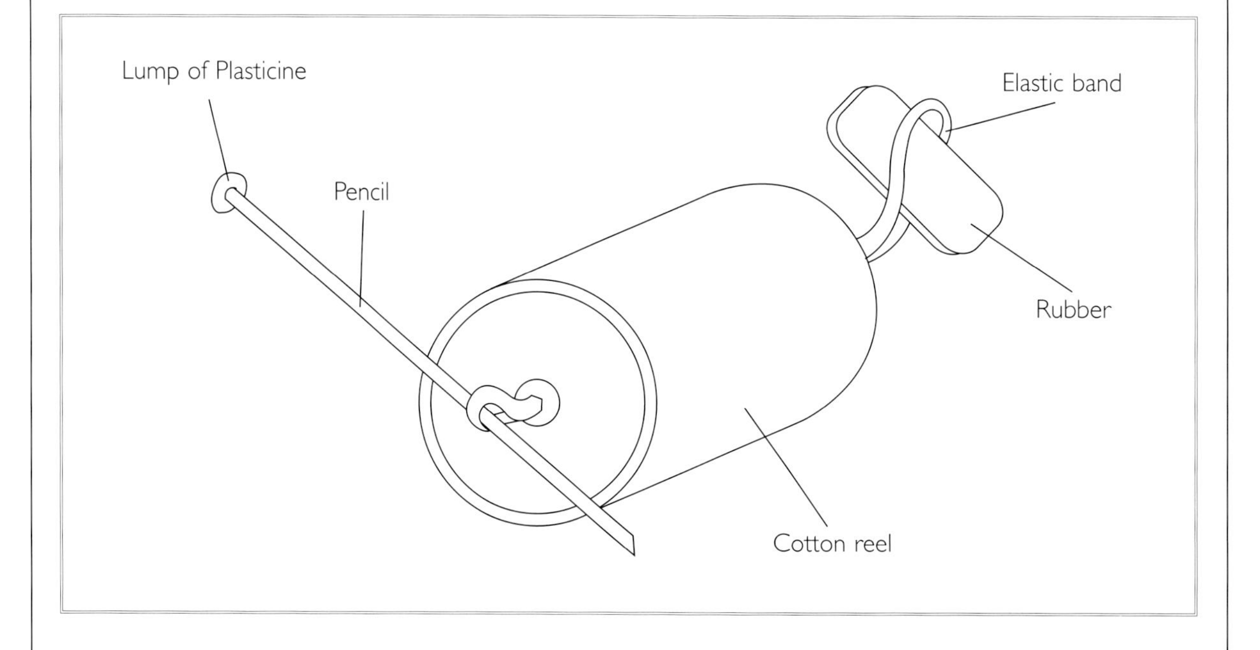

8. Build a go-cart

Why build a go-cart?

All the wheeled toys I have come across in outdoor classrooms have been commercial products. That's fine, but making your own will give children a lot of D and T learning as well as providing a new resource for the playground.

Learning objectives

This is quite a complicated task so you need to do the planning and get the children involved in the making. EYFS children will be practising using tools and techniques to assemble and join materials. KS1 children can measure, mark out, cut and shape a range of materials and assemble, join and combine materials and components.

Resources

Some improvisation is involved in making a go-cart, but here is a basic list of resources:

- Two pairs of wheels on metal axles – I have always used the undercarriage of a pram
- A length of wood 10cm by 5cm by 2.2 metres long
- The bucket of a broken plastic chair
- Ten U-shaped nails big enough to go over the metal axles of the wheels
- Four nails measuring 7.5cm long
- Four screws measuring 4cm long
- A length of rope 2cm in diameter and 2 metres long
- A bolt measuring 15cm long with a nut and thick washers.

Introducing the activity

Set up a street scene in your outdoor classroom with a traffic warden and motorists and role-play driving. Discuss with the children road safety and etiquette on the road. Talk to them about when they grow up and become motorists – what will they be like as motorists? Talk about the cars, bikes and trikes you have in your outdoor classroom and ask them if they think they could make their own. See what they come up with in the way of ideas.

Conducting the activity

- Cut your length of timber into three pieces – 100cm, 70cm and 50cm.
- Lay the 100cm piece on the ground. This is the body of the go-cart. Attach the 70cm piece to it with the 7.5cm nails so it forms a cross shape. This is the axle for the back wheels. Make sure the back wooden axle is centrally placed.
- Drill a hole through the body 15cm up from the front end. The hole needs to be wide enough for the bolt to go through.
- Drill a hole through the 50cm piece of wood in the exact centre lengthwise and widthwise. This is the axle for the front wheels.
- Place the front axle onto the body so the holes match up and attach the two pieces of wood together with the bolt. You need a couple of thick washers in between the pieces of wood so the axle will turn.

- Attach the wheels by laying them across the wooden axles and nailing them into place with four U-shaped nails for the front axle and four for the back.
- Turn the whole cart over.
- Drill four holes in the middle of the base of the plastic chair at the corners of a square measuring approximately 8cm by 8cm.
- Attach the bucket seat above the back axle with the screws so that it is securely attached to the 70cm-long piece of wood.
- Attach the steering rope to each end of the front axle with the remaining two U-shaped nails so that a person sitting in the seat can comfortably use it for steering the front wheels.
- Give your cart a name and paint it on the side of the body plank.
- Test drive your new go-cart.

Health and safety

This is a practical hands-on construction activity, which will require children to work in groups of four with an adult showing them how to use tools safely. When you come to use your go-cart, test it out first to check that everything works OK and that there are no nails or splinters sticking out.

Follow-up activities

Make two go-carts and have races. Have a go-cart challenge where each class makes and decorates a go-cart for a parade. Try making a storage compartment for the back of your go-cart so that you can use it to carry light loads.

See how far your go-cart will go with a single push on flat ground and down a gentle slope.

Teaching points
Look for similarities and differences between your home-made go-cart and a commercially produced wheeled toy.

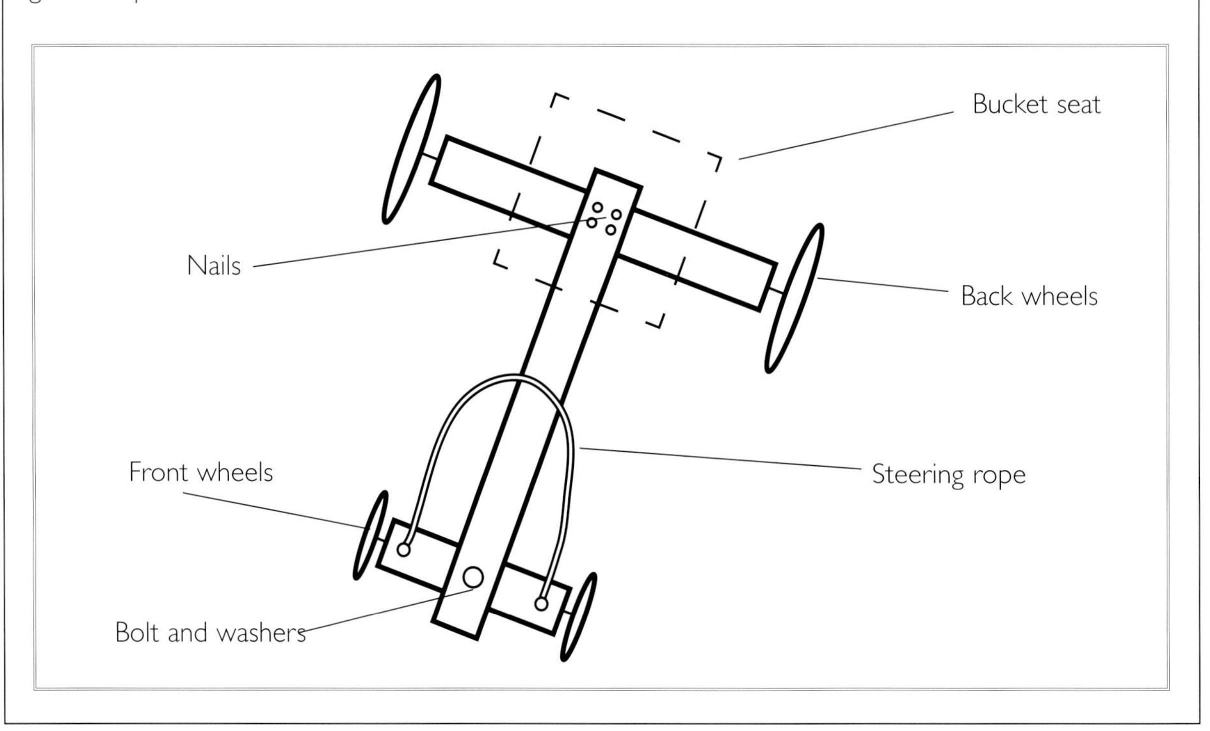

9. Making and flying kites

Why make and fly kites?

This activity will help to develop D and T skills and also give children a valuable insight into our weather systems. The kites we are making here are single-line kites, which are easier for young children to handle than the more powerful dual-line stunt kites.

Learning objectives

This activity supports the KUW curriculum of the EYFS guidance and will teach children to build and construct with a wide range of objects, selecting appropriate resources and adapting their work where necessary, as well as selecting the tools and techniques they need to shape, assemble and join materials they are using. For KS1 children the key focus of this D and T task is on evaluation and improvement of their design. Kites are quite fickle things and changes in design can reap rewards in flying enjoyment.

Resources

- Two pieces of thin dowelling rod, one 60cm long and one 30cm long
- A long length of thin string
- Sheet of strong paper at least 60cm by 30cm
- Scissors
- Sticky tape
- A spool – any sturdy stick approximately 2.5cm in diameter and 15cm to 20cm long will do
- Paints and crayons.

Introducing the activity

Carry out this activity in the autumn, maybe at a time when you are focusing on the weather. Talk about the wind with your children and discuss how it influences our lives. Talk about kites and ask children where they think a good local place to fly kites would be.

Conducting the activity

Making your kite

Here are step-by-step instructions to make a very simple diamond-shaped kite:

1. Make a cross with the two dowelling rods by placing the shorter rod horizontally across the longer rod. Check that both sides of the crosspiece are equal in length.
2. Tie the two sticks together with string.
3. Cut a notch in the ends of each rod and tie a length of string all the way around the outside to create the diamond kite shape.
4. Attach a length of string from tip to tip of the shorter piece of dowelling. This is where your flying line will be attached.
5. Lay the sheet of strong paper flat and place the stick frame on top. Cut out a kite shape by cutting around the outside of the string diamond shape. Leave about 2cm for a margin. Fold this margin over the frame and string and tape it down.
6. To make a tail, simply tie small pieces of ribbon along a length of string and attach to the bottom of the kite.

7. Decorate your finished kite.
8. Attach your flying line to the loose cross-string and take your kite out for a test flight.

Flying your kite

- Test your kite out on a moderately windy day.
- Choose a flat, open space that is free from obstacles such as trees.
- For a *short launch* stand with your back to the wind. Hold your kite out in front of you at arm's length and the flying line on a spool in the other hand. Release the kite into the air and let out the line a little at a time. Slowly let out more line as the kite is carried up by the wind.
- For a *long launch* stand with your back to the wind and let out the line as your helper walks backwards moving downwind and holding the kite. When your helper is about 10 to 15 metres away they lift the kite into the air for the wind to carry it up.

Retrieving your kite

- Simply wind the flying line onto the spool a little at a time to bring the kite back to you.

Health and safety

Do not fly your kite near power cables, in thunderstorms or when people or animals are nearby. It is advisable for children to wear gloves when flying kites to avoid string burn.

Follow-up activities

Watching a kite floating around in the autumn sky is a great way into descriptive writing and poetry.

This activity links in well with the activity about monitoring the weather in the science section (p87).

Teaching points
Children can throw a handful of grass cuttings into the air to find out which way the wind is blowing.

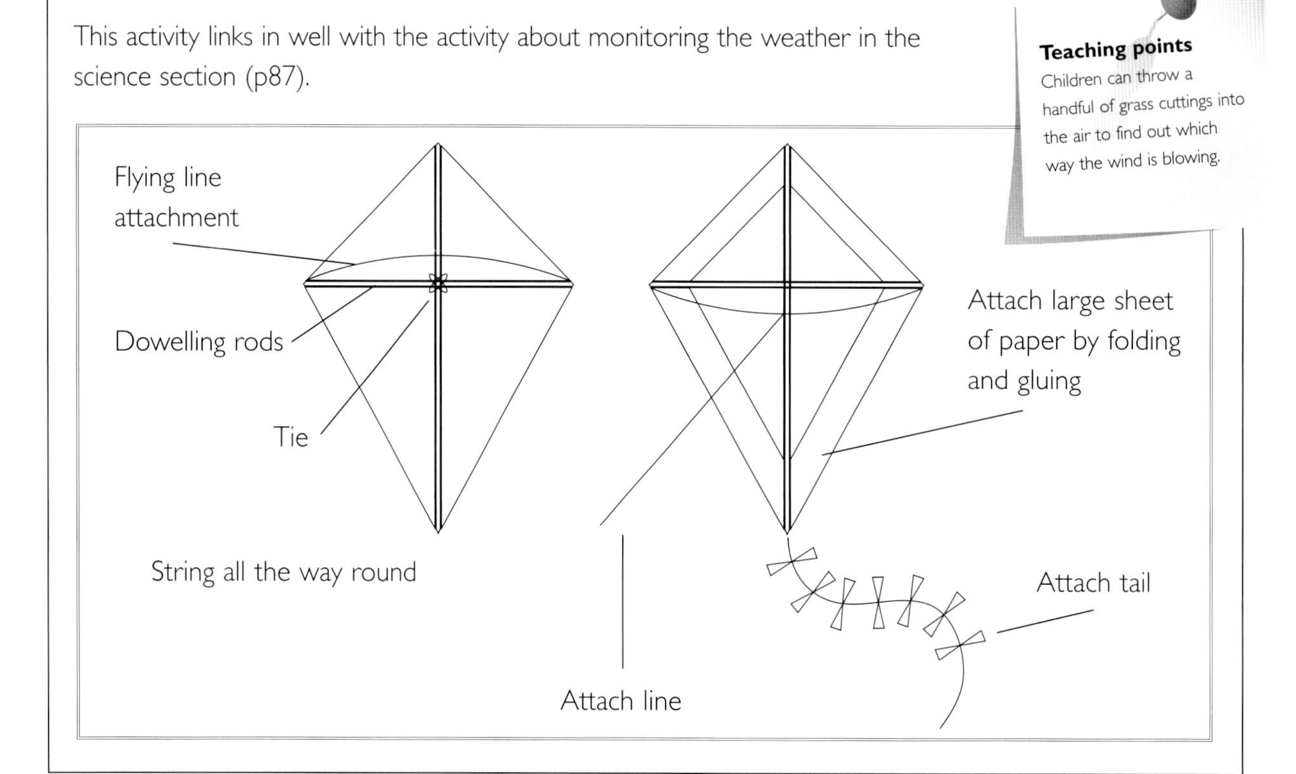

Theme: Gardening

Gardening: Introduction

Gardening in schools is a practical way in which you can tick a number of boxes and have lots of fun into the bargain. If you are working on the Eco-Schools Programme, an organic vegetable garden fed with your own homemade compost is a winner. If you are a Healthy School then supplying your school kitchen with herbs from your own herb garden and giving the children fresh fruit from your own mini-orchard are a big step in the right direction.

When I was a boy my grandad was a keen fruit and vegetable gardener. I didn't like his runner beans as they were too stringy! I did like his blackcurrants, which he would turn into a delicious blackcurrant crumble. I helped him in the fruit and vegetable garden, and as a teacher I have worked to pass on the skills of raising home-grown food to the children I have taught. I do believe that having a hand in producing your own food is an important life-skill.

As a way of really grabbing young children's attention and getting them to commit to a long-term project, starting a vegetable garden is a great project. I know schools where each class has a bed in the school vegetable garden – the skills just keep developing as children move through the school.

Learning objectives

A specific learning focus is given for each activity. Here is an overview list of learning objectives for gardening activities in general.

Early Years Foundation Stage

Personal, social and emotional development

- Be confident to try new activities, initiate ideas and speak in a familiar group.
- Respond to significant experiences, showing a range of feelings when appropriate.
- Work as part of a group or class, taking turns and sharing fairly.
- Manage their own personal hygiene (hand washing).

Communication, language and literacy

- Interact with others, negotiating plans and activities and taking turns in conversations.
- Extend their vocabulary, exploring the meanings and sounds of new words.
- Use talk to organise, sequence and clarify thinking, ideas, feelings and events.
- Know that print carries meaning.
- Attempt writing for different purposes.

Problem solving, reasoning and numeracy

- Count reliably up to 10 everyday objects.
- In practical activities and discussion, begin to use the vocabulary involved in adding and subtracting.
- Use language such as 'more' and 'less' to compare two numbers.
- Use everyday words to describe position.
- Use developing mathematical ideas and methods to solve practical problems.

Knowledge and understanding of the world

- Investigate objects and materials by using all of their senses as appropriate.
- Find out about, and identify, some features of living things, objects and events they have observed.
- Look closely at similarities, differences, patterns and change.
- Ask questions about why things happen and how things work.
- Build and construct a wide range of objects, selecting appropriate resources and adapting their work where necessary.
- Select the tools and techniques they need to shape, assemble and join materials they are using.
- Make short-term future plans.

Physical development

- Use a range of small and large equipment.
- Recognise the importance of keeping healthy and those things which contribute to this.

Creative development

- Respond in a variety of ways to what they see, hear, smell, touch and feel.

Key Stage 1

Science
Sc2: Life processes and living things
Knowledge, skills and understanding
Life processes

1. Pupils should be taught:

a. the differences between things that are living and things that have never been alive
c. to relate life processes to animals and plants found in the local environment.

Green plants

3. Pupils should be taught:

a. to recognise that plants need light and water to grow
b. to recognise and name the leaf, flower, stem and root of flowering plants
c. that seeds grow into flowering plants.

Variation and classification

4. Pupils should be taught to:

b. group living things according to observable similarities and differences.

Maths
Ma2: Number
Using and applying number

1. Pupils should be taught to:

Problem solving

a. approach problems involving number, and data presented in a variety of forms, in order to identify what they need to do.

Ma3: Shape, space and measures

Using and applying shape, space and measures

1. Pupils should be taught to:

Problem solving

a. try different approaches and find ways of overcoming difficulties when solving shape and space problems
b. select and use appropriate mathematical equipment when solving problems involving measures or measurement
c. select and use appropriate equipment and materials when solving shape and space problems.

Literacy links

Keep a gardening journal

Literacy activities are always appreciated more by children if there is a purpose to them. The purpose of a gardening journal is that you record the names of the varieties of vegetables that you grew, when you sowed and transplanted them, which ones tasted best and so on. This means that next year you have lots of experience to build on.

Gardeners' question time

This is a speaking and listening activity. Suppose your class is leading the way in your school in becoming vegetable gardeners and you want to encourage other classes to do the same. Stage a half-hour-long event where half a dozen of your most knowledgeable children sit as a panel and take questions on vegetable gardening from the rest of the school and the staff. Passing on information is a great way to learn.

Design a seed packet

Once you have collected some seeds from your own vegetables, why not package them up and give them away to parents who can take them home and get into vegetable gardening for themselves. Buy some appropriately-sized envelopes and children can draw pictures on the front. The important literacy bit is on the back where they give sowing, growing and harvesting instructions.

Become a compost champion

Around the country many local authorities are running schemes where local compost enthusiasts open up their gardens to allow members of the public to visit and find out about composting first hand. This is another speaking and listening activity. Invite parents and friends of the school to come along and learn composting skills from your children. Contact you local authority to see if they have a scheme.

Learning Latin

Every plant has a Latin name. Copy these onto your seed labels as well as the common name. It is good handwriting practice and children will like the unusual sounding names.

Health and safety

Gardening presents opportunities to teach children about using tools safely. Show children how to carry tools from the tool shed to the vegetable garden safely – hold the handle of the tool and have the blade or sharp end pointing to the ground and facing slightly forward so that if you trip no one will come to any harm. Never run with tools. The importance of washing hands after practical activities can also be reinforced. It is best to work in small groups of four or six with a dedicated adult supervising these activities.

1. Create a vegetable garden

Why create a vegetable garden?

Having a vegetable patch in school is the ideal way to deliver many aspects of the science curriculum and with a little imagination you can cross-fertilise this learning to many other areas of the curriculum too – such as maths and literacy.

Learning objectives

Life processes and living things in the science curriculum is the key curriculum area. A lot of maths work on measuring can be covered in the planning (scale drawings) and laying out (accurate measuring) of a vegetable plot. Children will also use their design and technology skills to build the surround for your vegetable beds. For Reception children, focus on planning sharing and working together.

Resources

- Tape measure
- String and four sticks
- Adult-sized garden spade, fork, rake and hoe
- Child-sized hand trowels and forks, rakes and hoes
- Two wooden planks measuring 15cm by 2.5cm by 3 metres long
- Two wooden planks measuring 15cm by 2.5cm by 1 metre long
- Four wooden posts measuring 5cm by 5cm by 50cm long
- Hammer and nails.

Introducing the activity

Start your initial discussions about this activity during fruit and drink time – especially on a day when you are having carrots or tomatoes. Ask the children where these foods come from and how they are grown. Ask if any of the children grow vegetables at home. There will be one bright little button who knows that a tomato is in fact a fruit and not a vegetable! Tell the children they are going to create their own vegetable bed and ask them what vegetables they would like to grow. Make a wish list and, as a class, agree a small selection to start you off.

Conducting the activity

Take your string and sticks and measure out a rectangle one metre by three metres. I find these are suitable dimensions for a vegetable bed for young children. It means they can reach the middle from the edge without the need for walking on the soil. They can also walk around the plot easily and are not tempted to try to step across and trample your young seedlings.

If you are digging into grass, this is a job for an adult and a spade. With the blade of the spade cut your patch into small squares the length and width of the spade blade. Now cut under the square of turf with a horizontal cutting motion and lift it out. Stack these squares of turf upside down in a corner and cover with black plastic. Over the next two years they will rot down to form a rich loam, which you can use to make your own potting compost.

Now you have a rectangle of bare earth. This is likely to be quiet firm so go over it with a garden fork to break it up before letting the children loose on it with hand forks and trowels. The children's job is to remove weed roots and stones. Explain to the children why you are doing this. Weeds will compete with your seedlings for light and water and stop them growing. Stones will block the path of roots growing into the soil. Break up the clods of earth into small crumbs. When the children go home you can give it another forking over to make sure the soil is really loose and well broken up. Your vegetable bed is now ready for planting. You won't need to add any compost or manure initially. If you have dug your bed on grassland, the soil will be fertile enough. In future years, add a wheelbarrow full of well-rotted manure per metre squared the autumn before planting potatoes and a wheelbarrow full of compost per metre squared to other crops.

Build a surround for your vegetable bed using the four wooden posts and planks. This defines the edge of your plot, helps give it an identity in the children's minds and can even stop them walking on it.

Health and safety

Children can use child-sized tools – make sure you teach them how to use them correctly. Explain to them that only you or another adult can use the adult-sized tools. The biggest health and safety issue I have found when gardening is over-enthusiastic digging by children leading to soil being sprayed around and going in children's eyes. I'm not advocating that they all wear goggles, but you might like to demonstrate careful digging before you get going.

Follow-up activities

Once your class has established its vegetable garden, invite other classes to come and have a look. Encourage other classes to establish their own vegetable plot. Each year at harvest you can have a vegetable competition and ask local gardeners to come in and be the judges.

Teaching points

As children pull weeds from your patch, look closely at the structure of roots, rootlets and fine hairs.

2. Growing potatoes

Why grow potatoes?

Potatoes are easy to grow and give a good yield, which children will thoroughly enjoy unearthing. They really do treat the harvesting of potatoes as a treasure hunt and there are squeals of delight at each spud they find. .

Learning objectives

Maths work involving measuring comes into planting out your potato tubers. The growing plant provides opportunities for scientific observations of living things.

Resources

- Seed potato tubers – one per child
- Plant labels – one per child
- String and two sticks
- Hand trowel
- A potato dibber – a long pointed stick about 40cm long
- Compost
- Tape measure
- Watering can.

Introducing the activity

Look at some packaging of potato products – instant mash, frozen chips, crisps, tinned potatoes and waffles, for example. Do any children know what all these foods have in common? Look at a real potato. Feel its firmness and texture. Have examples of red and white potatoes so children can appreciate that there are different types. Maybe show them a sweet potato and explain that this is a distant relation of the potatoes we are most used to. The tomato is also a member of the potato family.

Conducting the activity

Buy certified seed potatoes from a seed merchants or garden centre. These have been grown under special conditions, usually in Scotland, and are resistant to certain potato diseases.

Before you plant your potatoes in the ground you will need to chit them. It is the eyes of a potato that will grow into the new plant and these have to sprout before they are put in the ground. Take an egg box and cut off the lid. Place a seed potato in each egg space with one of the pointy ends up. Leave these in a cool place where there is light, but not bright light. A shed with a window is ideal or a cloakroom windowsill away from direct sunlight. Set your seed potatoes to chit in February. During March you will see small clusters of leafy growth emerging from the eyes.

Depending on where you are in the country, you will probably be ready to plant some time during April. Using a tape measure and string, mark out rows along your vegetable bed with 30cm between each row. Dib holes along each row with 30cm between plantings and twizzle your dibbing stick around to make the hole quite wide. It needs to be about 15cm deep. Place a handful of compost in each hole and a chitted potato on top with the sprouts pointing upwards. You want three good sprouts on a seed potato, so rub any extras off with your fingers. Cover the seed potato very gently with soil to avoid damaging the shoots then label with the name of the child who planted it and water.

As your potatoes emerge you earth them up. This involves dragging soil with a hoe from the side of each row to form a ridge over the green growth. This protects the growing plant from frost and you need to do it every week until mid- to late May.

Your potato plants will need watering if you have several dry days in a row.

Once your potato plants have flowered and the flowers have faded away, you can gently dig into the soil ridges to find the delicious treasure within.

Health and safety

Harvesting potatoes is usually done with an adult-sized fork. If you do the digging, children can then do the collecting once you move out of the way.

Follow-up activities

Boil your potatoes and let them go cold before serving coated in mayonnaise. Delicious!

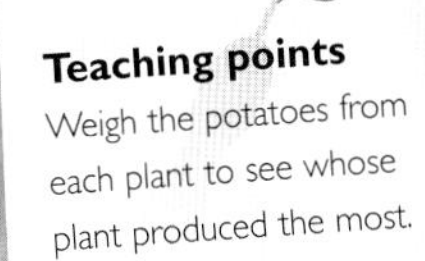

Teaching points

Weigh the potatoes from each plant to see whose plant produced the most.

3. Growing vegetables from seeds

Why grow from seed?

Sowing seeds and monitoring their growth lies at the very heart of life processes and living things. This activity has been a cornerstone of good primary practice since the year dot. Through sowing seeds for themselves, children learn so much about life, how it develops and is sustained and how it needs nurturing.

Learning objectives

Let's stick to the National Curriculum for science for this activity.

Green plants

Pupils should be taught:

a. to recognise that plants need light and water to grow
b. to recognise and name the leaf, flower, stem and root of flowering plants
c. that seeds grow into flowering plants.

Resources

- Vegetable seeds
- Plastic plant pots and seed trays
- Compost
- Hand trowels
- Watering can
- Labels
- Newspaper.

Introducing the activity

Bring some seed catalogues into school – you can pick these up for free in garden centres. Spend some time with the children going through them and choose some vegetable varieties to grow. You might even go online and order seeds from *www.gardenorganic.org.uk*. This national charity encourages schools in their efforts to promote vegetable growing and has an award system. It is well worth supporting.

Conducting the activity

Sowing big seeds

Broad beans, French beans, courgettes and pumpkins can be sown directly into the soil, but giving them a head start in pots gets an earlier crop and teaches some valuable horticultural skills. Start your seeds off in pots inside on a classroom windowsill during early April.

Start the seeds off in large yoghurt pots with a slit in the bottom to prevent flooding when watering. Fill your pot with ordinary seed compost and firm it down. Dib two small holes with your finger, plant two seeds, cover with compost, label and water. Cover with a newspaper to keep dark as seeds need darkness for germination.

Once the seedlings start growing, one will be obviously stronger than the other. One might not even grow at all and that is why you sow two. Pull out the weaker one and explain to the children that you are doing this so the remaining seedling can grow stronger.

Sowing small seeds

Small seeds such as tomatoes are sown in a similar way but sprinkled on the surface of soil in a seed tray and covered by sieving compost over them. Water and cover with a newspaper. Some small seeds such as carrots don't like being transplanted. Sow them directly into the ground in drills 1cm deep and gently rake the soil over them.

Transplanting seedlings

Beans, courgettes and pumpkins

Once your seedling has a stem and a couple of healthy looking leaves, it can be transplanted outside into your vegetable bed. The seedling will probably be about 10cm tall and will look strong; it can hold itself up. Dig a hole big enough to take the contents of the yoghurt pot. Place a finger either side of the young plant and turn the pot over so the whole root ball comes out and is cupped in your hand. Use your other hand to form a complete cup and carefully place the seedling and its root ball into the new hole. Firm the ground around the seedling to make sure its roots are in good contact with the soil and then water. Plant your seedlings outside after the middle of May, once the last frost has passed.

Tomatoes

These seedlings need transplanting twice. The first time they go from the crowded seed tray into an individual small yoghurt pot when they are about 7cm tall and have two distinct leaves. The second time is when they are about 20cm tall and look very much like a proper grown-up plant. At this stage they can be transplanted into grow bags or the soil of your vegetable garden and supported with a cane with a lump of Plasticine on top for eye protection.

Health and safety

One of the main reasons for growing food organically in schools is that you don't want to expose children to the dangers of pesticides. There are some natural pesticides used in organic gardening which are safer, but still make sure you read the instructions carefully before using them.

Follow-up activities

A summer picnic is the best way to celebrate your successes in the vegetable garden. Try out some different recipes and invite the parents along.

If you have grown different varieties of certain vegetables you can do some taste testing and see which one is the favourite with the children.

Save seed from your vegetables and use it again next year. This not only saves money, but also teaches the children more about the life cycle they have been working with.

Teaching points

Encourage children to adopt a scientific approach to their vegetable gardening by keeping records of what they have sown, where and when and the quantity harvested.

4. Plant a mini-orchard

What is a mini-orchard?

Some schools are beginning to plant the kind of apple, pear and plum trees that will develop over time to become large fruit trees and provide a considerable amount of the fruit intake of a primary school. Many schools, however, don't have the space for a full-sized orchard. Growing small fruit trees and bushes is a good alternative and these can even be grown in large pots inside the school building.

Why plant a mini-orchard?

There is nothing quite like the taste of a strawberry or a raspberry straight off the plant. The first fresh, home-grown apple of the year in late July is a long-awaited treat if you are someone (like me) who avoids the tasteless apples imported from New Zealand or Chile during our late winter and spring. All these pleasures can be yours if you establish a mini-orchard.

Learning objectives

As well as the horticultural work of actually planting the trees and bushes, children will learn some quite technical skills such as pruning. You can use the fruit you produce for cookery lessons.

Resources

Fruit trees and bushes

You can buy cheap fruit trees and bushes from supermarkets or DIY shops, but it is much better to go to a reputable nursery. They have generations of skill and will produce better quality trees and bushes. Brogdale, in Kent, is the home of the National Fruit Collection. Their website *www.brogdale.org.uk* has advice on buying good quality stock.

Other resources:

- A garden spade
- A large bucket of well rotted manure
- Garden compost
- A wooden stake
- An old pair of tights.

Introducing the activity

This is another activity to introduce while you are having your fruit time. Cut open the apple cores the children have finished with and extract the pips. Plant these in pots and grow your own apple trees. They won't produce fruit for a few years and might only produce shrivelled fruit or none at all. This is because the apple trees we get our apples from are grown in a special way called grafting, where a branch is cut from an existing apple tree and joined to the roots of specially grown trees.

Conducting the activity

Planting a small tree such as an apple

- Dig a hole in the ground bigger than the root ball of your tree.
- Line the bottom of the hole with well rotted manure and garden compost.

- Place the root ball in the hole.
- Place a stake next to it
- Fill in the hole and firm down the soil so as to ensure good contact between root and soil.
- Tie the tree to the stake with a loose figure of eight made from old tights.
- Dwarf fruit trees can be grown in large terracotta pots in a sunny courtyard area.

Planting a bush such as a blackberry

- Essentially the same as planting an apple tree, but no need for a stake.

Planting raspberry canes

- These are planted in lines and will need the support of four posts forming a long thin rectangle.
- Tie plastic coated wire around the posts to form a rectangular supporting structure to stop your raspberry canes from blowing over in the wind.

Planting strawberry plants

- Transplant strawberry plants into a freshly dug and manured bed leaving about 30cm between plants.
- You can also grow strawberries in a special strawberry pot that you can get from garden centres. This will keep the plants off the ground and stop slugs getting them. It is to keep slugs away that the ground beneath strawberry plants is traditionally lined with straw.

Health and safety

I don't like gooseberries myself, except in jam! If you do want to grow them there are prickle-free varieties available. Other health and safety issues are the usual gardening ones. Be particularly careful when pruning trees and bushes with sharp pruning knives and saws.

Follow-up activities

Apples in particular come with a whole cartload of folklore, myth, legend, traditional feasts and dances. This is a great opportunity to delve into the stories associated with apples over hundreds and maybe thousands of years.

There is an annual Apple Day on the 21st October that is promoted by an environmental charity called Common Ground. You might like to put on your own event to celebrate your harvest. Let them know and send them some photos for their website: *www.commonground.org.uk*

Planting an apple tree

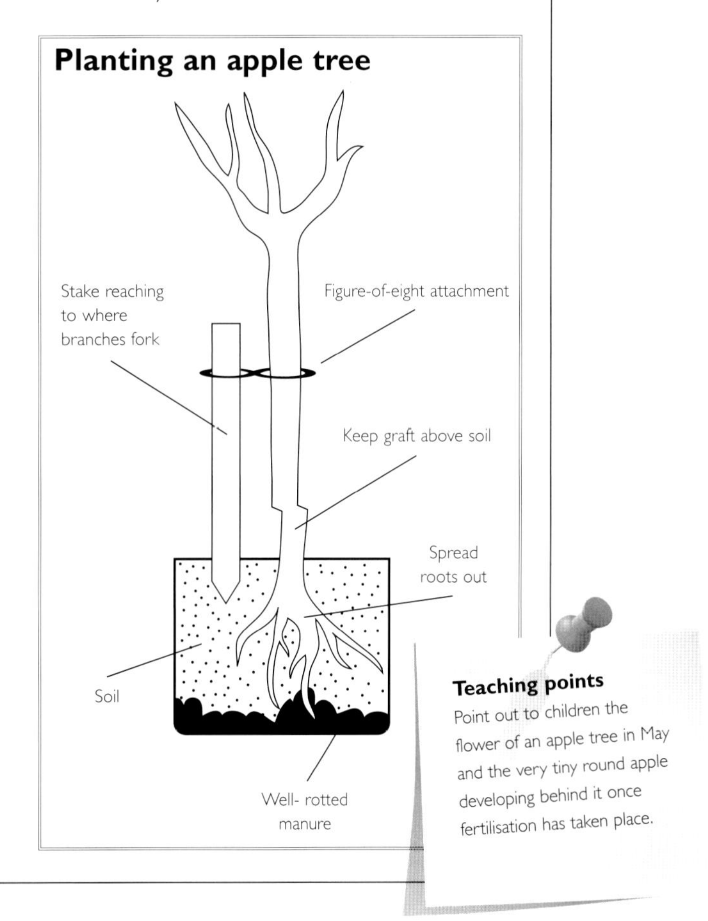

Teaching points

Point out to children the flower of an apple tree in May and the very tiny round apple developing behind it once fertilisation has taken place.

5. Make a wormery

What is a wormery?

A wormery is a purpose-built home for worms and allows us to study them close up.

Why make a wormery?

Making a wormery provides a great opportunity to talk about minibeasts, recycling food waste and the cycles of life. This is an exciting thing to do with children as it brings to their view a hidden world. They will be fascinated by the actions of the worms and the feel of them. They will also learn to take responsibility for living creatures.

Learning objectives

This is a construction project: as well as ticking boxes in the science curriculum, it will also link in with your design and technology curriculum. One way to make it even more D and T focused is to describe the conditions worms need to live in and then see what designs children come up with for themselves.

Resources

What you need:

- A 2-litre transparent plastic drinks bottle
- Plant pot filled with compost
- Masking tape
- Black paper, cardboard or material
- Horticultural sand
- Compost
- Kitchen waste
- Earthworms
- Magnifying glasses
- Marker pen.

Introducing the activity

Follow these tried and tested instructions to get this activity off to a great start with fully engaged children.

- Bring out a parcel wrapped in newspaper and ask the children what they think might be in it. Ask a child to smell the parcel and another to feel it.
- Open out the newspaper to reveal kitchen scraps .
- Identify each item of waste.
- Ask the children where we put our kitchen waste. Answers might include:
  - In the food waste bin that is collected by the council
  - In our own compost bin
  - Sometimes we are in a hurry and we put them in the wheelie bin with the waste that can't be recycled
- We don't eat these kitchen scraps. They are our waste. Who does eat them? Worms, millipedes, bugs, maggots, flies, etc.
- Tell the children they are going to meet some worms:
  - Give out worms in containers – one worm between two children
  - It is important to use Brandling or Tiger worms, which can be collected from a compost heap or bought from a fishing tackle shop. Ordinary earthworms are not the right ones for this activity.
  - Give out magnifying glasses

- ❍ Give children a couple of minutes to look at and talk about the worms
- ❍ What can they see? – segments, mouth, fine hairs
- Tell the children we are going to make our own special place where we can see what happens when we give our food waste to worms.

While engaged in this activity, talk with the children about each stage. Get them to describe what they are doing, what they can feel and smell and so on. You will be surprised by the contributions you get. One time I did this it led to a very wide-ranging discussion with a boy who went fishing with his dad every weekend and knew all about worms. More than me in fact!

Conducting the activity

- Cut the top and bottom off the plastic bottle, leaving a tall cylinder.
- Count out and put ten earthworms into the compost in the plant pot.
- Place the cylinder made from the bottle on top of the compost, tape the join and fill it with alternate layers of compost and horticultural sand – these layers need only be 1cm thick.
- Stick tape around the bottle and pot to join them securely.
- Mark the levels of the layers of compost and sand on the cylinder with the marker.
- Place some kitchen waste on top – preferably broken up into smallish pieces.
- Cover the cylinder with the black paper, cardboard or material to keep out the light.
- Keep everything damp – not wet – and leave for several days. Lift the cover and see what has happened to the layers of compost and sand.
- The wormery needs to be kept somewhere cool, and once set up can be left for one or two weeks. If you leave it any longer than this, there is a danger the worms will die. The worms can be released into your school compost bin.

Health and safety

Be careful when using scissors – teach children to use them safely. Wash hands after handling compost, food waste and worms.

Follow-up activities

Follow this activity up with minibeast related stories such as the *Hungry Caterpillar* by Eric Carle (1994, Hamish Hamilton), *A Worm's Eye View* by Jan Mark (1997, Mammoth) or *Diary of a Worm* by Doreen Cronin and Harry Bliss (2004, Harper Collins).

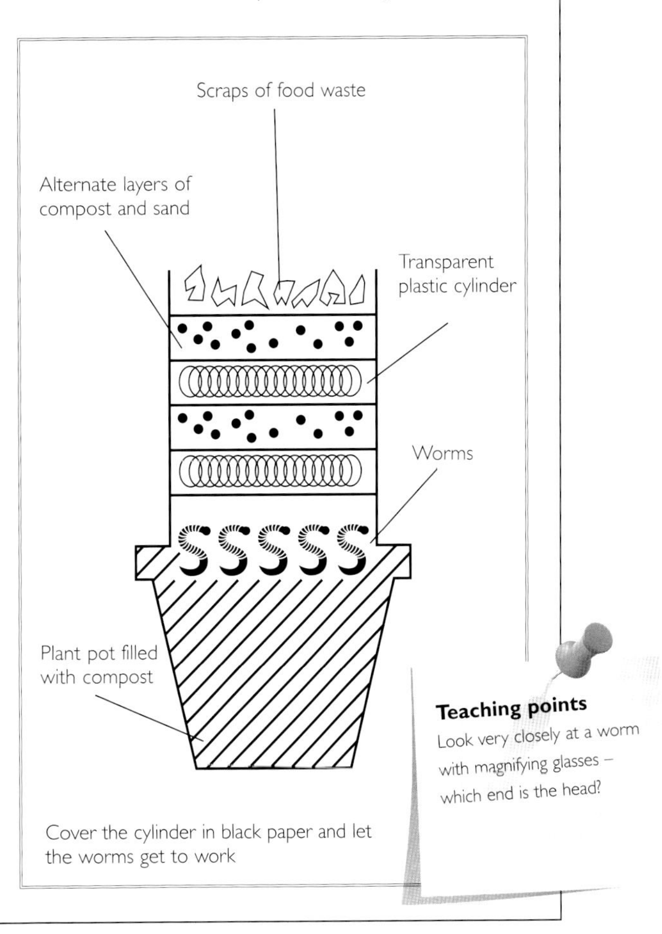

Cover the cylinder in black paper and let the worms get to work

Teaching points

Look very closely at a worm with magnifying glasses – which end is the head?

6. Make your own compost bin

What is compost?

Compost is partially decayed waste and can be made from uncooked kitchen scraps, weeds, grass mowings, bedding from vegetarian animals such as rabbits and so on.

Why make your own compost bin?

Many schools now have black plastic cone compost bins from their local council. These are fine, but a lot of learning takes place when you actually construct a bin yourselves.

Learning objectives

Maths and design and technology are the winners with this activity. There is lots of measuring, cutting and nailing going on.

Resources

- Uprights – four wooden posts measuring 5cm by 5cm by 90cm long
- Sides and back – 24 pieces of planking measuring 10cm by 1.5cm by 90cm long (waste pallet wood from your local industrial estate is ideal)
- Front – eight pieces of planking measuring 10cm by 1.5cm by approximately 80cm long (these will need to be cut more accurately in the finishing stages)
- Inside front – four pieces of wood measuring 1cm by 1cm by 90cm long
- Top front – one piece of wood measuring 5cm by 1cm by 90cm long
- Nails and a hammer
- Wood preserver – non-toxic to wildlife and children.

Introducing the activity

Introduce this activity by having all the materials and tools laid out in your outdoor classroom and asking the children to suggest what you might be planning to make.

Conducting the activity

- Lay two of the uprights on the ground parallel to each other and 90cm apart.
- Nail eight of your 90cm-long planks on to the uprights with 1cm between each plank to allow aeration of the compost.
- Repeat with the other two uprights and eight pieces of 90cm planking.
- Stand your two constructions up so they form the sides of the compost bin.
- While someone holds the sides upright, nail the final eight of your 90cm-long pieces of planking in place as the back of the bin.
- On the inside edges of the two front uprights nail the four 1cm by 1cm strips of wood so they form two grooves or channels.
- Into these grooves or channels slide your eight front pieces of planking. They may need cutting a little to fit exactly.
- Nail the top strip across the two front uprights – this gives the bin some rigidity.
- Paint the whole structure with non-toxic wood preservative and leave to dry for a few days before starting to fill your bin with compost.

All these measurements are a guide – if you are able to get hold of a load of free wood from a local industrial estate and it is not quite to these specifications then improvise.

Health and safety

Make sure children are fully supervised when engaged in woodworking activities. Preferably they will be working in groups of four with an adult and with only one child at a time using cutting or fixing tools.

Follow-up activities

In the middle of winter, poke a hole in the side of your compost heap and insert a thermometer.
Leave it in there for 15 minutes and then extract and read the temperature. Wow! How come it's so hot in there? Compare the temperature in the middle of the compost bin to the air temperature outside.

Teaching points
Once you have measured one of the pieces of side planking you can use it as a guide to cut the others rather than having to measure each one.

In the spring, dig out the compost from your compost bin. Sieve it and dig the sieved compost into your potato bed. Return the compost that was too big to go through the sieve to the bin for further rotting.

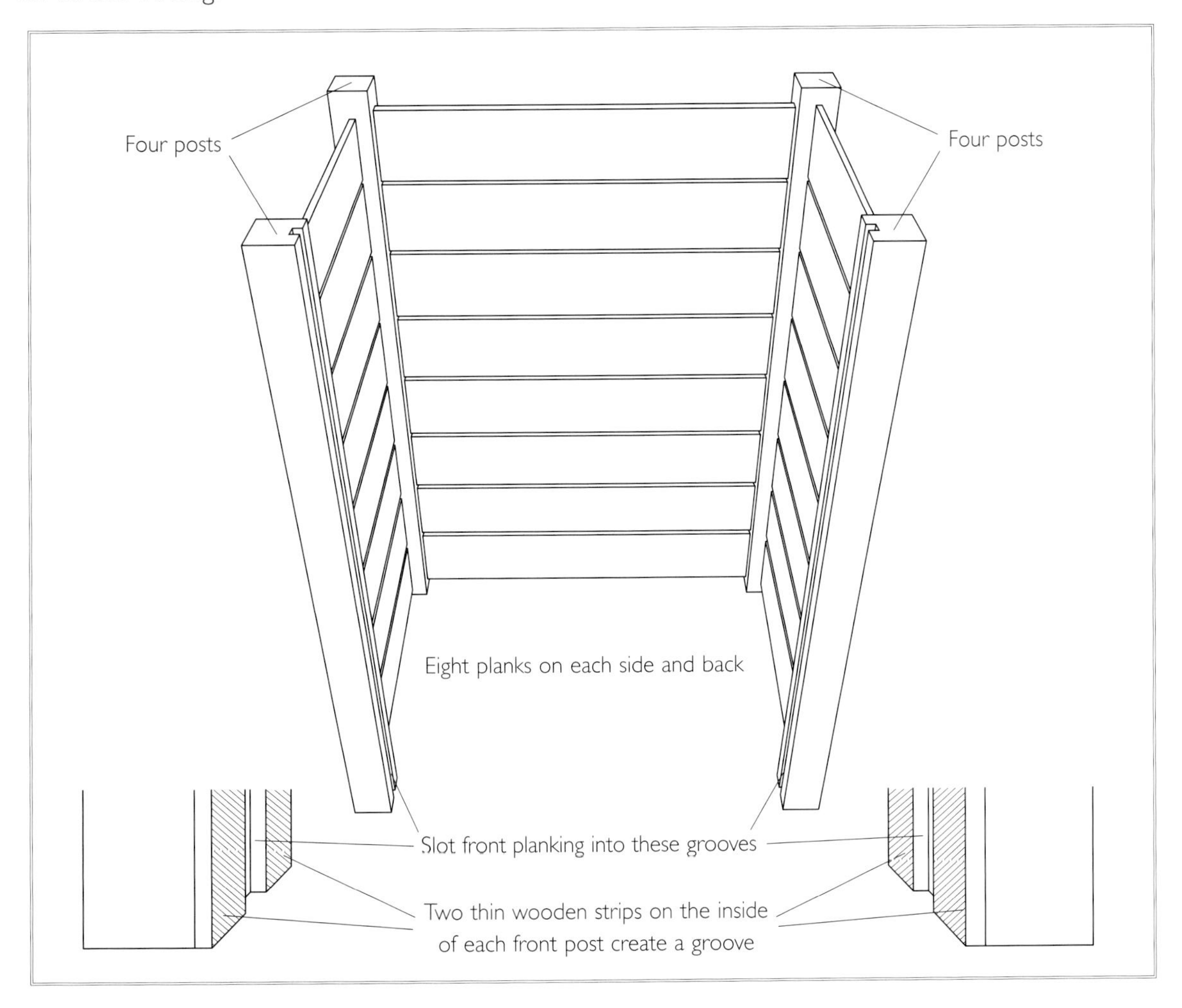

7. Keeping chickens

Why keep chickens?

You might think that there are just too many health and safety issues surrounding keeping livestock in schools, but if done properly, it can give your children a real sense of responsibility as well as providing fresh eggs for cooking, egg shells for painting, manure for your vegetable garden and inspiration for some great poetry and story writing.

Learning objectives

This is a big project and, if you tackle it as such and involve the children in the purchase of equipment and chickens, it can be a good way of developing planning and organisational skills.

Resources

- A chicken house (coop) and pen – available online or from a farm supplies outlet (you might need to fundraise for this)
- Feed container and water container – available from a pet shop
- Mixed grain and wheat straw – available from a pet shop
- Half a dozen chickens – see 'Buying chickens', below.

Introducing the activity

This activity could come out of a visit to a farm or you might invite a parent who keeps chickens to bring them in and tell the children what it entails. Chicken keeping is not just a rural enterprise; there are plenty of people who keep up to half a dozen birds in urban settings (my family included).

You do need to do your research before getting your birds. Check out suppliers. Get advice on keeping birds healthy with a visit to or from a vet. Get a good book that will take you through the process. I have found *The Complete Book of Raising Livestock and Poultry* by Katie Thear and Dr Alistair Fraser (1980, Martin Dunitz) to be indispensable.

Conducting the activity

Buying chickens

The first chickens we kept came from a battery farm and cost £1 each. They were a bit scraggy when we got them but soon perked up, grew back missing feathers and within days were scratching around in the dirt like they had always done it. Battery farmers will only keep birds for a year but ours kept laying for another three years. Look on *www.yell.com* (Yellow Pages) under 'poultry and game farmers and suppliers' and call a local farmer to see if you can provide a home for some unwanted birds.

Three of the birds we currently have are purebred bantams, and lovely they look too, but they did cost £20 each. Our fourth bird came from a fertile egg we popped under one of our other birds when she went broody. You might like to incubate and hatch out some eggs in the class. I have had mixed success with this over the years. You will also end up with approximately 50 percent cockerels and so you will have to find someone to take those off your hands.

Setting up

- Set up your chicken coop and pen on a patch of grass in a reasonably sheltered place.
- Line the coop and nesting boxes with straw.
- Fill the feed container with mixed grain – about 100g per bird per day.
- Fill the water container with fresh tap water every day.
- Introduce your birds and then leave them alone to settle in.

Daily and weekly maintenance

- Draw up a rota for feeding, watering and egg collecting each day – make sure you have someone to cover weekends and holidays.
- Another rota can cover the weekly clean out. You don't need to completely clean out the coop and pen every week, just remove the poo (wear rubber gloves) and put it on the compost heap. A complete clean out of all straw only needs to take place once a month.
- Every six weeks it is a good idea to dust birds with red mite powder. You can get an organic, herbal version of this from farmers' suppliers. Red mites are nasty little bugs that sometimes get in the scales of chickens' legs and cause great discomfort and ill health.
- Every three months, move the whole set-up onto fresh grass and don't return to the original patch for a year. This will help to keep pests down.

Health and safety

There are health and safety implications associated with keeping chickens but they are not insurmountable. Get your children and chickens into good hygienic routines and all will be well. For advice on the health and welfare of your birds, visit the Department for Environment, Food and Rural Affairs website at *www.defra.gov.uk*. Click on 'Farming' then 'Livestock' and then 'Poultry'.

Follow-up activities

Keeping chickens brings a whole new dimension to your work on spring and Easter. The chickens will not only provide eggs for you to use in your celebrations, they will also provide the inspiration for designing Easter cards.

If you do keep the full half-dozen chickens recommended here then the egg laying pattern over the year can provide an interesting subject for a data handling project. Count and record the number of eggs collected each day. Plot a line graph each day and see how egg laying increases and decreases over the year. Ask children why this pattern might occur (birds will lay more when the days are longer and they also go off lay when they are moulting, which they do quite naturally at certain times of year).

Teaching points

Children can handle the chickens occasionally if they are careful and this is a good chance to give the birds a once-over and check their health.

8. African gardens

What is an African garden?

In parts of Africa many young children are orphaned by war or disease and they find themselves having to grow food to feed themselves and their siblings. Through their own ingenuity and with the support of development charities they have found ways of vegetable growing which reduce the amount of space they need and use less water, while producing more food. These gardens come in several forms. A popular one is the bag garden and this is the focus of our activity.

Why make an African garden?

Making African bag gardens is a valuable way of introducing your children to the challenges faced by other children around the world. This is also a positive project, which shows how children are capable of solving their own problems. It can be a source of inspiration for your children. African garden making can be linked with fundraising for development projects, which will empower your children and help them to see that they can make a difference in their world.

Learning objectives

Both EYFS and KS1 children are finding out about living things through this activity. KS1 children can explore the similarities and differences between their lives and the lives of African children.

Resources

- A large hessian sack
- Several buckets full of small stones
- A wheelbarrow full of soil
- Trowels
- Various seeds and seedlings
- A two-litre drink bottle with the top and bottom cut off to make a tube
- Three sharpened sticks as long as the sack is deep, plus about 30cm
- A watering can.

Introducing the activity

Introduce your children to the continent of Africa through globes and maps, photographs and artefacts. Be careful to show that there are many faces to African life – it is not all drought and poverty. Show images of cities and transport systems as well.

Make use of *www.cowforce.com* from the Send A Cow organisation to gently introduce your children to the fact that life is hard for many children in African countries.

Talk to your children about the creative ways in which African orphans grow their own food and tell them that you are going to have a go yourselves.

Conducting the activity

Make your bag garden

- Place a layer of stones about 7.5cm thick in the bottom of the sack.
- Place the plastic tube upright on the middle of this layer and fill with stones.
- Fill the sack with soil all around the tube and up to the level of its neck.

- Pull the tube upwards to create another space to fill with stones.
- Once this is filled, place more soil around the tube.
- Continue upwards until the sack is filled with soil and has a column of stones running up the middle.
- Hammer your three sharp sticks down into the soil-filled sack and right through the bottom to anchor it to the ground.

Planting your bag garden

- Cut a dozen or so V-shaped slits at intervals around your bag.
- Sow seeds of radish, rocket, spinach, salad and so on into the soil exposed by the slits.
- Transplant seedling tomatoes and courgettes from pots into the top of the sack.
- Water your bag garden by pouring water down the stone column.

Teaching points
It is very important to show development work as a partnership rather than as a display of pity. African orphans are resilient individuals who just need a leg-up.

Health and safety

The sticks do need to have a sharp point on them in order to go through the soil and pierce the hessian bag, so it is best if you do this while the children watch.

Follow-up activities

The charity Send A Cow is at the forefront of this kind of positive development work. Check out their website at *www.sendacow.org.uk/schools* to find step-by-step instructions to create other types of African gardens including the particularly impressive keyhole garden.

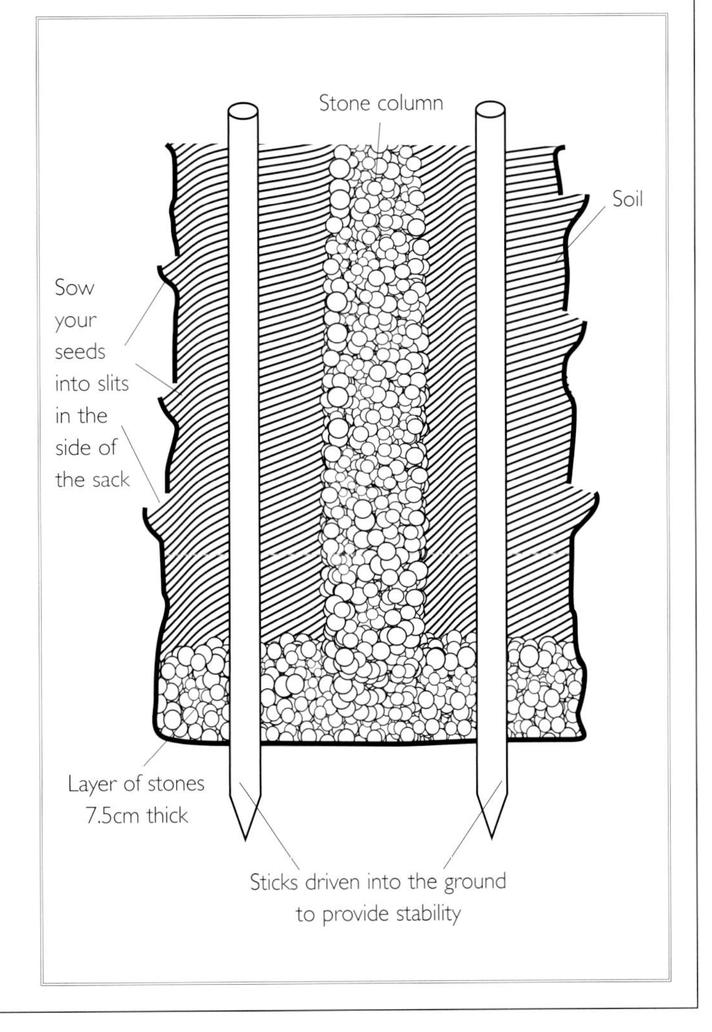

Theme: Our wonderful world

Our wonderful world: Introduction

History, geography and RE, what used to be known as the humanities, can all be taught in practical and exciting ways through the use of adventurous activities. These days I would add environmental education and citizenship to the list of humanities.

This theme is all about giving children a greater understanding of the world in which we live. I use the term 'our wonderful world' because I want to convey to the children what an amazing place we live in. My hope is that in giving them this appreciation of their world it will help them to grow up with a desire to take responsibility for the world and to play their part in making it a better place.

I often start with a globe. I take it off its stand and I hold it up and turn it around and tell the children what an amazing place I think it is. I then have a bit of fun with them and tell them to imagine it is a giant orange and that if I peel that orange and lay it out flat I have a map of the world. I then look at a large flat 2D map with the children. I say to them, 'Here is our little bit of the world' and I point to the British Isles. I'm trying to give them an understanding of the hugeness of the world. We then go on to name continents. We will always look at maps when we are studying history, geography or RE.

Learning objectives

Specific learning objectives are given for each activity. Here is an overview list of learning objectives for our wonderful world activities in general:

Early Years Foundation Stage

Personal, social and emotional development

- Be confident to try new activities, initiate ideas and speak in a familiar group.
- Respond to significant experiences, showing a range of feelings when appropriate.
- Work as part of a group or class, taking turns and sharing fairly.

Communication, language and literacy

- Interact with others, negotiating plans and activities and taking turns in conversations.
- Enjoy listening to and using spoken and written language, and readily turn to it in their play and learning.
- Sustain attentive listening, responding to what they have heard with relevant comments, questions and actions.
- Listen with enjoyment, and respond to stories, songs and other music, rhymes and poems and make up their own stories, songs, rhymes and poems.
- Extend their vocabulary, exploring the meanings and sounds of new words.
- Speak clearly and audibly with confidence and control and show awareness of the listener.
- Use talk to organise, sequence and clarify thinking, ideas, feelings and events. Attempt writing for different purposes.

Problem solving, reasoning and numeracy

- Use developing mathematical ideas and methods to solve practical problems.
- Use everyday words to describe position.

Knowledge and understanding of the world

- Find out about past and present events in their own lives, and those of their families and other people they know.
- Observe, find out about and identify features in the place they live and the natural world.
- Find out about their environment, and talk about those features they like and dislike.
- Begin to know about their own cultures and beliefs and those of other people.

Physical development

- Use a range of small and large equipment.
- Handle tools safely and with increasing control.

Creative development

- Respond in a variety of ways to what they see, hear, smell, touch and feel.
- Express and communicate their ideas, thoughts and feelings by using a widening range of materials.

Key Stage 1

Religious Education

Knowledge, skills and understanding

Learning about religion

1. Pupils should be taught to:

a. explore a range of religious stories and sacred writings and talk about their meanings
b. name and explore a range of celebrations, worship and rituals in religion, noting similarities where appropriate
c. identify the importance, for some people, of belonging to a religion and recognise the difference this makes to their lives
d. explore how religious beliefs and ideas can be expressed through the arts and communicate their responses
e. identify and suggest meanings for religious symbols and begin to use a range of religious words.

Learning from religion

2. Pupils should be taught to:

a. reflect on and consider religious and spiritual feelings, experiences and concepts such as worship, wonder, praise, thanks, concern, joy and sadness
b. ask and respond imaginatively to puzzling questions, communicating their ideas
c. identify what matters to them and others, including those with religious commitments, and communicate their responses
d. reflect on how spiritual and moral values relate to their own behaviour
e. recognise that religious teachings and ideas make a difference to individuals, families and the local community.

Geography

Knowledge, skills and understanding

Geographical enquiry and skills

1. In undertaking geographical enquiry, pupils should be taught to:

a. ask geographical questions

b. observe and record
c. express their own views about people, places and environments
d. communicate in different ways.

2. In developing geographical skills, pupils should be taught to:
a. use geographical vocabulary
b. use fieldwork skills
c. use globes, maps and plans at a range of scales
d. use secondary sources of information
e. make maps and plans.

Knowledge and understanding of places
3. Pupils should be taught to:
a. identify and describe what places are like
b. identify and describe where places are, recognise how places have become the way they are and how they are changing
c. recognise how places compare with other places
d. recognise how places are linked to other places in the world.

Knowledge and understanding of patterns and processes
4. Pupils should be taught to:
a. make observations about where things are located
b. recognise changes in physical and human features.

Knowledge and understanding of environmental change and sustainable development
5. Pupils should be taught to:
a. recognise changes in the environment
b. recognise how the environment may be improved and sustained.

Breadth of study
6. During the key stage, pupils should be taught the Knowledge, skills and understanding through the study of two localities:
a. the locality of the school
b. a locality either in the United Kingdom or overseas that has physical and/or human features that contrast with those in the locality of the school.

7. In their study of localities, pupils should:
a. study at a local scale
b. carry out fieldwork investigations outside the classroom.

History
Knowledge, skills and understanding
Chronological understanding
1. Pupils should be taught to:

a. place events and objects in chronological order
b. use common words and phrases relating to the passing of time.

Knowledge and understanding of events, people and changes in the past

2. Pupils should be taught to:
a. recognise why people did things, why events happened and what happened as a result
b. identify differences between ways of life at different times.

Historical interpretation

3. Pupils should be taught to identify different ways in which the past is represented.

Historical enquiry

4. Pupils should be taught:
a. how to find out about the past from a range of sources of information
b. to ask and answer questions about the past.

Organisation and communication

5. Pupils should be taught to select from their knowledge of history and communicate it in a variety of ways.

Literacy links

Questions and answers

The best way to get children enthusiastic about non-fiction research is for the questions to come from them. Spend time during the introductory phase of any activity stimulating children's interest and noting any questions they come up with. Then set about answering those questions through the various techniques detailed in the activities. It is important that you make use of the answers children find out – otherwise, what's the point? Share information with other classes or with your wider community.

Note making

Getting into the habit of making notes whilst out and about is good for the future development of writing skills. Take clipboards and pencils with you wherever you go and take time to stop and scribble down information and reflections.

Biography

History stays in the mind if it is associated with historical characters. Start a class file of interesting historical characters from world, national and local history. Draw up a standard template that children can fill in with a drawing of the character, dates, personal information and why we remember them.

Health and safety

Learning about our wonderful world involves going out into the world. Make sure you always follow your school and local authority procedures when taking children off site.

1. Festivals around the world

Why study festivals around the world?

Britain is a truly multicultural society and this offers many positive learning opportunities. Our wonderful world is diverse in culture and every month there are festivals to celebrate. Learning about different cultures through storytelling, cookery, dance, music, singing and so on helps children to grow up into adults who appreciate diversity. For the purposes of illustration we are going to look at the Hindu festival of Diwali – the festival of lights that takes place in late October or early November, depending on the phases of the moon.

Learning objectives

KS1 children are extending their knowledge and understanding of RE through exploring a range of religious stories and celebrations. EYFS children are learning about the cultures and beliefs of other people.

Resources

Resource requirements for different activities are given in the text.

Introducing the activity

Find out when Diwali will be celebrated and plan a week of activities for that time. Introduce the theme to your children by watching Diwali celebrations on the internet – there are many sites with video clips. Reading or telling the story of Rama and Sita is another good introduction. If your community is home to Hindu families then involve parents and grandparents in your activities. If your school is exclusively white, UK heritage then talk about a celebration the children are familiar with such as Christmas or Easter and compare/contrast the celebration of Diwali with this festival.

Conducting the activity

Storytelling – The story of Rama and Sita lies at the core of the Diwali celebrations. It is one of the richest and most beautiful stories in the world. My favourite version is available in the Usborne title *Stories from India*, which is written by Anna Milbourne and delightfully illustrated by Linda Edwards (2004, Usborne).

Cookery – Mithai are sweets that are synonymous with Diwali. These are made from semolina, wheat flour, chickpea flour or thickened milk. Grated coconut or carrots are sometimes added and the mixture is perfumed with sweet spices such as cardamom and nutmeg. Nuts and raisins are added and the mixture shaped into colourful squares and rounds. Recipes and information about food for celebrating Diwali can be found at *www.bbc.co.uk/food/news_and_events/events_diwali.shtml*

Music – You will be able to get CDs of Indian music from your local library and children can have a go at making their own music using percussion instruments.

Dancing – This is an important part of the Diwali celebrations. In Indian dancing the movements of the body, head, neck, stomach and so on, have particular meanings. Dance is used to put actions to stories.

Art – Make Diwali lamps using modelling clay and fill with olive oil. Add a string wick and light. Make Rangoli patterns out of coloured sand and rice. These are a form of traditional Hindu art and many examples can be found on the internet.

Fireworks – Organise a fundraising fireworks event at your school. Get the PTA involved and tick all the health and safety boxes to ensure a happy event.

Health and safety

If you are using candles and fireworks in your Diwali celebrations then make sure there is close adult supervision at all times and follow the firework code.

Follow-up activities

Colourfully illustrated poster-sized calendars of festivals throughout the year are available commercially. Look at one of these with your children. Build on the success of your Diwali celebrations and choose the next festival you want to celebrate. Plan the celebration with the children.

Teaching points

India has the second largest population in the world after China. Hinduism is the main religion in India with 930 million followers.

2. Travel the world

What is 'Travel the world'?

Most of us aren't going to get the chance to go to all the far-flung places we would love to visit but we can still visit those places through the wonderful childhood tool of imagination. This activity involves exploring a visit to another culture through drama.

Why travel the world?

Travel broadens the horizons. Giving children an insight into their wonderful world through imaginary travel ticks lots of boxes on the curriculum and also helps them to understand what a special place our world is.

Learning objectives

Both EYFS and KS1 children are learning about the cultures of other countries. KS1 children can describe what places are like and compare them with their own place, which is in the geography curriculum.

Resources

- Drawing and writing materials
- A suitcase containing objects needed for a journey
- Images and artefacts from the country you are visiting.

Introducing the activity

Choose a place you want to visit with the class. This may be a place that is on one of your schemes of work or it may be a place that you have visited yourself. Do your homework and gather together images and artefacts from this place. Introduce the location to the children by looking at a map of the world and looking at the photos/artefacts you have gathered.

Discuss with the children how you would go about visiting this place. Some of them will have experience of travel overseas and you will be able to make a list of the things a traveller needs to do in order to go on a journey: Plan the journey, make bookings, pack luggage, get injections, go through security and passport control and so on.

Another way to introduce this activity is to use a mystery traveller. Bring in a small suitcase containing several objects such as a pair of shorts, sunglasses, sun cream, shirt, sandals, a novel, a camera, a postcard and a pair of toy binoculars. Talk about each item and ask children what they can deduce about the mystery traveller and where he or she might be going. Do this with different suitcase contents for different journeys.

Conducting the activity

Making passports and tickets

Look at examples of real paperwork associated with travelling and make your own. For passport photos children can work in pairs and draw a picture of their partner. Borrow a rubber date stamp from the school office to stamp passports. Make a simple A5 template of a ticket for children to fill in information such as name, address, date of birth, etc. They can then decorate the ticket. Think of other paperwork you may need to prepare for your travels, such as maps.

Packing

Ask children to bring in a small bag packed with clothes and toiletries they will need for their journey. This just adds to the authenticity of the activity. You might even like to write a letter to the parents as if you were going on a school trip.

Build a plane

In the school hall lay out chairs in rows as if on a plane. Build screens around the plane with display boards, large sheets of material or card to give the sense of being inside a plane. Have your plane facing an electronic whiteboard and then you can run a slideshow of images from the country you are visiting during the flight.

Choose children to be the pilot, co-pilot and air stewards. Act out security and passport control. If you take the role of tour guide then you can accompany the children through each stage and welcome them aboard the plane.

Enjoy the flight!

Sightseeing

When you arrive at your destination, disembark and go on a sightseeing tour of the country you are visiting. Children can paint large pictures of places from the country and these can be displayed around the hall. Extend your visit with a meal of foods from the country. Watch some local dancing. Groups of children can create all of these in class before the flight. Make a day of it.

Health and safety

Sensible health and safety precautions when making and doing are all you need to take into account when making your plane.

Follow-up activities

You might like to turn your Home Corner into a travel agent for the duration of this project so that children have somewhere to role-play choosing destinations and booking flights. I have always found local travel agents are happy to give me lots of brochures, letter heads, pens, etc, to stock the office.

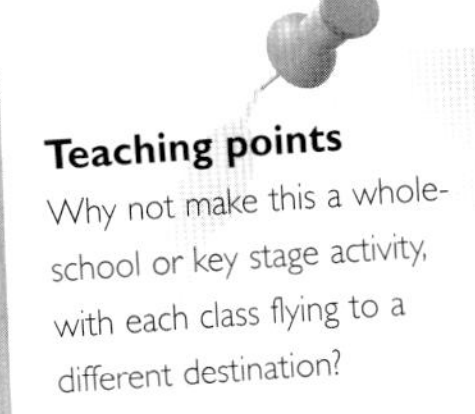

3. Making landscapes

Why make landscapes?

Physical geography can be quite an abstract idea; it is difficult for children who live in Suffolk, for example, to grasp the concept of mountains and looking at pictures doesn't always meet the need. Making your own 3D models of different landscapes can, however, make physical geography more real.

Learning objectives

EYFS children are finding out about the environment and extending their making skills. KS1 children are using geographical vocabulary and describing features.

Resources

- Two or three bags of builders' sand
- Rubber gloves
- Water
- Spade for mixing sand and water
- Four lengths of timber measuring 5cm by 10cm by 1 metre long
- Papier mâché mixture
- Paint
- Modelling materials such as Plasticine and cardboard.

Introducing the activity

Talk about the local environment in which the children live. Use terms such as hill, stream, valley, field, woodland and town or village. Talk with children about any holidays they have been on that involved seeing mountains or the sea – any features that do not occur in your locality. Discuss with them how you could go about making a model of any of these landscapes. Really promote geographical vocabulary.

Conducting the activity

Constructing a landscape

- Form a square with your four pieces of timber and nail together.
- Lay this frame on a large piece of polythene on a table or outside if the weather looks good for a few days.
- Fill the square with damp builders' sand. Play sand is too soft for this activity.
- Give children rubber gloves to wear and allow them to shape the sand into mountains, hills, river valleys and a coastline. Make the features bold.
- Carefully cover the damp sand in four or five layers of papier mâché and leave to dry for a couple of days.
- Lift the papier mâché landscape off the sand.
- Paint the papier mâché landscape in earthy colours.
- Add features such as trees, boulders, and houses using modelling materials.

Learning from a model landscape

- Use your model landscape for small world play – mountain rescue operations can be a fun way to learn about the geography of mountains.
- Practise sounding out and writing unfamiliar words to produce labels to identify the geographical features on your model landscape.

Health and safety

This is a construction activity but there are no sharp tools involved. Builders' sand is better for this activity than play sand but it can stain, so wear gloves and aprons.

Follow-up activities

Make a range of landscape features. See if you can build a waterfall or a coastal scene with cliffs and rock pools in an aquarium. These features can all be used for small world play.

You will find that once children have made one feature they will want to make more and will do so during their play in the sand or water tray.

If you have made a landscape that includes a river you can paint the river channel with PVA glue to make it waterproof. When the glue is dry you can pour water in at the source of the river in the mountains and watch it flow down the river channel to the river mouth at the sea.

Teaching points

Introduce your children to the concept of scale by asking them if the model trees and buildings they have made are too big, too small or just right for the model landscape.

4. Our local geography

Why study our local geography?

We don't have to put children on a coach and travel 50 or more miles to study geography. If you want to study a specific feature, such as the seaside, then maybe you do, but geography is all around us. Go out into the local environment with your children regularly and describe your community geographically. The key point here is about identifying geographical features – physical features such as streams and hills and also man-made, human geography features such as roads, footbridges and bus stops.

Taking children out into the local area will:

- Familiarise them with the geography around them
- Teach and reinforce geographical vocabulary
- Develop geographical skills such as surveying and recording geographical data – traffic levels or service provision, tourism and visitor satisfaction, prevalence of litter, recycling facilities and so on
- Allow children to identify and investigate local geographical issues
- Help develop spatial awareness and sense of direction.

Learning objectives

EYFS children are in the KUW curriculum. They will be observing, finding out about and identifying features in the place where they live and the natural world. They will also be finding out about their environment and talking about those features they like and dislike. KS1 children can develop their geographical fieldwork skills through studying local geography.

Resources

- Maps of your local area
- Clipboards, paper and pencils
- Digital camera.

Introducing the activity

Talk with your children about the community they live in. What do they like about it and dislike about it? Where do they choose to play? What sort of facilities are there? Do they have to travel far to do the things they want to do? If you are new to the area yourself this is a good way for you to get to know the community. If you have some new housing being built in your community you can always introduce this activity to the children by suggesting that you make a 'welcome pack' for when people move in.

Conducting the activity

When you are out and about in your local area consider the following aspects of physical and human geography.

Local landscape features

Identify, name and describe hills and valleys, coastlines, rivers and streams. Ask children to describe the area in words that would help conjure up a picture for a visitor who hasn't arrived in the area yet.

Transport
Look at how road junctions work. Identify different types of road and paths, bridges, car parks. Discuss the dangers of roads and safety measures. Carry out a traffic survey to find out just how busy your roads are.

Telecommunications
Look at all those poles and wires and talk about where they are going. Find your local telephone box and teach children how to use it.

Services
Pipes, drains, manhole covers and so on are all around us. Shops, offices, warehouses, manufacturing, storage and distribution facilities can all be found and discussed. If you are making a welcome pack then think about which of these services it would be useful for people to know about.

Food production
If you live in the country, there is farmland to visit and learn about where our food comes from. In the town there are allotments and gardens.

Land use
Identify with your children the different ways in which land is used in your local area: housing, industry, leisure, farming, quarries and mines, wildlife reserves and so on.

Take digital photographs, sketch pictures, interview local residents you meet about the features of their community. Gather lots of information. Take it all back to school and create a display to show off your local geography. Help other people to get to know and enjoy your local geography.

Health and safety
Follow your school policy when taking children off-site. For the youngest children, I always consider a ratio of one adult to two children is best – then each adult can have one child in each hand.

Follow-up activities
The next activity, 'Improving your local environment', follows on nicely from this one. Once you have a good understanding of your local area you can set about acting to improve it.

Celebrate your local geography by producing a *Town Trail* booklet.

Create your own local celebration. Some communities have long established festivities such as cheese rolling or singing to apple trees. Why shouldn't you do something for your local area?

Teaching points
The world is full of big and exciting geographical features. Help children to appreciate the features closer to home.

5. Improving our local environment

Why improve your local environment?

In the QCA schemes of work this theme is the preserve of KS2 children, but there are many ways in which EYFS and KS1 children can get involved in making their little bit of the world a better place. Children will feel good if they have done something positive to improve their environment. They are more likely to grow up respecting what they have created.

Learning objectives

EYFS children are showing that they are confident to try new activities, initiate ideas and speak in a familiar group (PSED). KS1 children are working in the geography curriculum and are recognising how the environment may be improved and sustained.

Resources

Resources for this activity will very much depend on what your children come up with for their project.

Introducing the activity

Build on the work you have done to get to know your local geography. Discuss with the children if there are any areas that could really do with a make-over. The welcome sign to the village might look a little tired and could do with a flower border around it to really welcome visitors to your community. The bench by the bus stop might need a coat of paint. A derelict corner could do with clearing out and would benefit from having trees planted in it. Once the children get going they will come up with loads of ideas.

Conducting the activity

There are several stages to any project aimed at improving your local area.

Discover what it is you want to improve. This has come out of your exploration of local geography.

Plan what you are going to do. At first, let your minds run wild with possibilities and then narrow the list down to what you can realistically achieve. Draw up a plan of action with stepping stones leading up to the final success. This helps children to see progress during a long-term or larger project. It is a good idea to involve any relevant local authorities. Don't just go out and paint the park bench! Check with the park authority first that it is OK.

Act! Get out there and do it. Involve parents in any heavy work such as disposing of large pieces of rubbish. Make a party of it with a break for refreshments and take lots of photos to show what a difference your project has made.

Evaluate and improve further

Once you have finished, don't rest on your laurels. Take the opportunity to take your improvements further or start on a new project using the skills you have gained on the first one.

Health and safety

Your health and safety issues for this activity will depend on what it is you aim to do. Think carefully about any issues and complete a risk assessment to show that you have thought of everything you can.

Follow-up activities

Make certain you involve the local paper in your project. Get a reporter to come along and interview the children and a photographer to snap them. Local papers love this sort of thing and from the children's point of view they really feel that their project is important if it makes it into the paper. Children could even produce their own front page for a school newspaper to celebrate their achievements.

Teaching points

Some local authorities have grant schemes available for local projects. Children can practise their letter writing skills and apply for them.

6. Living history – frozen pictures

What are frozen pictures?

This is a technique that is used in the theatre. It is known as freeze framing and is used to help actors learn more about their characters and interactions between characters. I have adapted it for use in schools and call it 'frozen pictures'. This activity involves creating a living photograph from a historical period using the children as the characters in the picture.

Why freeze frame?

This is a fun way to help children get a better understanding of any historical period you are studying.

Learning objectives

KS1 children are finding out about the past from a range of sources of information. EYFS children can use this activity to find out about past events in their family life.

Resources

- Historical pictures such as photographs, paintings or tapestry to act as a starting point
- There are no other resource needs for this activity although children will try to use whatever is at hand to improvise props!

Introducing the activity

Look at different visual images from the historical period you are studying. If that is Ancient Egypt, you might use tomb paintings. For the Great Fire of London, you might use an oil painting. For more recent history, including family history, use photographs. Discuss what is happening in the pictures and ask the children what they can learn about how people used to live by looking at pictures from the past.

Conducting the activity

In the school hall, split the children up into groups of five or six and ask them to create a scene from the historical period you are studying. Give each group a different focus. One group might create a scene showing how the rich lived in that time; another group can look at the lives of the poor. School, home and work can all be covered. Battle scenes are popular if they are appropriate to the period you are studying.

Once the children have created a scene that involves them all, ask them to hold it absolutely still for a few moments. Tell them to concentrate on what their faces are showing and what their body position is telling us. This is their frozen picture.

Now ask them to create a picture that comes before this one and one that comes after it. When the children are ready, ask them all to show you picture one, then picture two and then picture three. These are the beginning, middle and end of a story.

When I am doing this with children, I always tell them that in a story 'something's got to happen!' I think you will be impressed with the stories the children come up with. I have done this many times with children from Reception to Year 6 and have always been impressed with children's imaginative ideas.

Health and safety

There are no health and safety implications for this activity.

Follow-up activities

By all means ask children to write their story. I find a useful way to get them started on this is to ask them to draw the three pictures they created first and write a sentence under each.

Take pictures of everyday life in your time to create your own historical evidence. Think about how you can pass these on to future generations.

Teaching points

Share a range of historical images from different periods with your children to show how the use of pictures to capture historical moments has changed over time. Talk about how it might change in the future.

7. Historical drama days

What are historical drama days?
This is a really big, whole-school event where the children and staff dress up in costumes from a certain period and re-enact life in that time.

Why stage a historical drama day?
Drama days used to be very popular before the National Curriculum came along and it is time for them to make a comeback. The problem has been that we have become so used to the history curriculum being divided up into historical periods and being shared out to specific year groups. We have, to a certain extent, forgotten that it is possible to do some learning as a whole school and that this approach can work really well.

Learning objectives
We are in the history curriculum and EYFS children will simply be getting an understanding that there is a place called the 'past'. KS1 children will be developing a range of historical investigative skills.

Resources

- Appropriate clothing
- Artefacts from the historical period
- Different resources are required for different carousel activities.

Preparing for the activity
This activity requires a degree of whole-school planning and preparation. Decide which classes will contribute to which part of the day and allocate jobs to staff. You can approach this day in several ways. One way is to have a carousel of activities for classes to move around throughout the day. Another way is to take an epic historical story and re-enact that using all the children as characters in the story. We have recreated some amazing battle scenes in this way. Whichever approach you adopt, it will require as much or more planning than a good sports day and someone needs to have overall charge of the event.

Introducing the activity
If you are taking the carousel approach it is a good idea to start with an assembly to explain the ground rules of the day – expectations as to behaviour, how people will move around and so on. You could get the day started by reading or telling a story from the historical period. I have also done it before by transforming the hall into a giant time machine to take us all back in time.

If you are using an epic historical story as your theme, such as Jason and the Argonauts if you are looking at the Ancient Greeks, then go straight into the story. With a whole school of characters, drama days are best conducted outside and this restricts them to the summer term.

Conducting the activity

Let's take as an example a drama day based on Ancient Greece. Here are some possible carousel activities you could set up:

- Food – make a selection of simple Greek-style dishes to contribute to a great feast as part of your re-enactment
- Costume accessories – Ancient Greek costumes are quite easy for parents to provide for the drama day. One of your carousel activities could include making jewellery to adorn the simple costumes
- Art – pottery making and decorating
- Storytelling – one teacher can spend their time telling classes of children different stories from Greek mythology
- Philosophy – older children stage a debate based on the politics surrounding the abduction of Helen and the Battle of Troy.

One approach to a carousel of activities is to have the children in mixed age groups rather than single age classes; family groupings work well for this.

If you are going down the route of an epic story then the story of Jason is a good one. You need to have one storyteller directing the whole event. Key characters act out the story under the direction of the storyteller and whole classes undertake the role of citizens, sailors, Harpies, etc.

You can combine these two approaches by having some of the storytelling approach with occasional breaks for carousel activities.

Health and safety

With large numbers of children on the move you do need to be organised so as to ensure they don't all end up in a heap! Have a system of signals to ensure that everyone knows when it is time to move and how that is to be achieved.

Follow-up activities

Children will be talking about your historical drama day for weeks and months afterwards. Take advantage of this enthusiasm to get lots of research and story writing done. In fact, if you have your drama day as part of a themed week you will find the children will produce masses of good quality work simply on the back of all that excitement.

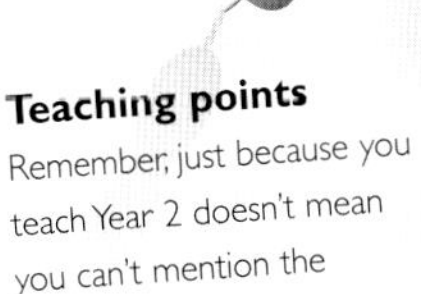

Teaching points

Remember, just because you teach Year 2 doesn't mean you can't mention the Ancient Egyptians!

8. Local history timeline

What is a local history timeline?

This activity involves travelling back in time within your own school and community to find out what life was like over the last 100 years. It is all about chronology and a step-by-step journey through the story of the area in which the children live.

Why make a local history timeline?

Young children need a clear focus for their history studies. Looking at their own families, holidays and homes, learning about major characters and events such as Samuel Pepys and the Great Fire of London gives them this focus. Using your local area as a focus for history adds another, exciting dimension to all of this.

Learning objectives

EYFS children are finding out about past and present events in their own lives, and those of their families and other people they know. KS1 children are placing events and objects in chronological order and learning how to find out about the past from a range of sources of information.

Resources

- Old photos
- Record books such as a school log
- The anecdotes of local people.

Introducing the activity

Start with some old photos from your own life. Talk about your childhood and your family. Invite children to bring in pictures of themselves when they were younger and pictures of their relatives. Peg these photos onto a simple timeline made of string with the most recent on the right-hand side and the oldest on the left. Write dates on pieces of card and peg these alongside the photos to show children how these images are helping you to go back in time. Finish by telling the children that you are going to create a timeline for the area in which they live.

Conducting the activity

You will need to collect a variety of evidence from your local area.

Collecting old photographs

Somewhere in your school there is almost certainly a cupboard containing old school photos. Looking through these is great fun – even if only to see just how much clothing and hairstyles have changed over the years! Put out an appeal through your school newsletter and local papers for copies of any old photos of your school, local shops and other buildings and street scenes.

Search for images on the internet by entering the name of your town or village and the words 'old photos'. Compare an old photo to a recent one. Look for similarities and differences.

Interviewing local residents

Invite grandparents who have lived in the area for many years into school. Get the children to draw up a list of appropriate questions and see just how much you can find out about the history of your local area from this very valuable source of primary evidence.

School records

Many local authorities now store historical school records in the county archive. A quick call to your museum's service should locate these and you can arrange to have copies. These records will tell you names of former pupils. If yours is an old school the school log may tell you how many children were away from school potato picking in the autumn of 1897!

Church records

- Ask a representative of your local church to visit the class to show children the births, deaths and marriages records.
- Visit the local churchyard or war memorial and see how many of the surnames are recognised by the children.

Buildings

Get out in the local area and draw buildings. Ask around and find out when they were built so you can add this detail to each picture.

Your local history timeline

Once you have gathered all this evidence together, display photos, drawings, anecdotes and dates on a timeline stretching across your classroom.

Health and safety

The health and safety implications of this activity are to do with taking children out of school, so make sure you follow your school and local authority policies.

Follow-up activities

One aspect of the KS1 geography curriculum is to study a contrasting locality in the UK. Why not do the same with history? By using email you can quickly and simply hook up with a school in a different part of the country and exchange text and images about the local history of your two areas.

Local newspapers often have a section devoted to images from past issues. Talk to the editor about running a piece on your school with class photos from down the ages and interviews with grandparents who attended the school in the past.

Teaching points

Counting backwards in tens from 100 is particularly helpful in rooting the concept of a timeline in young children's minds.

Theme: Small world play

Small world play: Introduction

Small world play is well known in the Early Years. It involves setting out familiar scenes such as a farmyard, a printed road carpet or a model house. Children then explore the setting with model characters, animals, toy cars and lorries, etc. The purpose of this play is to give children the opportunity to explore and develop an understanding of the worlds that they will be interacting with as they grow up.

There is no reason why small world play should not be used in KS1 and beyond. It is also quite possible to make this play more adventurous by directing the children's play to a certain extent.

In my experience, girls will tend to go for houses when engaging in this kind of play and boys will go for road carpets. This is not a problem, but we can extend the possibilities dramatically by creating small world play opportunities that are non-gender specific. We can also encourage boys to find play opportunities in 'girls'' themes and vice versa.

Several of these activities bring together adventurous construction activities from elsewhere in the book to create the scene. Suggestions are then given on directing children's play to maximum learning effect.

Learning objectives

Specific learning objectives are given for each activity. Here is an overview list of learning objectives for small world play activities in general.

Early Years Foundation Stage

Personal, social and emotional development

- Continue to be interested, excited and motivated to learn.
- Be confident to try new activities, initiate ideas and speak in a familiar group.
- Work as part of a group or class, taking turns and sharing fairly.

Communication, language and literacy

- Interact with others, negotiating plans and activities and taking turns in conversations.
- Extend their vocabulary, exploring the meanings and sounds of new words.
- Use language to imagine and recreate roles and experiences.
- Use talk to organise, sequence and clarify thinking, ideas, feelings and events.
- Use their phonic knowledge to write simple regular words and make phonetically plausible attempts at more complex words.
- Attempt writing for different purposes.

Problem solving, reasoning and numeracy

- Recognise numerals 1 to 9.
- Begin to use the vocabulary involved in adding and subtracting.
- Use developing mathematical ideas and methods to solve practical problems.
- Use everyday words to describe position.

Knowledge and understanding of the world

- Ask questions about how things happen.
- Build and construct a wide range of objects, selecting appropriate resources and adapting their work where necessary.
- Select the tools and techniques they need to shape, assemble and join materials they are using
- Make short-term future plans.

Physical development

- Use a range of small and large equipment.

Creative development

- Respond in a variety of ways to what they see, hear, smell, touch and feel.
- Explore colour, texture, shape, form and space in two and three dimensions.

Key Stage 1

Geography

Knowledge, skills and understanding

Geographical enquiry and skills

1. In undertaking geographical enquiry, pupils should be taught to:

a. ask geographical questions

c. express their own views about people, places and environments.

2. In developing geographical skills, pupils should be taught to:

a. use geographical vocabulary

c. use globes, maps and plans at a range of scales

e. make maps and plans.

Knowledge and understanding of places

3. Pupils should be taught to:

a. identify and describe what places are like

c. recognise how places compare with other places.

Design and technology

Knowledge, skills and understanding

Teaching should ensure that knowledge and understanding are applied when developing ideas, planning, making products and evaluating them.

Developing, planning and communicating ideas

1. Pupils should be taught to:

a. generate ideas by drawing on their own and other people's experiences

b. develop ideas by shaping materials and putting together components

c. talk about their ideas

d. plan by suggesting what to do next as their ideas develop

e. communicate their ideas using a variety of methods, including drawing and making models.

Working with tools, equipment, materials and components to make quality products

2. Pupils should be taught to:

a. select tools, techniques and materials for making their product from a range suggested by the teacher
b. explore the sensory qualities of materials
c. measure, mark out, cut and shape a range of materials
d. assemble, join and combine materials and components
e. use simple finishing techniques to improve the appearance of their product, using a range of equipment
f. follow safe procedures for food safety and hygiene.

Evaluating processes and products

3. Pupils should be taught to:

a. talk about their ideas, saying what they like and dislike
b. identify what they could have done differently or how they could improve their work in the future.

Knowledge and understanding of materials and components

4. Pupils should be taught:

a. about the working characteristics of materials
b. how mechanisms can be used in different ways.

Literacy links

Talking

The key area in which small world play helps develop literacy skills is through the huge amount of talking that goes on during the construction stage of any project, as well as during the subsequent play. These scenes help children to develop their imaginative interaction with places they may visit as they grow older and some that they may never visit. This play talk is very important: as children mature it becomes internalised and fuels the development of thinking strategies. The more children talk together while they are young, the better they will be at a range of thinking skills.

Signposts

Not all writing is in sentences and part of a story or a report. We need to give children every opportunity to explore text in everyday situations and small world play is great for this. Children can design signposts to show the way in their scene or larger signs to adorn the fronts of buildings. Make one big sign out of modelling materials with the title of the scene on it and the children won't even realise they are practising their literacy skills!

Directions

Encourage children to plan journeys through the scenes they have created by leaving a clipboard, paper and pencils alongside. Write a list of directions yourself for children to follow with their play characters. Give instructions for specific tasks to complete on the journey.

Health and safety

While the making of small world play models and scenes may have health and safety implications in the use of scissors and so on, there are no real hazards associated with the play. Just check that very small children are not putting little toys in their mouths.

1. The Pirates of Volcano Island

Why play Pirates of Volcano Island?

Pirates are a very popular theme in children's play. This play scene incorporates some historical learning with fantasy play and is a great way into storytelling and story writing.

Learning objectives

EYFS children are developing their PSED skills through working together on creating the scene and their problem-solving skills (PSRN) during their time playing with the scene. KS1 children are using geographical vocabulary and describing what places are like. These are in their geography curriculum. They can also develop the full range of designing, making and evaluating skills in the design and technology curriculum.

Resources

- A builders' mixing tray
- A model volcano (see Build an erupting volcano, p94)
- Play sand
- Black plastic bin bags
- Compost
- Lolly sticks and twigs.

Making Volcano Island

- Lay your builders' mixing tray on a table where there is all-round access
- Fill the tray with play sand
- Place your model volcano in the middle of the island
- Scoop out an area for the sea and another for a lake. Line these with pieces from a black plastic bin bag and fill with water to create additional features
- A swamp can be made in the same way by creating a lake and filling it with a mixture of water and compost
- Add trees made from pipe cleaners and tissue paper
- Place a model ship in the sea
- Add some scary labels by writing on jagged pieces of lolly sticks stuck on twigs and placed next to features.

Directed play in Pirates of Volcano Island

- Link this small world play in with activities described in the Pirate Day activity in the role-play section of this book (p147)
- Set problem-solving tasks such as following a pirate map to find buried treasure
- Actually bury some treasure in the sand so children are not disappointed at the end of the journey
- Give children challenges such as building a bridge over a river or getting their toy characters across the swamp without sinking.

Health and safety

If your island contains messy play, such as a swamp, get the children to wear aprons and emphasise the need for personal hygiene by washing hands after playing.

Follow-up activities

As pirates are such a popular theme, it is worth capturing the opportunities for learning in the key areas of literacy and numeracy. Follow up play time on Volcano Island with drama and story writing, reading stories about pirate adventures and talking about life in the past. Draw maps and teach simple coordinates to bring in a maths dimension.

Teaching points
A lot of informal learning will take place through the discussions you have with children while you play alongside them.

2. Superhero HQ

Why play Superhero HQ?

Because it is great fun and it really gets boys into small world play in a big way! I was amazed at just how keen boys were to get a turn on the small world play table when we came up with this theme.

Learning objectives

EYFS children can build and construct a wide range of objects, selecting appropriate resources and adapting their work where necessary (KUW). In the same area of the curriculum they can select the tools and techniques they need to shape, assemble and join materials they are using. KS1 children can also develop the full range of design and technology skills.

Resources

- Lots and lots of Lego
- Cardboard boxes
- String
- Glue and paint
- Plasticine
- Strips of wood.

Making Superhero HQ

- Place a great pile of Lego in the middle of a table and let small groups of children begin to build their fantasy Superhero HQ.
- Encourage children to be ambitious and build space stations or underground bunkers.
- As ideas begin to emerge, develop them in a more creative way through model making using cardboard boxes to create vehicles and technological gadgetry for your superheroes to use.
- Use string to add zip wires and high ropes for the superheroes to train on.
- Make ladders out of strips of wood.
- Create bizarre monsters out of Plasticine for your superheroes to fight.

Directed play in Superhero HQ

- You don't need to provide model superheroes for your children – simply ask them and they will bring them in from home.
- Your superheroes need something heroic to do! Give them a challenge to tackle through playing with their characters – rescue a stranded group of scientists from a cave, capture and cage a huge creature that has emerged from the sea or prevent the lava from a volcano from destroying a city. Make sure any challenge you come up with has a degree of problem solving built in so that children need to talk to each other and reach a solution.

Health and safety

Superhero play, even on a small scale, can become quite boisterous. Negotiate the rules of play with your children before they get started and review these regularly to ensure that the children can enjoy their superhero play safely.

Follow-up activities

When it comes to getting some literacy learning out of superhero play, boys will suddenly realise they want to go and play elsewhere! You have to be cunning. As you are playing alongside the children, develop a story together. This by itself develops speaking and listening skills. After your play session, make a floor book together where you scribe the story and the children add illustrations. Gradually encourage your reluctant writers to add a word or sentence in writing here or there in the story.

Teaching points

Watch extracts from old Thunderbirds episodes to further stimulate ideas for building secret bases.

3. The Underwater Kingdom

Why play Underwater Kingdom?

This is an extension of water play at the water table. Creating a scene and bringing in characters broadens the opportunities for children to learn around the water table and to create all manner of imaginative stories. It is also an opportunity to learn about real life under the sea through playing with models of sea life.

Learning objectives

This is a great activity for creative development for EYFS children. They can explore colour, texture, shape, form and space in two and three dimensions. They can also respond in a variety of ways to what they see, hear, smell, touch and feel. KS1 children can develop geographical vocabulary.

Resources

- A transparent water table or large transparent plastic tank
- Gravels, stones and one or two rocks
- A model shipwreck
- Plastic packaging boxes
- Model sea animals
- Plastic replica underwater plants, which can be bought from a pet shop.

Making the Underwater Kingdom

- Make your scene before filling your water table or tank with water – it just makes the construction phase easier.
- Lay gravel, small stones and a couple of rocks on the bottom of the tank to create a seabed.
- Make your plastic sea plants stay on the bottom by embedding them in Plasticine.
- Make a palace for a merking out of transparent plastic packaging boxes. Make this as a diorama and then weight it down to the bottom of the tank with stones so it doesn't float away.
- Make furniture for your merpeople out of plastic packaging materials.
- Use plastics of various colours to really bring your underwater scene to life.
- Slowly add water to flood your scene.

Directed play in the Underwater Kingdom

There are all sorts of possibilities in an underwater kingdom:

- Use plastic model mermaids and mermen to create your own underwater tales.
- If you can't find plastic mermaids in your supplier's catalogue, make your own out of plastic packaging materials cut out and sewn together using plastic thread.
- Use your underwater scene for non-fiction learning by providing model fish, whales, octopuses, crabs, sharks and so on. Children can play out sharks hunting fish and fish hiding among rocks to get to know more about life beneath the waves.

Health and safety

There is the potential to get very wet indeed while playing in the Underwater Kingdom, so make sure children are wearing aprons and that an agreed code of play is in place.

Follow-up activities

- Read or tell stories about mermaids and underwater kingdoms. Make up your own stories around these themes.
- Bring in model divers to explore the shipwreck and look for sunken treasure.
- Make a non-fiction book about sea life to display alongside your underwater play table.

Teaching points

Scottish culture is particularly rich in stories of people who turn into seals and marriages between mermaids and mortals.

4. Lost in Space

Why play Lost in Space?

Space is a fascinating subject and children are never too young to start learning about the universe in which we live. This small world play activity is actually quite big and creates a model solar system for children to explore with their small world play characters. Very exciting!

Learning objectives

There is a lot of making going on in this activity. EYFS children are building and constructing a wide range of objects, selecting appropriate resources and adapting their work where necessary. They are also selecting the tools and techniques they need to shape, assemble and join materials they are using. KS1 children will develop the full range of design and technology skills and can begin learning about the Earth and space, which is in the science curriculum.

Resources

- An enclosed space such as a play house or play shed
- Lots of black sugar paper and black sheets
- Nine balls of different sizes to represent the planets of our solar system
- Newspaper and wallpaper glue
- Craft knife
- Masking tape
- Paint
- String
- Kitchen roll tubes
- Cardboard
- Scissors, glue and sticky tape
- Torches
- Astronaut characters.

Making Lost in Space

- Line your play space with black sugar paper and cover in black sheets so it is lightproof.
- Paint small white dots on the black sugar paper to represent stars – make the patterns of some of the constellations.
- Cover the balls in papier mâché and leave to dry. Cut around each papier mâché ball carefully with a craft knife to remove the ball. Stick the two halves back together with masking tape. Paint each ball to represent one of the balls in our solar system. Make these as realistic as possible by using images from the Hubble telescope – *www.hubblesite.org*
- Attach the planets to the roof of your play space with string.
- Make model space rockets out of kitchen roll tubes.

Directed play in Lost in Space

Give your children a mission such as to be the first people to land on Mars. Give children torches and magnifying glasses to explore space. They can use their model spacecrafts and astronauts to discover new worlds.

Health and safety

Only have a couple of children at a time in your dark play space to avoid accidents. Normal precautions apply when making models with scissors and glue.

Follow-up activities

- View images of our solar system, our galaxy and beyond with the children on the amazing Hubble telescope site.
- Talk about possibilities for the future of space travel and ways in which a knowledge of space can help us here on Earth – weather satellites are a good example.

Teaching points

Space is all about large numbers, so take the chance to see just how big your children can go with numbers.

Appendix 1: Resources

Nature

Publications

Baker, N (2004) *The New Amateur Naturalist*, Collins.

Bharat Cornell, J (1999) *Sharing Nature with Children*, Dawn Publications.

Oddie, B (2008) How to Watch Wildlife, Collins.

The Field Studies Council produces an excellent series of laminated fold-out charts covering birds, mammals, pond life, spiders, butterflies and so on. These can be ordered through their website at *www.field-studies-council.org*

Equipment

Many of the small tools such as spoons, pots and brushes that you will need for collecting wildlife can be gathered from household or school sources. It is also good to build up a small collection of specialist equipment. Certainly every child should have a magnifying glass when you go out exploring. Other equipment such as binoculars can be shared among a group of children.

Science

Publications

Harlen, W OBE and Qualter, A (2009) *The Teaching of Science in Primary Schools*, David Fulton.

Equipment

Most of the activities in this section can be carried out with ordinary everyday equipment and simple materials and chemicals, which can be found in the school science cupboard.

Art

Publications

Callaway, G, Kear, M and Leach, A (1999) *Teaching Art and Design in the Primary School*, David Fulton.

Equipment

As well as all the consumable art resources that you buy from your educational supplier make good use of natural and recycled items. These materials really help children to develop their imagination as they respond to the individual qualities of each item.

Woodcraft

Publications

Iggulden, C and Iggulden, H (2006) *The Dangerous Book for Boys*, HarperCollins.

Martin, S (2007) *The Curious Boy's Book of Adventure*, Bloomsbury.

Equipment

You will find most of the equipment you need for woodcraft activities lying around out in the woods.

Role-play

Publications

Featherstone, S and Williams, L (2007) *Role Play: Progression in Play for Babies and Children*, Featherstone Education Ltd.

Equipment

Build up your own school collection of role-play resource boxes on different themes. Make good use of parents for this and put out occasional appeals for clothing and equipment under particular themes.

Design and technology

Publications

Morgan, P and Morgan, H (1992) *The Book of Kites*, Dorling Kindersley.

Equipment

Most of the resources you need for D and T projects can be sourced from recycled or reclaimed materials. It does help raise the profile of these activities if you have decent tools to work with and it is worth building up a small collection of woodworking tools of an appropriate size for children.

Gardening

Publications

Clevely, AM (2008) *The Allotment Book*, Collins.

Larkcom, J (2002) *Grow Your Own Vegetables*, Frances Lincoln.

Popescu, C (2003) *Hens in the Garden, Eggs in the Kitchen*, Cavalier Paperbacks.

Wilde, K (2005) *Gardening with Children*, Collins.

Equipment

See what you can get for free from local garden centres and DIY stores. The end of each season is a good time to pick up freebies as the stores are in the process of changing their stock ready for the next season.

The garden is a great place to promote recycling – reclaimed timber for building compost bins, yoghurt pots for growing seedlings in and cut-up margarine tub lids for plant labels.

There are some very stylish (and expensive) chicken coops on the market. Keep an eye on your local free ads to pick up a much cheaper second-hand one.

Our wonderful world

Publications

Kindersley, A, Kindersley, B and Copsey, S (1995) *Children Just Like Me: A Unique Celebration of Children Around the World,* Dorling Kindersley.

Equipment

Build up a whole school collection of artefacts from different cultures, places around the world and historical periods to enhance children's learning in this area.

Your local authority library or museum service will have available resource boxes that you can borrow on different themes.

Small world play

Publications

Ward, S, Featherstone, S and Ingham, K (2005) *The Little Book of Small World Play*, Featherstone Education Ltd.

Equipment

There are some great model figures available from educational suppliers and these will really help to bring to life the scenes you build.

Children will also want to bring their own figurines to play in the small world arenas you create.

Child development

Publications

Fontana, D (1995) *Psychology for Teachers*, Palgrave Macmillan.

Piaget, J (1952) *The Origins of Intelligence in Children.*

Piaget, J and Inhelder, B (1956) *A Child's Concept of Space.*

Piaget, J and Inhelder, B (1969) *The Psychology of the Child.*

Schaffer, HR (2003) *Introducing Child Psychology*, John Wiley & Sons.

Wood, D (1997) *How Children Think and Learn* (2nd edition), WileyBlackwell.

Appendix 2: websites

Curriculum:

The National Curriculum can be accessed online at *http://curriculum.qcda.gov.uk*

Nature:

British Trust for Conservation Volunteers *www2.btcv.org.uk*
Providing practical skills and advice for wildlife projects.

Botanical Society of the British Isles *www.bsbi.org.uk*
Runs national surveys of wildflowers, which your class may like to join in with.

Cheviot trees *www.cheviot-trees.co.uk*
Specialist growers of trees and plants for forestry, woodland, hedging, reedbeds, erosion control and marginal areas

Hedgehogs *www.sttiggywinkles.org.uk*
A hospital for hedgehogs with advice on how to make them welcome.

Herpetological Conservation Society *www.herpetofauna.co.uk*
The national organisation for saving reptiles and amphibians.

The Invertebrate Conservation Trust
www.buglife.org.uk
For everything you need to know about a diversity of minibeasts.

Royal Society for the Protection of Birds
www.rspb.org.uk
Find out all about bird feeding and nest box building. Wildlife Explorers is their youth branch.

Sharing Nature Foundation *www.sharingnature.com*
Initiators of many imaginative wildlife games and practical learning ideas.

The UK Rock Pooling Club *www.uk-rpc.org*
Providing practical advice for fun days out by the sea, including identification photos.

Wildlife Trusts *www.wildlifetrusts.org*
Umbrella organisation for the 47 county-based trusts around the country.

Wildlife WATCH *www.wildlifewatch.org.uk*
The youth branch of the county wildlife trusts with loads of practical ideas.

Woodland Trust *www.woodlandtrust.org.uk*
For identifying and planting trees.

Science:

Electricity *www.learningcircuits.co.uk*
A glitzy website with Macromedia imagery that will capture children's attention.

Hubble telescope *www.hubblesite.org*
Look at some amazing images!

Royal Astronomical Society *www.ras.org.uk*
Has a useful resource database for teachers.

Royal Meteorological Society *www.rmets.org*
Practical weather projects and information for schools.

UK Fossils *www.ukfossils.co.uk*
Practical advice on where and how to find fossils.

Art:

Natural dyes *www.wildcolours.co.uk*
Practical advice from someone who does it for a living.

Sculpture *www.goldsworthy.cc.gla.ac.uk*
Photographs of natural sculptures made by Andy Goldsworthy.

Willow *www.englishwillowbaskets.co.uk*
The website for PH Coate and Son in Somerset who know everything there is to know about willow.

Woodcraft:

Knots *www.animatedknots.com*
Watch the knots tie themselves in amazing animation.

Map reading *www.ordnancesurvey.co.uk*
The experts on mapping with practical advice on not getting lost!

Practical skills *www.forestschools.com*
Lots of schools are getting involved in this exciting initiative.

Role-play:

Drama skills *www.makebelievearts.co.uk*
Creative approaches to help you develop your skills so you can help children develop theirs.

Design and technology:

Cookery *www.bbc.co.uk/food*
Hundreds of online recipes searchable by ingredients or culture.

Kites *www.kite-festival.org.uk*
The website for Bristol International Kite Festival with some fantastic visuals in the press section.

Lego *www.lego.com*
The original construction kit – try the big, soft blocks.

Quadro *www.quadroplay.co.uk*
For building really big structures.

Gardening:

African gardens *www.sendacow.org.uk*
The people behind the inspiring bag gardens that help African orphans feed their families

Common Ground *www.commonground.org.uk*
The environmental and arts charity that promotes Apple Day.

Compost *www.recyclenow.com/home_composting*
All the advice you need to make rich soil conditioner for your veggie patch.

Fruit trees and bushes *www.scottsnurseries.co.uk*
A very informative catalogue.

Garden Organic *www.gardenorganic.org.uk*
Practical advice and a popular schools scheme.

Keeping chickens *www.poultry.allotment.org.uk*

Worms *www.wigglywigglers.co.uk*
Check out their excellent Can-O-Worms composting system.

Our wonderful world:

British Council *www.britishcouncil.org.uk*
Promoting cultural links with other countries.

Geographical Association *www.geography.org.uk*
Lots of links to other useful resource websites and a great magazine full of practical ideas for promoting geography.

The Historical Association *www.history.org.uk*
Downloadable resources to inspire little historians.

Recycling *www.recyclenow.com*
You'll be amazed just what can be recycled.

Small world play:

Farming and Countryside Education
www.face-online.org.uk
Resources that will hopefully ensure every child knows milk comes from cows!

International Talk Like A Pirate Day
www.talklikeapirate.com
19th September every year.
The website has lots of advice on becoming a pirate.